The Early Diary of Anaïs Nin

Volume Three

1923-1927

WORKS BY ANAÏS NIN

With a Preface
by Joaquin Nin-Culmell

———

A Harvest/HBJ Book
Harcourt Brace Jovanovich, Publishers
San Diego · New York · London

THE EARLY DIARY
OF ANAÏS NIN
VOLUME THREE *1923-1927*

✿

Library of Congress Cataloging in Publication Data
(Revised for vol. 3)
Nin, Anaïs, 1903–1977.
Linotte, the early diary of Anaïs Nin.
Vol. 1 translated from the French by Jean L. Sherman.
Vol. 3 has title: The early diary of Anaïs Nin.
Includes indexes.
Contents: v. 1. 1914–1920—v. 3. 1923–1927.
1. Nin, Anaïs, 1903–1977—Diaries.   2. Authors,
American—20th century—Biography.
PS3327.I865Z522   1978   818'.5203 [B]   77-20314
ISBN 0-15-652386-8 (v. 1) (Harvest/HBJ : pbk.)
0-15-127184-4 (v. 3)
0-15-627250-4 (vol. 3) (Harvest/HBJ : pbk.)

Printed in the United States of America
First Harvest/HBJ edition 1985
A B C D E F G H I J

❧ *Editor's Note* ❧

The third published volume of *The Early Diary of Anaïs Nin* is drawn from her journals numbered nineteeen to twenty-four, covering the years 1923–1927. Up to this time Anaïs had written in inexpensive "date books," but she now began to use genuine diary books bound with red leather and marbleized paper, perhaps in recognition of her new status as a married woman. Journal twenty-one is an exception. It was the first that Anaïs kept in Paris, and it appears to be a French school notebook.

This volume, like the earlier one, was prepared from Anaïs's own typescript, but although she had found reason to cut a number of passages from the 1920–1923 journals—much of which was restored in final publication—here, she censored nothing, faithfully copying all contained in the original handwritten journals. One journal was lost, together with a suitcase, during her first return trip to New York, in 1927, but unlike the 1918 gap in *Linotte: The Early Diary of Anaïs Nin, Volume One*, this missing portion was reconstructed by Anaïs from memory, during her sea voyage back to France. So once again the material is presented in a continuous chronology; and again it has been edited to delete repetitious and routine entries and to clarify doubtful passages.

The previous volume of *The Early Diary* ended in February 1923 (in the middle of journal nineteen) as Anaïs waited for Hugh Guiler's arrival in Cuba, where they were to be married. A month elapses before the next diary entry is made, that of March 20th, which opens the present volume. Anaïs has already settled down to married life in Kew Gardens, New York, near her family. She will hereafter sign her journals "Anaïs Nin Guiler," and she acknowledges her new identity by calling this portion of her diary "Journal d'une Epouse," just as she had called the earlier portion "Journal d'une Fiancée." It is not until 1931, however, that she begins to use titles on a regular basis and to more dramatic effect.

The diary as a whole Anaïs called "Mon Journal" when she was writing in French, from 1914 to 1920. This becomes "My Diary" in journals nine through seventeen; eighteen and nineteen, as I have said, carry individual titles; while twenty through twenty-three are called simply "Journal and Notebook." But in journal twenty-four, which ends this volume, Anaïs returns to the language of her heart and again calls her diary "Mon Journal." Possibly it is a mark of her growing acceptance of France, but it will be the name of her diary for the rest of her life.

Rupert Pole
Executor, The Anaïs Nin Trust

Los Angeles, California
April 1983

LIST OF ILLUSTRATIONS

🌿 *Preface* 🌿

Anaïs often gave titles to her diaries, titles that set goals or established new relationships. Volume III of the Early Diaries dwells on the initial years of her marriage to Hugh (Hugo) P. Guiler and her return to Paris as a married woman; hence she titled it *Le Journal d'une Epouse* (*The Diary of a Wife*). In fact, it went far beyond that, for it involved the rediscovery of her idealized father, the disillusionment of life in Paris and the cultural shock of a Europe she had forgotten. It also involved the discovery of contemporary tendencies in art, which both she and Hugo had chosen to ignore hitherto, and the eternal struggle between reality and realism.

Certain common denominators remained. Of these, the foremost was Anaïs's vocation to write, closely followed by the workings of an imagination that never capitulated, though it often wavered, in the search of herself and of the meaning of her relationship to those she loved. Anaïs wanted something greater than human happiness, something beyond the frontiers of human relationships; however, her thirst for the innermost core of experience alternately raised her spirits to soaring heights or relentlessly dashed them to the ground. Long before she ever met Antonin Artaud, or even knew of his existence, he had acutely expressed this febrile state of mind in a line of his poem "Extase": "Recherche épuisante du moi" (exhausting search for self).

Anaïs was compelled to write because she suffered and because the joy of writing was "so intense, so pure, so all-absorbing and free and all-encompassing, flooding the soul in mystical ecstasy, elevating and sanctifying, infusing beauty in the humblest subjects and a purpose in the most wayward life." And yet she had little confidence in herself as a writer, apart from her diaries, which she regarded as the most intimate, if not the most complete, of the reflections of her changing self. She reread them, made copies, evaluated their accuracy, and defended them from the frontal attacks of those around her who felt that too much introspection was a hindrance to her development as a writer. She attempted to translate them into fiction but soon realized that she was not ready for the exchange, nor had she found the form and freedom of her writing. She wanted to rely on her impulses and instincts rather than follow the more stabilizing advice of others. She wanted to remain at the heights of life every moment, to penetrate the past and to divine the future. But above all, she wanted to write as a poet.

It would have taken more than writing as a poet and even more than the introspection of her diaries to deal with the repercussions of her meeting with her father and of his quest for happiness in his second marriage. Even though she thought she immediately understood him, he was still a stranger, if not an intruder in her life. And yet she thought of him as patient and reasonable, particularly when she compared his reactions to her mother's "ugly emotions" upon being served what Anaïs dismissed as the mere formality of divorce papers. The fact that the papers came unexpectedly on her mother's arrival in Paris, and moreover were designed to favor her father, never seemed to bother Anaïs, or so it appears by her comments. She firmly believed that she could steer her mother and control her father, even though she had little confidence in her father's ability to evaluate his actions and her mother was not the kind to be steered. She felt strongly that she must compensate her father for his restraint and that all should be forgiven.

Anaïs enjoyed meeting her father's new wife, María Luisa Rodriguez (Maruca), again. They had last seen each other in Arcachon in 1913, when Maruca was a teenager and Anaïs a child, but now Maruca was Anaïs's stepmother. Anaïs found her father at his best when Maruca was present, but the "Problem," as Anaïs called him, remained unsolved. There was no question that he was an artist, and Anaïs literally worshiped artists, but he was also the idealized father who had abandoned and disappointed her as a child. Eventually, she would abandon and disappoint him, but on her own terms.

Reading still gave Anaïs a fever, which day by day burned her more violently. "It is the fever of life, the consuming desire to live intensely, to create something strong and great, to understand all things, to possess every knowledge and every experience. . . ." Once more she decided to search for her education "in the very thorough *chewing* of books." Books rather than people and their limitations sent Anaïs, as Hugo wrote in her diary, "well on the way to the true knowledge of herself and the full expression of her rich mind. . . ." The list included Balzac, Flaubert, Rabelais, Anatole France, the inevitable Dumas and Victor Hugo, Meredith, Henry James, Marcel Proust (whose influence lasted well beyond the Paris years), John Erskine, Edith Wharton, Pierre Loti, d'Annunzio and his imitator Nicolas Ségur, and Anaïs's old friends the Goncourt, Maurice de Guérin and Amiel.

For the first time, thanks to the beneficial, albeit disconcerting, influence of a middle-aged lycée teacher of English literature and translator of American writers, Hélène Boussinescq, Anaïs began to take a lively interest in modern novelists and dramatists such as Waldo Frank, Sherwood Anderson, Pirandello and Ferdinand Bruckner. At first, modern writing seemed as discordant, harsh, disjointed and mad to her as Stravinski's music. Although Mademoiselle Boussinescq mildly disapproved of Erskine's writing, which both Anaïs and Hugo greatly admired but with increasing qualifications, she fascinated Anaïs with the overwhelming scope of her varied interests, which went from an intimate knowledge of the cathedral of Chartres to a most discerning and stimulating curiosity for the dramatic presentations of Jouvet, Pitoëff, Dullin and other heroic avant-garde directors of the 1920s.

"Boussie," as we all called her, was a French Protestant from the south of France and perhaps the first and only stalwart socialist Anaïs ever encountered. More than a guide to Chartres and a literary influence, she was a catalyst and an active one at that. To what extent Anaïs depended on her at first is hard to pin down. It would seem likely that Anaïs shared her impressions, hopes, ambitions and even tentative literary efforts with her. And knowing Boussie, I am sure that she was supportive in her own dry, matter-of-fact way, school-marmish at times to be sure, but never lacking in foresight. Of all Anaïs's French friends of that period, Boussie was the only one who brought something substantial for Anaïs to *chew* on and who understood in her own way Anaïs's struggles in English. Her contributions were soon to be exhausted but perhaps less quickly than with most people Anaïs knew.

Although Hugo called on Anaïs to live in the present, she was really interested only in the future. She was maturing day by day, by leaps and bounds, and even the diary had a hard time keeping track of the ground covered. She began to avoid certain subjects and longed to write about one subject in particular, which she never openly identified. Her open letter to the world was beginning to explore the dark confines of the unknown, and for the first time she realized that she must get a locked box for her diary.

The realities of life in Paris became, for Anaïs, a nightmare. It wasn't so much the sensuality of the city that shocked her (who hasn't felt the exquisite feminine lure of Paris?) but rather the open sexuality of everyday life. French books and publications, French plays and movies, public experiences and social events all contributed to her feeling of not belonging, of looking from the outside in. She hated salacious talk, and her puritanical concept of life, largely the result of her readings or misreadings of Thoreau, Carlyle, Emerson and other idealists, hardly prepared her for the concept that there is no life of the spirit without the senses. She confused the senses and sexuality as she confused reality and realism. She wrote long tirades against life in Paris and what she thought it stood for, noting at the same time "how undefinable is the change Paris makes in one." The eternal Spring of Paris finally cast its spell, and by the time Anaïs returned to New York for a short visit, she realized that the magic was more effective than she had anticipated. New York was the Past; Paris was the Future. Outgrowing one, she had yet to take her place in the other. (This was the moment Richard Maynard captured in his portrait of Anaïs.)

But what about her life as a married woman? For the first time she understood her life, her love and even Hugo. Yet Anaïs, who thought of herself as a "clinger," felt that she was the stronger of the two. Stronger perhaps, but also less unified. And so she questioned herself: "Would I like to be either purely woman or purely writer, purely mind?" The word *either* indicates a choice, for she felt she could not have both. Hugo, who loved her more than himself, helped her find the solution to the dilemma and because of this was the only one she could love wholly, the only one who could be everything to her every day. As she wrote in her diary: "How can I put in so many words what I owe to Hugo?"

Hugo's work at the bank enabled her to "create" for both of them, and yet Anaïs was sharply critical of his chosen profession. Hugo's criticism of Anaïs's writing, on the other hand, was always constructive and encouraging. She was inordinately sensitive to criticism, *any* criticism by *anybody*, and Hugo was no exception, even though his help was essential in overcoming the feeling she had of being an "outsider in English." She nevertheless tormented him with the reproach that he did not love her, that he did not understand, that *nobody* understood and threatened "never to write again, to destroy the book, my Journal, myself, anything."

Hugo shared Anaïs's reading, her enthusiasm for people and places, and grew and matured along with her. The "humorous banker," as she dubbed him, was also a loving husband and an unswerving supporter of the family obligations Anaïs had taken upon herself, such as helping Mother and me to survive the economic strain of my musical studies in Paris. Hugo was extraordinarily attentive to my mother and acted as my own "big brother" in many important and critical moments of my life.

He kept his own journal, albeit sporadically, and in order to present Anaïs with the complete works of Amiel, he even found time to write a poem in archaic style to his "faire ladye." Of course Anaïs wanted him to write more and work less, or at least be less absorbed by his work than he appeared to be. In some ways, she did not understand to what extent her restless inventiveness was inspiring his own work at the bank. Perhaps he did not feel as keenly as Anaïs did the pain of lettings others speak for him, but his growth continued nevertheless, and of all the things he dared to do, the most daring and the most dangerous for the well-being of their marriage was to encourage Anaïs to be herself.

Joaquin Nin-Culmell

Berkeley, California
March 1983

The Diary of a Wife
(Journal d'une Épouse)

1923

March 20. Richmond Hill. In the same room which held my youth's virgin dreams, bathed in the same soft light which threw a rosy radiance about my fancies, reflected in the same mirror into which I gazed in girlish expectation, questioning and wondering, now sits Hugo,[1] my husband.

A little more than a month ago I was in Havana, still taking part in social life, still the butterfly with gorgeous colors on her fluttering wings, inwardly beginning to tremble at the approach of half-veiled changes.

Somehow, out of a confusion of practical reasoning, romantic impulses, decisions forced by circumstances, Hugo and I emerged one morning, married. . . .

Social pleasures, adulation, luxury and idleness, the last fragments of a brilliant and short season of girlhood, all seemed to melt away as our ship sailed out into the open sea. Days of traveling, our arrival in New York, were all steeped in unreality, which nothing could dispel. Now we live under the shadow of Mother's[2] sorrowing spirit, and our life is difficult, but we are strong together.

March 26. In one room I may spend the most honeyed hours with my Love. Youth vibrates in both of us; our confidences, our growing knowledge of each other, steeped in glowing tenderness, are infinitely sweet and wondrous.

[1] *Hugh Parker Guiler—called "Hugo" because his father was also named Hugh.*
[2] *Rosa Culmell de Nin.*

Regretfully I close the door upon my heaven, and I steal softly into another room. Mother lies there, weeping. I fall upon my knees—with a sorrow so piercing that it effaces all other feelings.

Mother clings to me. She murmurs vaguely that she has lost her little girl. Of life, which has been all hardness and pain for her, she expected a sole compensation, and she does not have even that. She tells me through her tears that her life is useless, that she has lost the desire to live. Her faith is broken, her courage, her health, her very heart. The unspeakable cruelty of it overwhelms me. There are times when, in horror of the grief I am causing the mother I love beyond words, I think myself mad.

My Love opens his arms; his eyes shine with love of me and the need of me. Behind him Mother's sorrow looms, immense and terrifying. I see her tear-stained face, her weak, worn figure. I am torn by the choice, torn by conflicting reasoning, by irrepressible sentiments, by pity, by rebellion, by bitterness and self-reproach.

I am impotent to preserve those I love from sorrow. Shall I be permitted to alleviate it? Why has God allowed me to be the instrument of Mother's unhappiness when I prayed night after night to be allowed to suffer for her?

Evening. The Hugo I have described in the past is not the one whose wife I am now. In the first place, I described him as I saw him with my girl's eyes and misplaced idealism. I did not know him then. Now he has truly changed. Whatever I write now alone counts and is alone true. I need to say this because I love to muse on his character and disentangle the diverse discoveries I make day by day.

And Hugo has above all else the quality of constant variety. He evolves continually, so that I can understand him without knowing all of him.

I foresee the exclusion of one generally accepted misfortune befalling the married ones—we shall escape monotony.

March 27. Clinging to Carlyle's teaching and seeking to do the work before me well without thinking or questioning. But I must write because I suffer.

My work is done; and just as I so often sat to rest and dream, writing to fill my aching emptiness and vain expectation, I now sit listening for the sound of Hugo's footsteps upon the gravel path. How sweet it is to meet after a day of separation.

I long for evening, when I can hear his voice again and be

folded in his arms. It is only when he is with me that I am contented. As I sit here watching the twilight and waiting for him, I can now say I want nothing else, my life is complete, I know its purpose now.

Evening. Too often now I hesitate before my opened book, tempted to retrace the broken web of my most wondrous past. There is not a day, however bright, which does not suffer from the fading touch of time.

This makes me regretful. I am one who respects the past, who reveres it. A thousand pictures return to me. I see Havana once more; I see society and luxury and beauty of environment; I pass again by the seaside in our soft-rolling car; I move again in that ease and idleness in the brilliant sunshine; I gallop again along the white road at dusk, seeing the palm trees outlined against a fire-colored sky; I meet the peasants and answer their humble greetings; I visit their little huts and witness their abject poverty; and then I again dress in fine, delicate, colorful things and set out to a tea in some luxurious place, deeply struck by the contrast— outwardly the fluttering butterfly, inwardly passing from one deep thought to another.

Through the mist of recollections Hugo's voice reaches me, and as I look into his face I hear something calling to me: Live in the present, live in the present!

March 28. I used to lay great stress upon Hugo's quality of decision, of character. In my hours of profound discouragement I looked up to his strength and self-confidence. It is a curious example of the irony of fate to find that he does not possess these things. I, in my weakness, am the stronger of the two. He gives me happiness, understanding, devotion, the truest companionship, all that I have ever wished for and dreamed of, all but *support.* I had hoped for that support and leadership; when it failed me, like some frail plant I swayed and trembled, then suddenly I held my head high and held myself straight and firm, and in one moment realized that I had learned to stand alone and struggle alone. Where shall this lead us? I, who believed myself made to cling, thrown upon my own strength.

March 29. I am struck by the manner in which love transforms the most humble work. What once revolted my far too sensitive "artistic sense" has now become invested with sacredness, not for what it is, or means in itself, but for its ultimate end. Whatever I do is done for Hugo. And I love him, so that the ugly becomes beautiful and the coarse fine, only because it is for him.

What joy for me to prove that a mind inclined to occupy itself with elevated, creative thought, to dreaming and solving, to philosophizing, can yet hold sway over the necessary "machinery" of life and equally apply itself to the humbler labor.

This is new language you are listening to. You have listened to my ravings and my raptures. So shall you listen now to my wise and sober discourses upon my preoccupations and interests as woman (still a "prosateur" and still enamored of her books and her pen).

Hugo often talked of these things which he does not possess, and I now understand it is because he thought of them so continuously and strongly. And I used to feel intimidated by his emphasis on them because, as I looked into my own heart, I found them lacking.

Is it not perhaps after all a blessing that it should be thus? What he might have had in his nature he might have expected of me, exacted. Now he admires what is in me, and perhaps I love him more when he confides and clings to me than when he seemed apparently so self-sufficient and self-assertive. How strange the contrast between what I believed of him and what truly is.

How strange our marriage, where union is based on likeness and accord. We begin with similar roots; we both feel deeply, think continuously; we have moods and dreams and visions—and there the similarity ceases, for the results of these, the effects outwardly, the actions and manner of living, are strikingly different. Thus we begin by *understanding* each other. We meet in a feeling or thought. In acting, we branch out, each in his own way, but we do not lose each other. We criticize and explain each other, we reason, we seek to influence each other—we understand even when we do not approve.

April 3. Now after days of unspeakable torment, I watch on Mother's ravaged face the first signs of fleeting happiness. Her expression too often clouds at mention of the future, but at least the excruciating pain of the first days is softened into the first awakenings of resignation.

Evening. Hugo teased me the night I wrote of Havana, for he said I did it because I loved to dwell on the warmth, it being so cold here. So, without knowing it, on a cold, crisp March night I wrote about Havana to keep myself warm! If I could be happy by writing about happiness.

But for some reason or other, I always come to your pages cold, and I write of warmth to forget. . . . Oh, it is sweet to be contented, but it is far more thrilling to be ever dissatisfied and reaching out, for who knows how far and where a great thirst may lead you.

I look up to see Hugo smiling reproachfully at me. He is a little jealous of you, little journal. It is true I should tell all things to him, and I am willing, but how can I when we are together so few hours and when I have so much to tell that even you are not enough, and most of it is turned into soliloquies?

April 7. Hugo was teasing me and among other things said that one could not spend all one's time writing in a diary. He little knows how near that phrase lies to the truth, which torments me. Why can I not do anything else? Why can I not find the class of writing that I am suited for? Am I like Amiel,[1] only capable of *this*?

Our life is slowly being molded into a close resemblance to our dreams. We have spent two evenings listening to entrancingly fine music. We have renewed our literary talks with Eugene[2] and John.[3] We have taken walks in the woods. Our evenings are restful.

The thought of Mother alone enshadows me, and I can have no taste of happiness without intolerable pangs of regret and self-reproach. I should have sacrificed love for her sake.

April 13. Above all else I have desired death these past days. Not even my love of Hugo could alter my despair; it even deepened it, because I could not surrender to the charm of it wholly—always the thought of Mother, Mother holding sway over my feelings.

Hugo begs me to control these feelings, and I could if it were *one* feeling, but Mother's despair calls out all of them, the deepest, the most enduring and the most heartrending. There is my love for her; there is the pity I always feel strongly even towards strangers and more so when it is my mother who suffers; there is the helplessness to sustain and live for one who needs me, as Mother does;

[1] *Henri Frédéric Amiel.*
[2] *Eugene Graves, Hugh's closest friend.*
[3] *John (Johnnie) Guiler, Hugh's brother.*

there is the intolerable pain of causing suffering. And Mother sees in our separation only the ruin of all her dreams, her hopes, her needs, her very life.

Sometimes I find strength to communicate my faith to her; at others I am carried away, and together we follow the road of our calvary. And to think that I wrote, some time ago, in the ignorance of my idealism, in the blindness of my dreams: "I see the way to a truer happiness for Mother." I did not know she wanted only me, free of obligations, free to devote myself to her completely.

April 14. Among a thousand other things, I ask myself if it is possible to find completeness in human companionship. In contemplating love, I foresaw the abandonment of my diary. In fulfilling love, I still cling tenaciously to these pages. The reason I need you is to receive the emotions and ideas which overflow from my being.

With mind ravaged by the devouring monsters of revolt, I attended Mass—an offering on the altar of my mother-worship—and was struck into awed and humble silence by a simple sermon on simple faith. With eloquent, contagious trust, the priest laid healing fingers on the burning pulse of my doubts. He made faith beautiful, and he made peace holy and precious.

I did not question my attitude. I knew that at the moment I was *good*.

"It is not a question of being good or wicked," said Hugo, analyzing this. "It is a question of being right or wrong."

I reflected for a moment. The hesitation was provocative. "I was wicked before, but I was *right*. And now I am *good* but I am *wrong*." He took it humorously. But this is a case of the grain of truth in humor.

April 18. Eugene, Johnnie, Hugo and I the other night discussed religion, superstition, faith and mysticism, and weighed the distinction between thought and feeling.

We agreed there was no distinction, but I well know that the balm on my agonized emotions [I experienced at Mass] was of a different nature and superior sphere.

Detachedly I watched and marveled. Eugene, Johnnie and Hugo were gently puffing their pipes, and through the mist of smoke I could see all our books and, as if arising from them, our discussions and the weighing of one another's ideas. The little room was warm with animation and earnestness.

In the intellect alone there is a strength, balance, happiness . . . but there is no peace.

Does peace come only with the death of the flesh? Why can we not have it when the intellect is all-powerful and it is allowed full freedom and sway?

April 20. Eduardo[1] arrived from college. He invited Hugo and me to the performance of Ibsen's *Peer Gynt*, and before that, we renewed our former talks, marveled at the change in each, aired our new ideas, exchanged unexpected impressions. Eduardo is still essentially charming, and even his dealing with a more palpable existence is clear, fresh and pure.

Jesting, I begged Hugo to break me of the vice of diary writing. He objected. It was rather a privilege to be endowed with the habit of writing. Besides, he added, it was exercise and preparatory practice.

No. I am caught in a circle. At first I wished only to exercise, to develop, to attain ease and fluency, but now *I cannot cease*. I cannot fit myself to any kind of writing after so much arduous and sincere preparation. And then I long to give myself wholly to my writing, if at all. A diary is a polite work and easily adaptable to the fragmentary quality of time I have for it.

To willfully ignore sorrow, to guide the thoughts into detached channels—that is the acme of mental weakness, and yet sometimes the result of unbearable pressure. To steady myself, to retain my evenness, I sometimes avoid the subjects closest to me. But now I may again approach them.

It appears as if the solution of our numberless troubles is to be found in a total change, and realizing the state of Mother's mind as I do, I hail as our salavtion a change of country and environment such as we are threatened by. Hugo's affairs may take him to Paris,[2] the city of my most secret and cherished dreams, long thought lost.

And as the feelings surge within me, I again come to you to unburden myself of them. Dearest diary, you are the living symbol of my failure, as the world sees failure, but you are the representative of all I hold most sacred, which is the subtle transi-

---

[1] *Eduardo Sánchez, a cousin with whom A.N. had been in love.*
[2] *He worked for National City Bank and had asked for a transfer to the Paris branch.*

tion of thoughts and emotions into words, which are to me invested with the holiest of joys.

Oh, the joy, the joy of writing, a joy so intense, so pure, so all-absorbing and free and all-encompassing, flooding the soul in mystical ecstasy, elevating and sanctifying, infusing beauty in the humblest subjects and a purpose in the most wayward life.

April 23. Eduardo has gone, and again the loss of his enchanting presence creates a void.

I had the joy of feeling harmony between Hugo and Eduardo —a joy mingled with gratitude, for Hugo not only sanctions my devotions but *participates* in them. Eduardo's personal merit perhaps largely influenced the continuity of this response, but not the first expression of it, which is what touched me.

Accepting the theory that I am composed of many selves, of many opposing forces, moods, even reasonings, I shall proceed to classify them as high and low, for this in itself is suggestive of the feelings which accompany the passing of one state into another.

Thus in my highest moments, which I believe to be inspired by a sudden and mysterious kindling of the divine influence, I make statements and laws and utter righteous truths. And in my lower moments, I do not abide by them. I forget. I become an empty skeleton into which, so to speak, no ideas breathe.

These days I have blindly struggled with myself and hungered for purer thoughts and nobler sentiments, for that state I remembered vaguely having visited, in the past, which was beautiful compared with the present one.

Today I remembered my own words, which I wrote with a quivering, triumphant pen: "Happiness is a small consideration and seems of little value. I feel a joy beyond joy in the midst of my sorrow, and what I feel while suffering is far beyond contentment —beyond peace—it is something nameless which approaches the divine. . . . In agony, in torment, in despair, through burning tears, I thank heaven that I am suffering, because through the purifying fire of sorrow I shall see the ideal, and I see God. I repudiate ordinary happiness. I want martyrdom and sacrifice, I want something greater than human happiness!"

April 25. I cannot write of my love. Each time I approach it, I seem to melt in pity and reverence. But it is joy to be consumed by flaming adoration.

Hugo and I have long and heated discussions on all topics. Last night he said half in jest that I was too materialistic for him. Fatalism and materialism, these are what I have swung towards, pendulumlike, and it will be curious to observe whether I shall swing once more away from them or remain enmeshed till the end of time.

It cannot be; I shall pass through materialism as I have before passed through all unworthy states. But I fear that fatalism is more deeply rooted, for it is not a mere conclusion reached by reasoning; it is beyond that—it is a *feeling*, as clear and as strong as any faith, that scorns and evades all proofs and weighing.

I read somewhere an enlightening definition: "Mal de siècle, dégoûté de la vie, cette maladie nait, comme on le voit, de la prépondérance dangereuse que prend l'imagination dans une vie desoeuvrée!"[1]

It took me so much paper, pen and pains to reach the same conclusion!

It is at once inspiring and discouraging to discover that "Michelangelo aimait s'entourer de gens differents à tous."[2] The human being is pleased to find support. The creator is distressed to find himself preceded. Perhaps that is why I can never be wholly satisfied with anything. There is no *unity* in me, I am not *whole*. It is amusing to be composed of fragments; there is always the hope that some of them may be lost. But would I like to be purely woman or purely writer, purely mind?

I might become bored. At least I now may experience the enchantment of eternal variety—not forgetting the agony of perpetual conflicts—which, as some say, also exist for the purpose of saving us from *boring* perfection.

The writer feels perhaps more grateful than others for that mercy which provides for a new life with the beginning of each day. I say the writer because his faults are doubled in comparison with those of ordinary mortals, and they are more difficult to efface. He sins in act, and sins in the writing of his sins, which magnifies and fixes them.

I often think of the man who was thought great by his fellows, deeply reverenced and intensely praised, and all because *he did not talk*. His silence permitted others to interpret him. Often when

[1] "*Mal du siècle, distaste for life, this illness is born, as one can see, from the dangerous preponderance of imagination in a person who leads an idle life.*"
[2] "*Michelangelo liked to surround himself with people different from all the rest.*"

silent, I have won the deepest appreciation, have heard many interpret my ignorance as wisdom, my indolence or indifference as a wondrous calm or depth of thought. Were I to remain silent, I might retain these opinions. Instead I thoughtlessly write my own condemnation and reveal my faults to those who love me. Is this not the first step in the renunciation of self and vanity, and do I not owe this tribute to Truth, which I profess to worship?

It is a pleasant feeling to reach a limit in a talk when the intelligence can travel no further. It gives one the sense of having traveled some distance and reached something—even if it be a limit.

May 1. This day marks the beginning of a new development in my writing. I have earnestly begun a play and completed the first scene.

To Eduardo:

For a moment, as a keen contrast to your kind of life, mine seems to be evolving outside the bounds of literature. Yet no, it seems rather to remain permeated with the intense coloring of literature, but to have ceased breathing within it. By that I mean that we are so absorbed in the living of our own dreams, thoughts, emotions, that we cannot read. Think of it, we are making a home. We are creating our own story henceforward. We are creating the setting and the background. . . . For now the time has come for us to be and have and give all we had dreamed and read about. Now we have a life to lead such as those in the books we love. The moment for which our studies, readings, imaginings, were but a preparation has come, and we realize the importance of it and strive to succeed. . . . Weekends we spend far away from here, in some woods where we find peace and can worship nature. We take books along but never read. We either sit silent, drinking in the tender sunlight filtering through the leaves, or talk quietly of deep, absorbing things. . . .

June 30. A dream fulfilled. We have at dusk sat with hands clasped, Hugo's head upon my breast—he listening and I reading from my old journals.

We have once more lived through the entire past. From the moment of our first meeting, and our discoveries, difficulties, joys and disappointments, fears and doubts, until the present moment, still unwritten . . .

July 4. My aunt has come.[1] She brings many stories of those people I once was so deeply interested in, and a flood of memories.

With her coming, the ever increasing tension and agony of my contact with Mother is brought to a climax. Last night the pain became overwhelming; I felt a chasm opening between us such as no material separation can equal. I slept with my head on Hugo's breast, and only the realization that it was as much my obligation to live for him as it was before to live for Mother, prevented a mortal despair from crushing me.

Mother no longer grieves over my loss. She grieves over the will and dominance I do not submit to. I made her happy before by living a subdued, submissive life, and now, although I give her more materially and spiritually (for I am able to help her and be with her more), she is not satisfied. I write bluntly, out of the bitterness of my soul, for I am crushed by the cruelty of her unreasoning.

I have spared no effort; I have been thoughtful of her every need. She has, if she truly loved me, the assurance that Hugo is as good to me as she could dream.

Her will alone, her unbending will, towers above her truest feelings and blinds her to the crime. For she breaks my health and poisons my joys, and Hugo suffers with me.

July 6. My aunt's good sense and masterful, convincing expressions of it are working upon Mother's mind. I owe her more than all those visible gifts the world can see . . . so much that I will wait for a peaceful day when I may tell you about it with a clearer mind.

July 7. My thoughts do not linger now on lofty subjects or universal problems. They do not concern themselves with all-embracing principles and laws or truths. It is a curious phase, to study this transition between the high-pitched voice of earlier years, criticizing, philosophizing, concluding, dealing with things large, wide, abstractedly; and then, after much converse, much disquietude and loud expressions of intentions, opinions and decisions, to be placed in the heart of true life itself and set to act.

July 9. Musing on a book review from which I gathered a curious definition of genius: "excess of vitality or of emotion or of imagination . . ."

[1] *Tia Antolina, a sister of A.N.'s mother who lived in Cuba.*

This suits as well the one who writes without talent—who writes urged by a nameless pressure—a creature such as I myself might be. With this difference: that I know what urges me—the excess of feeling and imagination, the overflowing, at which I wondered when I believed it unnatural, nay, condemnable.

Today I was gripped by the sharp, stunning sense of unreality and paused in the midst of my life and work, suspended as it were.

Looking upwards, I was flooded in my old dreams, my half-spoken dreams of love and home and life. Looking down, I was dazzled by the realized picture. I saw Hugo dreaming from the pillowed depths of his armchair, watching the smoke curling from his pipe. A jet-black kitten with glossy fur, a yellow bow around his neck and yellow eyes lay on a black-and-yellow pillow at his feet. A soft breeze quivered through the soft-green curtains. Sunshine lay in patches over the Persian rug and the dark furniture, and its light was reflected in a large mirror over a bureau, and with it the books within the bookcase and the books on the table. In the mirror, too, I saw the reflection of a vase of yellow flowers, the yellow and black lampshades.

Not far off is our bedroom—warm, rose-walled, gray-curtained, soft as a nest of softest feathers. We sleep in the very heart of a velvet-petaled rose, whose stem and leaves we live in when awake and wish to read or write.

Extending from midway up the stem are the little kitchen and bathroom. The first, white and dazzling, has a window with red curtains, framing boxes of red geraniums and trailing ivy. We eat there mornings, and the sun pours into it, cheerfully.

July 13. I read of women who give as a reason for their continued interest in work after their marriage the fact that they become restless and bored and lonesome in their houses. I could scarcely believe my eyes. I find an ever deepening joy in solitude and have too much with which to fill my time—to read, to study, to write, to sculpture, to sing and dance—so much, I wish my days and life were longer, and I envy those who have too much time on their hands.

Enric[1] played for us at Mother's house and played to perfection. He shall some day receive the tributes due him; some he has

[1] *Enric Madriguera, a young violinist who is in love with A.N.*

already, in Spain and Havana. I marvel too at his mental growth. He has gained remarkable understanding and breadth of vision, and also a firmer hold on solid things and facts. The vague dreams in which he continually indulged when I knew him have dispersed like mists. This was no surprise to me. I have seen the same change, in principle, take place in Eduardo's character.

Enric is also more interesting and even more charming. His eyes, gestures and voice are expressive of the multitude of emotions which move his bow. His temperamental irregularities are no longer perplexing and mysterious, but they deepen the color of his individual character and strongly influence those around him, attracting and holding interest.

He is no longer a talented boy whose place in life and whose fate are subject to vague suppositions—he is a genius who, whether recognized or ignored, will place an ineffaceable stamp of his passage in the world. I bow before his achievement. He has done more than I. He has already given to the world a glimpse of the inspirations and visions that visit him, and he has the power to enrich others' lives with hours of beauty.

His music roused my longings to pour out in writing all that comes to me in such overwhelming fullness; this grows day by day until it will become stronger than I, and I shall be swept away, joyfully. What retains me now are such worldly and human considerations as should dissolve in the white heat of so divine a calling.

August 31. I come to you, dear journal, with an apology. I have mangled and cut into you mercilessly, have left you deprived of half your belongings. I have no longer added pages to your book; rather, I have torn them from you. And even in your poverty you have still that elusive and inexplicable way of retaining your power and your character. You are still alone and unsurpassed in that you are the most intimate, if not the most complete, of the reflections of my changing self.

All because I have written a book,[1] which on the 24th of this month, having been begun on the first, reached its 184th page.

During those long days of unbroken and copious overflowings, I had no time to turn to any other writing. Mind and soul, like a sunflower, pointed only one way, which I followed so intensely that I reached the climax and may therefore rest.

[1] *A novel called* Aline's Choice.

September 1. I will someday write a story of how a woman can love two men; how she can receive one kiss while dreaming of the other's lips; how she can gaze into one face with love while remembering another face; how she can fall asleep in the arms of one and dream of the other. How one letter may evoke the most exalted devotion, and she may a moment later open the door to the other and receive him with tenderness.

Such a thing is possible.

September 7. I have moments of doubt and discouragement. At such times Hugo has faith and strength for me and he supports me. He listens to me when I read him what I have written at night, and sometimes I am thrilled to find that I can lift the weight of weariness from his shoulders, that I can excite his imagination and touch his soul.

So has love risen above my devotion to writing, for I find that the latter depends upon the first and draws its élan and inspiration from it alone.

Eugene approves of my work. Eduardo is breathless with surprise and expectation. While I work I think only of those who have faith in me, although ultimately my writing is directed at those who have no faith in what I uphold.

I would like my book better if someone else had written it.

September 17. West Shokan, Ulster Co., N.Y. Once more among the mountains and not far from Woodstock. My Love and I are going to visit the place where I was at once so happy and so sorrowful, but we are now interested because I have written of it in my book.

Its nearness keeps me in constant remembrance of my writing, which is a cause of pain, for often I do not have the heart for it, and yet it seems criminal to waste one day, nay, one hour, through sheer laziness.

September 25. The desire returns; the book progresses now, and it is in its last phase of retouching and perfecting. I have crowded into it a young woman's whole life and many ideas, many moods and numberless emotions—also characters that have flitted about me. If I were asked to name my greatest difficulty, I should unhesitatingly say: omission. To omit was my problem, for I had too much of everything, including adjectives and split infinitives!

The labor of it was tedious enough—that I cannot deny—but I cannot describe, on the other hand, the joys I derived from my own book's favorite passages. I have privileged chapters which thrill me, even though I have written them myself.

Somehow now my entire literary life hangs on the fate of this book. Its failure would destroy it; its triumph would mark the beginning of endless production, for I feel it in me to produce generously, at least, if not wisely.

Oh, that someone might pick it like a wild flower and see in it not the perfection of the hotbed rose but the vivid color of spontaneous growth. For this I pray, and also that the world and the critics and the editors might not detect my twenty youthful years—as I detect them and self-consciously turn up my nose at the sight of them.

Why am I ambitious? Why am I no longer content to write in my journal and for my own ears? Why has my voice swelled and increased in volume, as have my once timid desires and purposes?

First, because the time is ripe to fulfill my mission. Second, because I want to bring happiness to Mother.

October 14. Eduardo came from Harvard to read my book, and again his charm delighted me, and I find the hours short.

Eugene, the other night, read us a written criticism of the book, and the criticism was a far better piece of writing than you could find in any of my chapters.

Alas, I am again turning to my old ways. For a long time I was sustained by my Love's praise and reflected the faithfully burning flame of hope my writing has aroused in him, but now I am descending gradually and sadly, and I no longer believe in my book.

October 16. I have heard it said that the sign of an artist in literature is one who loves his writing. Can it be then I am more of a writer (I cannot say artist, though the definition suits me) than a woman? For when all comfort fails me, when even the tender watchfulness of my Love is not sufficient, then I feel that unreasoning sadness. Hugo has his crises too, and they return at almost regular periods, but they react upon his health, his work, his love. Mine are inward, silent, and they consume my soul, they gnaw within me constantly, progressing fearfully like a ravaging fever.

October 18. Maurice de Guérin describes the feeling which assailed him after a long conversation in which he participated whole-heartedly. It was as if he had lost something which he had until then retained in himself, as if he had thrown away part of his heart. That same feeling comes to me as a result of having written a book. You give so much of yourself, you share so much of your soul, and it all goes to people who do not understand, who are waiting to criticize, to dissect your style, to measure the ticking of your heartthrobs.

But I suppose this is one of the writer's pains, and no mission is fulfilled without labor and suffering.

This sense of loss, of having revealed secret and intimate thoughts, of standing naked before the world, would be unendur-able to me but for the consolation of my journal, in which I know there are still feelings that shall never be discovered or misinter-preted. Somehow I can shut my door upon the entire world and find an inviolable shelter still, and the depths of my soul are mine and virgin yet.

This is indeed not the true emotion of an artist. An artist gives without thought of himself; his whole soul he offers to the world. I must learn. It is that I am not yet trained in endurance. Criticism and misunderstanding, although my mind accepts them, pushes me into my shell again, wounded and quivering. I must forget myself and my sensitiveness. I am here to serve the world. I want my written words to resound far and wide, I want to speak what I have been sent to speak and give all that I have in myself, which is not mine but given me to communicate and to share. I want to write until my mission is fulfilled.

But meanwhile I shrink from the pain. I pray for courage. At night I sorrow with the weakness of a woman, when I should exult in the struggles of mind reaching out towards its visions.

October 23. One time, when I was pressed for work while posing because I had been forced to refuse an artist who disappointed me by his coarseness, I attempted to visit a painter who, I had heard, painted only his wife and had written a successful story for Scribner's. Encouraged and interested by the latter statement, I disregarded the first, and it was thus I met one afternoon a man whom I count now among my friends.

I was dazed and shy at the time, and the first quality with which Richard F. Maynard impressed me was his gentleness. Then, too, on his large studio walls hung portraits of many women, as I would have liked to paint them, and there were many books. The pleasing surroundings inspired an instant sympathy in me towards the man whose character they represented.

He engaged me, and I posed for a little statuette.

When I first met him he struck me as a man much drawn into himself. Yet something in me inspired his confidence, and without introduction, the flow of our conversation was directed at the very things I understood and liked to talk about.

He was experiencing a certain isolation, which troubled him, for he felt the desire to mingle with people, to find a comfortable friendship, a free intercourse on the subjects dear to him. He felt the suffocation I knew when a certain quality of talk is long repressed, and he told me he was grateful to me for the spiritual freedom I was giving him by my very presence.

We showed each other our writing. He, gray-haired and older in experience, and I, still sounding the facts of life, met however on a common ground of interest and answered each other's questions and gave each other the sum of our knowledge and points of view.

I listened to his more practicable philosophy of life, his solutions to problems, his manner of overcoming obstacles of a material kind.

He, on the other hand, admired my freedom from actuality, which he thought left my spirit marvelously free and strong. He compared me to a lantern shining in so transparent a holder that one could forget the form and color of it and see only the light. In short, he thought of me as more of a spirit than a human creature. He was certain that my spiritual life, developed and cultivated, would influence those around me.

And then he gave me these four words to ponder on, as holding in themselves a vast plan of life: Attention. Purpose. Faith. Love.

Attention to purpose, which should lead to success, faith in self; and love, in the general sense of the word, as a virtue through which we should judge our acts and by which we should give the whole course of our life. That is what I made them out to mean.

At a time when I was so troubled and perturbed by outward events, his calm was soothing and his ideas illuminating. I felt that although he did not know all of me, he knew perhaps the most important, and that is what moved me to ask him to paint my portrait when I returned.

Incomplete as this description is, it may give you an idea of the man in whose company I spent three mornings a week. And now that I have the outline, I can more carefully attend to the details and the shading.

Even when studying my Love in the coolest light, I cannot modify a quality which is constantly and vividly intensified by contrast with ordinary men: it is his finesse and delicacy of thought, such as one would find in beautiful poetry. He is sensitive like a woman, possessing the quick discernment and sympathy usually attributed to women, by comparison with that toughness of texture found in man. When I watch his eyes I see in them feelings subtle and uncommunicable, which stir and tremble faintly and continuously. Delicacy in woman is in character with her nature; in man it is one of those rare and priceless qualities which make him such a lover as are described in legends and fairy tales and which are entirely unbelieved and unexpected in a husband.

October 25. One accusation brought against Mother and which in the same breath serves as an apology for the meagerness of her achievements is that she is first a woman and then an artist. I would so desire my life to be a refutation of this. Does this not seem inconsistent with my past ideas?

Woman is asked to remain wholly woman by finding love all-sufficient, devoting herself solely to it, while in a corner the artist weeps with shame, and failure peers at her.

Yet Hugh is of all men the least selfish in this respect. He urges me to write, he helps me, he inspires me, he dreams of making it possible for me to write all day if I so desire. Yet if I told him that my mental activity is a source of unearthly exaltation to me, he would ask me: "Is it so great a joy to you as our moments together?" And I would surely kiss him and say: "No, my darling, nothing can equal those moments."

Yes, I am woman. Yet in my moments when the artist reigns supreme and the ecstasy of creation carries me to unbelievable spheres, then I know that my soul belongs to Art, that it is Art I worship and Art I live for. Writing holds my entire being in the palm of its hand.

The woman artist sees at last the dawn of her achievement grow near. Then love slips his hand around her hand, she drops her pen and he leads her quietly away, murmuring: "Come away with me to watch the stars and the pale moon."

That is why woman remains woman while man can be an artist.

October 29. Richard Maynard believes the artist to be the most practical of all men, for he knows what he wants, seeks it and attains it, even if it is not the same thing that the so-called practical man is seeking. Of these men, few know what they want and most follow the herd blindly.

Returning to Maynard, he is most interesting when he talks of painting, for then he is inspired. He is more of a scholar when he refers to writing, for he is dominated by what he has learned of writing and writes accordingly rather than by inward urging.

It is when he is in his studio that I best understand him, for he expresses himself fully in painting, in writing and in his surroundings.

The studio itself is characteristically harmonious. The bronze or burnt-gold walls, soft-green pillows and velvety couches, a long, narrow table in the center with a blue candlestick at each end, old-fashioned chairs, the books all about, the fireplace, the gold-framed mirrors and paintings, the soft-green hangings—all these are of flawless taste and quiet, soothing charm.

October 30. (Written while traveling in the subway.) Journal writing is the cause of bad habits as well as good ones. Perhaps because of the usual human weakness which urges one to lay the blame on others for one's blunders, I, today, thus accuse you of the fault I have been reproached for:

"Make your people walk in a real world," some beg me.

"Give us more concrete, pictorial writing," cry the others.

"Give us tangible background," etc.

Despite all my minute descriptions, I have yet allowed myself to float over these pages in a most ethereal manner. To all appearances, I never eat, I have no bed to sleep on. No one knows where I live or whether I do live as human beings do. Mind, mind alone, has seemed to evolve and struggle.

This fleshly body of mine also walks upon the earth and with no light step. For a while it had its abode in a small apartment and traveled forth from Forest Hills to Kew and from Kew to the city.

I must mention, in continuation of the Forest Hills episode, that there my soul had found a home, but that it could not remain because the rents were too high.

Then for a while we again floated—no, I forget, we stayed at West Shokan two weeks and ate at a boardinghouse and from there came to Mother's house—but now comes the transformation. For the first time I shall feel truly settled, with my feet firmly rooted into the ground. My whole shiftless nature will be riveted to the earth, and joyously so.

Because we shall have a home, a true, true home. It is situated about a block away from Mother's house, and it is little and red-roofed and only one story high. Properly speaking, it is a bungalow. However, it has a fireplace and a patch of garden and a dollhouse porch and gables. Anyone in a house like this can assuredly be very happy, provided she has a dog, a typewriter, wood for the hearth (and food, of course) and, last, a husband, a nice, tall man with kind eyes and a protective air, who comes home at night and kisses her fondly and tells her he loves her more today than yesterday—that would complete the home. And I have all these things.

The entrance of our dog, Laddie (a collie), into the family I have inexplicably failed to record. We bought him during our vacation. He is like a giant fox, with long gold-brown and pure-white hair and a fine, pointed head and ears that stand up straight like attentive sentinels.

There you have it all, husband, house, dog and fireplace—all concrete, pictorial, substantial, earthly—a heart-satisfying page for those who lament my unbalanced descriptions of things and people.

December 21. A year ago I was a girl—and all Christmas night I danced, sang and drank wine with the others. And at midnight, when the hour was struck on a gong, my heart filled with sorrow, regret and longing.

All the things I then desired I have today. This Christmas at midnight I shall be in church upon my knees—a woman, a wife—with my mother on one side and my husband on the other. And · afterwards we shall come home and give to each other such things as we have obtained through our own labor. Our lives are beautiful and active. Whatever difficulties Mother has to bear are but because of money, and we help her bear them.

Heaven has indeed blessed me, I, so unworthy. It has filled my life with indescribable riches. Yet it is not to rejoice that I mention its blessings. Fatalism has entered irrevocably into my soul. I look upon my happiness with awe and silent fear. Heaven, which at once metes out cruel punishment and undeserved charity, how shall it play with me?

December 28. It seems to be in my nature to resist joy, yet I suppose it is consistent with my creed of sorrow. But even when my creed was first formulated, it was followed a few hours later by my rejoicing over some pleasure or other.

Today, then, I wish to confess another. This morning I had just finished dusting and ordering and was standing in the parlor, surveying the appearance of the room, when an ineffable joy overwhelmed me and I had to sing. Was any girl ever so blessed as I?

Hugh during the night kissed me in his sleep and woke me.

"What do you want?" I asked vaguely.

"Love, love, love," he murmured in his dream and kissed me again.

And then this morning, early, he left me, as he does every morning, his last words always tender and his last kiss remaining with me the whole long day.

Loving husband, little house and sweetest home—Oh, I am happy, so, so happy! My Love is happy, too. I can see it in his eyes and in his eagerness to come home at night. He has told me that I have given him more than he ever dreamed of, that I have filled his life with sweetness. Some evenings he does nothing but sit by my side and whisper pretty phrases. His poet's soul has made an eternal lover of him; his detachment from his family has allowed me to cherish him as a mother and sister—and I am alone in the care of him, and his entire heart belongs to me.

December 31. Each year I have felt more keenly the unimportance of time and dates. Solemnity on the occasion of the New Year appears to me more and more ridiculous. In some way life has become so vast, so limitless, so eternal to me—the years have become so full—that they seem like many thousand lives in themselves.

Another year? What of it? Do we live and grow by the hour? Do we not in a moment sometimes age years through an experience? Do we not in a year sometimes move not a step further than where we stood before?

I was not sixteen when I met my Love—I was a child. The

five months I spent in Havana did not make me five months older, but a woman.

Last night my Love was happy, for I read him of our life together, as my journal writing has pictured it. Fired by my example, he again wrote in his own journal, which he keeps but fitfully, and I grew tired of waiting for him to finish and fell asleep.

Eduardo was here and we were with him Friday and Saturday. In my heart of hearts I sometimes fear for our friendship. When Eduardo loved me his romantic nature was satisfied. He is still devoted to me, but time is slowly molding our devotion into one of a purely mental character. My marriage has stamped it definitely as such. And Eduardo is not all intellect. As I watch his character grow, I notice the ever growing strength of his emotions and I wonder . . . for I see it as certain that he will slowly turn towards the fulfillment of his romantic impulse—that this will occupy his life to the exclusion of all other interests. I even doubt he will seek the union of intellect and beauty in his love. The latter is continually blinding him to the former. I see it in his choice of books and of poetry. Thought, philosophy, color, movement, form, sound, beauty of word—to these his nature is keenly attuned.

Woman is symbolical of these. I represented them to him, even though he liked to spiritualize me. Today I am only mind and spirit. Lately he told me I had beautiful eyes. And then he was embarrassed, and he lowered his eyes and said: "I should not notice these things any more. Read to me from your book."

Yes, Eduardo, I shall read to you from my book until the princess comes—not I, whom you once thus designated, not the storyteller, but the story itself.

And so like [Oliver] Goldsmith I shall sing of love and of one love in which I can have no share.

Nothing hurts Hugo more deeply than for me to speak of the day he will no longer love me, nor I him. He cannot understand that I should doubt, when I am in love and so certain of his love for me today. He does not understand that half-mystical, half-cynical lack of faith I have in the endurance of anything beautiful.

He sees wells of unfathomable and boundless sorrow in my eyes. I have heard of nuns who retire into the convents merely to pray for the sins of the world. I must have been made to sorrow over the passage of beauty and the loss of all the things the poets love, and to sorrow for the agonies of the world. That is why my eyes are so infinitely sad that everyone notices it, comments on it and paints it. . . . The spirit of Marie Bashkirtsev[1] has taken possession of me, lingering so long upon myself as a subject for description. For the resemblance to be complete I need only to do so flatteringly. But I can't go far.

❦ 1 9 2 4 ❧

January 4. The passage of time works a strange alchemy out of the drugs of the mind, and it makes memory something like a sieve through which experience passes—the subtle and fine, like a powder, runs through and is lost while the stronger impressions remain. I was thinking today of Havana and of how all I remember of it these days is the beauty—which invariably raises in me a joyous emotion.

And in my books I want to fix the beauty to which my memory clings, for it has seemed to me today as if this selection is what makes poetry. I want to write, first of all, as a poet. I want to make just such a selection, cast a mist about the molded thing. I want things to appear not as if I had seen them but as a vague picture into which the ugly and the weak had crept, unperceived almost, and taken their place—as they do in life.

January 16. My mother has gone to Havana!

How unexpected and how revolutionizing. In five days she was ready, after receiving a telephone call from Tia Antolina, who does not feel well and wants Mother to help her with an asylum[2] she has built. And Mother, who has suffered through long winters of cold and poverty and worry, has turned as I turned to lovely Havana, with all her hopes and faith. I am happy for her sake, though I miss her so that I have not slept for several nights, thinking of her. I am happy because *she* was happy to leave her gloomy house, her debts, her persecutors (creditors, etc.) and the cold.

---

[1] *Russian painter and diarist.*
[2] *The Asilo Rafael de Cárdenas was a day school for underprivileged children that A.N.'s Aunt Antolina built on her ranch property in Havana.*

Everything is bearable but the separation—but it will last six months and we shall fill them well with work, and Mother will return with the summer roses.

Joaquin[1] has gone with her. Thorvald[2] and I have charge of her house, and he eats with us in the evenings. I want to make a success of my charge for Mother's sake, and the managing of the house (renting the rooms, etc.) will henceforward be one of my chief occupations. My beloved little mother—if she could only find happiness there and the means to make her burden lighter.

January 27. The shadows have returned. I have to struggle against the old crises of despondency which used to alter my life so frequently. Again the feeling of infinite weariness and physical helplessness, more acute even, more hopeless. I lie in bed thinking of all I want and must do and feel the malaise of my physical being slowly penetrating my mind and dragging my thoughts into dark abysms.

Yet I love activity. I have driven myself for days and accomplished unbelievable things, and while the spirit sustains me I work with feverish intensity. Then suddenly it leaves me, and the world seems to grow dark and oppressive, and nothing seems to hold me to life any longer. I drift, I feel weak and agonizingly tired.

I am ashamed and don't want to write, yet I must write because it helps me, and then I have no need of burdening any loved one with my black hours.

January 31. The same influence that Mother's big house had on her spirits, oppressing her with interminable labor, worrying her, now affects me. I had been freed of it, I had my little house, my Love to care for. Now the care of Mother's house wears my strength away. I have to rent the rooms. The occupants of the apartment have turned out to be fiendishly trying and inconsiderate. People came all day today; each one is a problem, and those problems are increasing. When you think things will run smoothly, another evil breaks out in the most unexpected corner. The upkeep, renting, watching of that huge house, are maddening. Today I reached the climax of discouragement. Creditors press us on all

---

[1] *A.N.'s younger brother.*
[2] *Her older brother.*

sides. The promised money does not come. The rooms are all empty, and I have done so much to make them attractive.

Outwardly, little journal, things go well. That is why you must suffer my lamentations. I can act before everybody, but not for *myself*, which is what *you* are.

In a little while I shall be serving my husband and brother dinner and we'll lightly talk over things and pass from them to other subjects.

I wish I had more courage. The big house with all its cares has made me feel small and weak, although until today I had been active and tremendously stubborn, and although tomorrow I shall be just the same. It is only during these wee, lost minutes that I despair, and in a moment I will be strong again.

I think the cause of this weakness is that added to the struggle against ordinary defeats, I have to master a disgust towards all struggles of this kind—practical, financial—which involve contact with people, counting money, and demonstrations of strength for the benefit of those who watch for an opportunity to trample you.

I would rather be struggling over my book. If I succeed with the house, what will it mean? I will have carried on the business at a profit, paid off debts. There is a vast difference. But I suppose the noble is always the loathed task. I wanted to do something for Mother. Am I now going to cry out?

February 2. I cried myself to sleep last night while my Love whispered the tenderest words he knew and kissed my tears and stroked my burning forehead. Today I am strong again and wishing I had enough energy to give some time to my poor, neglected book.

Mother writes, hurried and not too happy, and her situation but confirms my resolutions.

These are strange days, when I look at them calmly. My Love leaves me early in the morning, and by 9 o'clock I have finished my housekeeping. The rest of the day is divided among many things: I have to embellish the rooms not yet rented, show them continually, answer mail, do some accounting and book-keeping, do marketing for both houses, make beds in both houses, half prepare Thorvald's breakfast for the next day, interview creditors, return to my house when I have time and wash clothes and iron and mend, and then it is time to prepare dinner and wash more dishes. In between, I wash and sew curtains and light the fire in our furnace when it goes out, water and tend my seeds, brush Laddie's long hair and feed the canary bird.

By evening, when my dinner simmers and waits, I am agonizingly weary and I wait eagerly for my Love's footsteps on the path, his familiar rapping on the door, and for his kisses, which make me forget my weariness.

This reunion after a long day of absence is indescribably sweet. Hugh,[1] while he eats, tells me about his day of business, pausing when he comes upon an agreeable morsel, to chew on it more leisurely, and his eyes shine and he smiles like a boy and tells me what a good cook I am.

We always make elaborate plans for the evening: we either expect to finish the book, or write in our journals, or write several letters we have on our conscience. But exactly what becomes of these plans it is difficult to tell, for we invariably do nothing. We sit on the divan in the studio and talk and dream and play, or I dance for him, or we figure out how long it will take us to pay off our first mortgage and speculate on how soon my Love's salary will be raised, and then we permit ourselves the luxury of making plans for the future and tell each other what we shall do with our wealth. And then I sew on a button I had forgotten and we wind the alarm clock, undress, open the window and go to bed, to wake again at 6:30 a.m.

February 4. In a few days I shall end a whole year's story in one volume. This alone is a proof of my neglect, for at one time I could fill a larger book than this in one month.

The discovery has bewildered me. Again the thoughts I had the other day while I sat mending by my sunny window return to me. My journal lay near me, on the desk, and the sight of it set me wondering, for I sometimes doubt that this can be considered a complete record of a life. Not because I have not written every day, but because I have not written *all* day, every hour, every moment. Only thus could it be complete. The moment I catch and fix, when I can spare a few minutes and sit down to write, is only one of the thousands which go into the making of a day. Thus I miss completeness. And also because there is so much that never occurs to me to write of. This unconscious selection and elimination is the result of character. I am inclined either to dwell on what I love or to seek remedy against the things I do not love.

[1] *From this point, A.N. refers to her husband by his true name, Hugh.*

But life is not composed of extremes, and it is usually under the power of such an extreme that I run to my journal. Too often it is the overflow of either joy or sorrow and too seldom the calm flow of these many things which stand between the extremes.

Some things I cannot conceive writing of because they are so obvious, so closely knitted to my being that I cannot look at them. One of these, for instance, is a thing seldom mentioned and which yet does influence my life perhaps more strongly than anything else—my love for my mother.

My pen travels through the darkness like a firefly. But all around it is space, of which no one knows the limitations, the meaning. There is more around the firefly than those little spots of light which its passage betrays. The whole of a human being, however much he may write or talk, still remains hidden in the space and darkness.

February 5. It is true that I have abandoned my book. When I have a little time that I might give it, I do not have the power to suddenly adjust myself and attune my mind for a task so different, but it truly seems as if the selfsame creative spirit which so ardently moved me to write now flows into other forms with as much fire.

I want to make my home so beautiful and my Love so happy. I create now with my fingers, with every stitch of sewing, every touch of a painting brush, with scissors and cardboard, with pots and brown earth and seeds—and as I work, my thoughts revolve around the picture of my home as it will be soon. Every room has thus been born of careful thought, and I have thought of each room as a little work of art upon which I have spent as much imagination and labor as I would upon a book.

Every detail I have lovingly planned. My luxurious tendencies have been checked by my limited allowance, but then I have had to use ingenuity and trickeries, for I would not surrender the "effect" my mind first created, the picture I sought to achieve.

And when I survey the results, the harmonious colors, the curve of a pillow, the placing of a chair, the swaying of a tassel, I wonder how people can speak of homemaking as a drudgery.

Now and then my hands grow roughened and scratched, and my fingers worn with needle pricks. These are only the pains attending creation. When I write, my fingers also ache and my body grows weary and my head burns and my eyes are filled with mists. Yet I would not give up my writing. Neither would I abandon the creation of our home, in which our love exists.

February 21. My twenty-first birthday! I was just wishing that my writing were larger. I am eager to finish this notebook so that I might write in a new one my Love has given me.

Yesterday I again took up the work on my novel, which, when I *do* work, progresses at a terrifying pace. John Erskine is going to read it. He was Hugh's teacher at college, and my Love and I admire his writings intensely. I just dread the day he will read my book, and I wonder whether he will denounce me publicly as a defiler of the pure English language.

Hugh helps me so much in my writing. At first I used to question his opinions and have sham quarrels. Now I have grown to rely on him. He gives me the freedom I want, but he also knows how to restrain me, how to express my thoughts better sometimes.

Always these few minutes to dream over the day—while I wait for my Love's footsteps on the path, while my dinner simmers on the fire. And my home is clean and neat and there is something I have made to show Hugh, a bit of sewing, and a new chapter to read him. I am living a life full and complete, as a wife and as an author.

February 29. I have only a few minutes before I leave for the city, where I shall pose for Richard Maynard. He always says that I make him think. I am not quite sure that this is exactly what he means, for I have analyzed his influence upon my own self and find that he *reawakens* my thoughts when they are dull and sleepy. By this I may be insinuating that neither one tells the other anything new, which is, accidentally, exactly what I do mean.

I first thought of that the other day while he was speaking to me, and I suddenly wondered whether, after all, *reminding* people was all we could do now if we believe that all things have been thought and expressed in the past. This set me wondering about what exactly takes place when we read, or listen to a talk. It seems to me that a vast source of knowledge and half-conscious learning slumbers continually within us. Certain writing, certain talks, have the power to revivify. Past a certain age, one comes again to the point where one needs to be reminded, where the first, old paths must be retraced. Is this really so? Is the human mind capable of infinite retention? Or, if limited, by what qualities is this power of retention either weakened or strengthened?

March 1. I used to mock the word "concrete," write parodies about it, smile wryly when it was mentioned, and even get impatient when I was plainly told that I lacked that quality in my writing.

Yesterday I had a revelation. I discovered that I really had never understood the word in its broadest sense. I discovered that Hugh was all along thinking of something which I did not grasp at all. I stumbled upon my discovery when I began an entire revision of my novel, which I had not done for some time, and I was struck by a glaring, appalling lack of *something* I did not name then. I set to work and inserted some new passages. When I read them to Hugh, he said simply: "That is what I meant when I asked you to be more concrete."

It seems strange, but it is a fact that I was not able to write like that until I *became* that. I did not understand "concrete" writing until I experienced, independently and spontaneously, a certain definite emotion. Hugh himself says that lately I have become more concrete in my character. Now that I have it in me, I shall at last be able to give it out. This certainly proves that writing emanates from what the author *is*. Simple conclusion! But what a long time it has taken me to reach it!

March 3. A year ago today, my Love slipped a gold ring upon my finger and promised to cherish me and to be true to me. He has filled my life with tenderness, has blessed my days with kisses and the nights with dreams, and a year has passed unclouded by even the smallest misunderstanding. There was never a more devoted husband, a more eloquent lover, a truer friend and companion. So strong, so humble, so loyal he is! I cannot help looking back and in every day I find some sweetness, every day he has loved me. And now I hope that I have made *him* happy, that I have made him feel how loved he is, that I have been to him as much as he has been to me. I am happy today only because he has told me, his eyes have told me, how truly happy he is.

It is in the little things that he is so tender. He remembered this date even before I did. He not only understands sentiment in the way woman does, but he feels it. Again I repeat that the poet in him is what draws him so close to me, for it has given him certain qualities by which our understanding of each other has reached perfection—sensitiveness, delicate sympathy, the power to express emotion—for now the Hugh of today is expressive and warm to a degree I had never dared imagine.

This morning early, as soon as we opened our eyes, we thought of the other morning, a year ago. We asked each other what we had felt and thought then upon awakening, and discovered we had both been dazed, that our hearts beat so fast and our thoughts leaped so, that we hardly knew what we were about.

I dressed myself in the white silk things my godmother made for me. I wore a black dress embroidered with white, a white fur and a white hat with a long veil. When I came out to find Hugh I wanted him to tell me how I looked. But he was silent and I asked him: "Don't you like me?"

"Oh, my darling," he almost cried out, as if I were asking a question he could not answer because he felt so much.

I think we were both equally childish in our tremors and excitement. My hands were cold, and when I signed my name in the big book they trembled fearfully. It was then Hugh gave me my ring.

At the pier, apart from my aunts and uncle, there were only Alfredo Belt and Ramiro Collazo[1] to bid me farewell—I had not wanted more, since my little mother was not there. I remember someone saying a bride should not weep, because I did when I had to say good-bye. Hugh took my arm firmly and we stepped on the ship.

Ah, why should I look back on these things, when I regret that they should be over. I wish I could have them forever—all those emotions, those experiences, those old, faded things, which, only a year ago, consumed us.

April 1. The more I see of other men, the better I appreciate the one to whom I have consecrated my life, the one who has been destined to spare my heart. He is at once so boyish and cultured, so fresh and unspoiled and pure, and yet intensely romantic, intensely loving.

Secretly I always feared the crude, brutish qualities of man, his blundering ways in handling woman's feelings, his sincere but *insensitive* love. Hugh knows when to coax, when to command, when to praise; he is thoughtful and patient; he forgives; he gives in. He has all the ways of the most studied lover; he worships now the queen, now the child. He relies on the knowledge and power of the *mind* and forgives the whims of capricious moods. He listens to and answers the words woman's lips utter when woman wants to speak and kisses them when they want to be kissed. If he displeases me, he is humble; if he makes me happy, he is elated. And

[1] *Apparently friends of A.N.'s during her stay in Havana.*

how sweetly conscious he is of every moment of our love, not as a thing which, by uniting our lives, has served its purpose and can now be discarded, but as the quality that is behind his every act and thought and word.

April 5. There is nothing I desire so fervently just now as the success of my book, for it seems to me that I could in this manner bring joy and peace into my little mother's difficult life. Each time I get a letter from her in which I read discouragement, I pray eagerly that I may soon finish my work.

The greatest of my difficulties has been the constant change that has kept flowing within me in such a way that each day I write differently, and each day I look on the day before as an older critic. The thing I must do now is almost rewrite the entire book quickly enough while one phase lasts, and then leave it for what it is, and not laugh at it.

I am glad of one thing, and that is that I have had the courage to do in my book what I did not have the courage to do in the past, either in my journal or even in my own mind. I have laughed, not too loudly and rather sympathetically, at many foibles, weaknesses and ridiculous traits of people and have made none of my characters angelic and stainless.

Mr. Maynard says that there are two classes of writers, those who destroy false and bad things and those who construct ideals. He seems to fear I belong to the former by right of irony—though I had never expected to develop into a realist, as seems to be the case. That is, I create or reproduce people as I see them, not as I wish them to be. What a wide abysm has sprung between my present attitude and those far-off days of girlhood dreams, when I lived in a world entirely my own, conversing with ideals, with imaginings, not with real people.

Here ends the truest book of all—one written for no human eye and for no human purpose, and because it is such a rough, impulsive, unstudied reflection of life itself, it will prove perhaps those very things I am putting in my formal books—that life is not one thing or another but changes constantly, that character has not one face but a thousand, changing as these pages change, growing as these books have grown, with all the pettiness, inconsistencies, bursts of passion, fits of dejection, periods of exalted activity and of revolting idleness, which these books reflect; with the same egoism, the same weaknesses, the same fears, the same mysteries.

Turn these pages and see whether one spirit pervades them all or whether a different mood each time has left the trace of its passage on a soul which sings and weeps by turn and never truly knows itself in this confusion.

April 9. Having spent nearly a whole afternoon extolling the charms of diary writing to Richard Maynard, it is with renewed vigor that I embark on my new volume.

From this you must not infer that I go about praising and advising diary writing to the masses—far from that. It is just that I have come to the point where I feel that this is the form of expression with which I am most familiar and the one I am most strongly attached to, so that here and there, when I find a nature wasting itself in a "repliement sur soi-même,"[1] through lack of expression of some kind or other, or a man who stands in danger of wrecking his precious inner life through a false attitude towards communion with self, looking inward, I feel that I have tested my own journal long enough to know that it can save a character from both evils. R. Maynard, in a way, suffers from both. No one around him seems able to receive the overflowing of his emotions, and these, with a poetic feeling for many things, he drives back into himself (as Hugh did in the past), and it makes him feel all the pangs of loneliness that it is possible to feel. And besides this he has been acting all his life under an exaggerated principle of inordinate thoughtfulness for others, past the bounds of reason, which has nearly obliterated his own individuality.

An ordinary creature, so self-contained and yet so selfless, might be allowed to pursue its existence with the certainty that it will end a martyr to some cause, or simply a victim on the greedy altar of unselfishness, but R. Maynard is not an ordinary creature—he is an artist and he owes it to art to extricate himself from this life (which in either case leads to oblivion) so that he can create.

I thought the best way I could help him was by teaching him the way to find himself and to gain a freedom from the unuttered thoughts that crowd within him—for these are only a few of the blessings I have derived from these seemingly useless scribblings.

Someday I want to write about this, as a tribute to a much despised form of literature, as an answer to those who have shrugged their shoulders when they saw me bending over a mere

[1] *Withdrawal into oneself.*

diary. I shall try to give diary writing a definite character and a definite place in life, and for the sake of the practical people who have wept over the wasted hours, I shall demonstrate the uses, the purpose, the visibly beneficial effects, of the much deplored habit.

Meanwhile, I am content to enjoy you, and though my manner of enjoyment may have changed considerably since the days when I fancied you a handsome prince visiting me on my mother's porch, the deeper qualities of our intimate talks and association only grows deeper with years, and perhaps I prize you the more.

R. Maynard fears to write things which might be read by others. He asked me if I locked up my books to prevent their falling into other's hands. Unconsciously I have used a sort of protection by generalizing and mentioning not people but abstract ideas, by vagueness when my criticism or judgment was unkind, by maintaining a peculiar impersonality. Of course, I do this less and less now, and there are one or two things that I have not written about (one subject I often long to write about particularly) because they might cause a great deal of trouble. You have to choose between doing harm and your own gratification. Such a choice is rather simple. The freedom gained by writing what must otherwise be stifled is certainly not worth more than the happiness of those around you.

I don't know what I would do if Hugh made me unhappy and I had only my journal for comfort. I guess I would lock you up and write all I needed to write and make a will begging that the journals should be burned unread. Or I'd send them to Eduardo as a birthday present—it is his birthday today—as he gave me most of the books in which I wrote, and he might utilize them for decorative purposes in his library.

April 16. Have spent the day on my book, and my hand aches and my eyes smart and yet I felt an uncontrollable desire to write here, even if but a few lines.

Mother may return any day now and I am anxious to finish the book before she comes. It will soon be almost a year that I have worked on it, on and off, mostly the latter, unfortunately. But I have come up against a serious problem. My writing has changed so tremendously since I began the book that I practically had to rewrite it. There is nothing left of the original copy but two or three chapters! My ideas, feelings, attitudes, philosophies, have changed. Mr. Maynard thinks I am maturing day by day, growing a few inches taller overnight, so that he is wondering what I will grow into within a year or so.

I grow older by the minute—I feel it myself. I see so clearly what I want to write and how I want to write it. I don't feel indecision about anything, somehow, and I tremble to observe my own assurance, the strength I feel while I create, the determination with which I reach out for certain things, the cool way I regard life when I write, the curious way that my idealism has been mixed with my fatalism, so that I can possess the soul of a dreamer and that of a cynic at the same time. Mind and spirit no longer quarrel to rule me—they have so closely united that I judge with my emotions and feel with my mind. Pretty soon I shall believe that there is no distinction between reason and emotion, that ultimately they are one and the same thing.

Meanwhile, I end my book with a note of cynicism, after making my heroine an idealist—she remains one, but I do not.

Hugh often speaks of the things he wants to give me—comforts and luxuries and clothes—and I invariably beg him for only love and the time to write.

He has the most beautiful expression in his eyes sometimes, of utter, infinite goodness, and they are so limpid, so soft, so bright. His eyes are blue when he looks at the sky in the morning, and they are gray-brown at night, and dark when he bends over to kiss me. His eyes and his mouth are what I like best of his exterior. His smile is at once boyish and manly, frank and open and trustworthy.

Another woman might love him some day for all these things, but I think no one will ever understand him as I do. Nor will anyone ever understand me better than Hugh does.

"Why don't you believe our love will last forever?" he always says when I tell him such things as I just wrote. "Because it is too beautiful, too beautiful . . ."

I made him promise to tell me when he did not love me any more, and he chides me for it. This is probably what all lovers have said to each other throughout the ages, but we are as serious about it as they were. I hope my love and I will live long enough together to laugh at these fears of youth. I hope, and I fear.

Did I not waver before promising to be his wife, with the fancy for another[1] blinding me? And memories still haunt me,

[1] *A.N. is referring to her relationship with her cousin Eduardo.*

still rouse me with an inexplicable power. I turn them into literature, but they still live.

April 30. Mother is here! She arrived Friday and since then we
have spent most of the days with each other. The excitement of
the first talks has somewhat subsided, and again life seems to be
flowing on, unevenly and capriciously, but more like the old,
before Mother went away. We want to make her forget the disappointment that the trip has been in a broad sense, for in little
ways it helped her considerably. And that is not so difficult, as
Mother is happy with her children, and I think if it were not for
the financial side of it, our life could be said to be very satisfying.

May 3. As I grow older I become less of a poet and turn to pure
philosophy. Color and sound and scent I feel most keenly always,
but I cannot rave of them as I did before. I am preoccupied with
ideas, with problems, with human nature and the world in general,
with the story I wish to write after my first book.

I have lost the power to enjoy blissfully and thoughtlessly.
Irrevocably now my nature has chosen its serious consciousness—
consciousness of a kind so unspeakably sensitive that there is not a
moment when my mind rests and ceases to think.

Kneeling by my flower beds, I have transplanted tender
seedlings, and with my face almost touching the ground, I have
watched to see that no little stone or hardened earth should bruise
them. And I thought of children, and of the child we want and
must wait for.

June 1. Again I stand by the milestone on the road and hesitate,
not knowing whether I should look backward or forward.

When [Robert Louis] Stevenson mentioned the necessity of
distance and detachment from experience, he should also have
mentioned peace. And this last I lack sorely. I am seated on a
wicker chair in the front part of the white boat which is to take
us to Kingston Point, and from there we are bound for Woodstock.

Behind me a group of musicians plays the latest jazz and the
oldest sentimental tunes known to men. At my right a child dances
on his mother's knees. All around me there is the constant buzz of
wagging tongues. And as a climax, a black-coated man urges us to
join in a Sunday service, giving us pamphlets with songs, such as
"Sunshine in the Soul," etc. And we are now expected to fall into
a religious mood.

It is no wonder I have left the contemplation of my actual life and fallen to musing on the appearances, the ridiculousness and the coarseness of things in general.

Now we pass by the well-known scenery of the Hudson River —so widely advertised in the subways. Some people think it the appropriate time to spoon, and the girls' heads fall on the men's shoulders and the latter's arms encircle waists of varied dimensions. Others have taken to photography, or else to sentimental musing on the scenery.

Hugh, at my left, is distinguishable from other men by the fact that he has dropped the Sunday papers to read Walter de la Mare's *Memoirs of a Midget*.

Fearing to fall into one of Eugene's critical and perhaps intolerant moods or, if not that, fearing a return of the eternal sorrow which is always dormant in me and so easily aroused, I willfully turn my eyes back into the bright and well-filled past.

Oh, dear, the religious service is on, and it was started on its way by an inspiring burst of patriotism—Jews and Christians shouting in falsetto and husky voices the melodious "America." After this tribute to our wonderful country, we now encroach upon our heavenly father's patience by a moist hymn, urged on by the now red-faced black-coated man. In a little while he will expect us to fall into each other's arms.

But I'm getting hungry and do wish we could have our lunch with the nice muffins Mother made for us, the cream cheese, and everything.

This experience I would particularly like to preserve in a little tight-closed jar with a label, for Eugene, on whose keen appreciation I can count.

People on their way to an artists' colony, one a famous banker and the other a novelist, should not be expected to behave like either Jews or Christians on a Hudson River Daylight Boat while a perfectly lovely thermos bottle rocks in our valise.

Poughkeepsie! The orchestra attempts Gounod's "Ave Maria," and then, as the boat partially empties itself, I wearily inquire the time and wonder why it is we can never have anything without trouble and hardship. Woodstock, once we reach it, will compensate us, I suppose.

June 2. Woodstock. It did. We have already enjoyed a peaceful night, a calm, fresh morning, a hearty breakfast, and we visited the pottery shop. Hugh is comparing the real Woodstock with the one of my descriptions.

We have followed a road aimlessly and reached a point where we dominate a view of the village, and here we sit in the shade of a bush, each giving his journal a little attention. I am so happy here with Hugh, and he wants to go over every place I visited alone that year I came and efface the memory of my solitude and the letter he wrote which disappointed me so much. Our life together is more beautiful than I ever dreamed, and I realize it when we do together what I did alone. The love that makes us one enables us to enjoy solitude together. In silence we sit and muse and dream, and the same emotions pass through us, and we do not even seek to explain them to each other.

We are resting, and he calls this freedom, just as I did, and he too finds it beautiful. Our little bungalow and our other life there have receded far into the past. Though we love it, though it was joy to work, is it not this, after all, we work for? Two weeks of idleness among the mountains. Two weeks of peace.

We had reached the point at home when our activities, our engagements, the petty obligations, had formed an endless circle, narrower and narrower each day until we felt stifled and infinitely weary in body and spirit. Nothing could free us but to absolutely break away.

We had an interesting lunch with the talented John Erskine, Professor of English at Columbia and at one time President of the Authors' Club, whose presence intimidated me so much that I could neither talk nor eat, much to the distress of our host, George Gillette, the superrefined product of an exquisite education.[1]

We received and returned visits—the Dubles, a typical modern couple, rich and childless, the man cheated of his desire to give, the woman exulting in her new-found power in business— domineering, intelligent, capable, delightful as a man, not as a woman.

I spent a week nursing Mother, to whom the constant rain and cold gave a severe cold and earache, and feeding my brothers. In between, I posed for Maynard and planned a little party for Ruth Morgan, the young girl who has been stopping at Mother's house all winter and one of the few women I have sincerely admired. She will be back in her home in Canada by the time I return, so I

---

[1] *He was a classmate of Hugh's at St. Paul's School in Garden City, New York.*

spent an exhausting week beautifying our home, hanging lanterns, sewing pillows, and finally, on Friday night we had the little dance, which Ruth, Frances,[1] Johnnie, Thorvald and Boris Hoppe[2] attended. Seeing Boris again set me wondering: how awful is the way in which woman chooses a life, according to the man she marries, each life entirely distinct from others, each so appallingly powerful in the way it swallows her, fixes her in the vast chaos—and, if she makes a mistake, returns her to herself.

With all this, we planned and achieved our garden, enjoyed several intimate evenings with Eugene and saw Johnnie often. Towards the last days I worked with my mind in a haze, weary, weary, and longing for this that I have now.

Just this moment three cows that were grazing nearby came to explore our more immediate surroundings and, incidentally, to give us a once-over. My Love and I appeared quite harmless to them and they walked on, the little bells around their necks jingling in time with their pace. To watch them wander away made us curious as to what lay behind this hill. And so we are off again and shall adopt the same peaceful walk.

Above all, we seem to need rest. We neither think nor feel too much—we vegetate, we feed on the silent beauty of the site and ruminate. I write because I have the desire to write—not because I feel there are any brilliant thoughts in my head which I think worthy of preservation. Therefore, these will be so many pages to be torn off someday when I fall into a critical mood.

We are occupying the same little room in Mrs. Snyder's house, and my Love has just been sitting at the same little table, before the same little window, writing in his journal. He looked up from his writing as I used to do, out into the little street, and watched the passers-by and the mountains and listened to the song of the birds, but he would not let me see what he wrote, saying it was poor. So was what I did, yet I had the courage to put what I thought of Woodstock in my book. It is a matter of boldness. People with no talent and plenty of initiative—of which I am one—seem to get all the work done, while others, Eugene and Hugh, are both silent and do nothing. I told them so one night, and they both smiled—but that was all.

---

[1] *Frances Schiff, a former classmate of A.N.'s with whom she shared the ambition to be a writer.*
[2] *One of A.N.'s former beaux.*

Yet Hugh today spoke of beginning his book here. How happy he would make me! Why are not the best qualities united in the same person? I have the fluency of a chatterbox, the inexhaustibility of a well, and could ramble on uselessly forever. Hugh has none of these, and yet I have faith in his talent. But he writes falteringly, he hesitates, he ponders. On one word he wastes hours. I have the impulse, the energy. Eugene and Hugh, the one with limitless knowledge, the other unique in his thoughts, both stand watching *me*, willing to help me, to redress my crippled phraseology, willing to judge and encourage me.

June 3. The crowing cock woke us at dawn, and after a long night of fragrant peace we rose, not too early, and started to climb Outlook Mountain. Halfway up, the thought of our lunch brought us swiftly back. But not before we had discovered the most shaded and clear-toned brook and the sweetest honeysuckle.

I keep my book and my typewriter under our bed and wish I did not have to see either for a long time.

June 4. On our way home from a trip to the very top of Outlook Mountain, seeing that our feet were sore from walking, we chose to sit under a tree. Hugh, according to a promise he made me, began to write in his journal, while I dozed. But the insects vexed me and I was driven to writing, that I might forget them. At first I thought of begging my Love to resume our walk, but I saw that he had become interested in his writing and I resigned myself to this.

I had hoped that the description of our trip would fall to Hugh. And as it is, I believe I shall refer you to page 19 in his red journal, since I cannot write of our long walk as idealistically as I should. The stones on the way hurt my feet. Once there, my strongest emotion was one of hunger. The precipices at our very feet alarmed me to such an extent that I scarcely raised my eyes to view the delectable valley, but kept them on the narrow trail. And now, though valleys, wide sweeps of abundant vegetation curving upward into the hills and the hills melting into the mountains stretch before me, though a brook swishes somewhere below and the fragrance of many flowers rises from the meadows, though the field at our left slopes gently to the road and invites my thoughts to glide peacefully, a mere handful of vicious insects prevent me from joining the harmonious stillness and from writing. Thus I see life now, watching the valley yet feeling the insects.

June 7. I accomplished two things with great effort—wrote to Mr. Maynard and worked on the Woodstock chapters of my book.

Hugh bathed in the pool—I was too cold to dare it—and just like a boy, when he came out and felt the delicious exhilaration he sang and laughed and teased me, and it made me happy to see him, to watch the color of his face, the new vigor of his body.

He bought me a pitcher of Kentucky pottery, which is of a fascinating blue, an object I had coveted since I came. And now we lie in bed and he is reading, and I watch the light fading with regret, knowing that the pale flicker of the oil lamp is not enough for me to write by. I had so many little things to write. Nothing yet seems to have taken the place of these little confidences, though Hugh and I talk all day and lie awake at night whispering things to each other for which we had no time in Richmond Hill. We have amused each other by going over each step of our story since the first night we met. "And what did you think of me that night? —Did you like me for my face?—When did you first know you loved me?—Did you used to pass the house on purpose, just to see me?—How often did you dream of me?—Did you expect me to be as I am? Or were you disappointed? No? Well, agreeably surprised, then?"

June 15. Our last day—our last hour rather. I sit on a flat rock by the stream, while Hugh bathes. We have just been talking about Woodstock, about the feeling we both have that we want to *realize* the place, return home with a satisfying certainty that while we were here, we knew we were here and we noticed everything, that our minds did not travel within a hazy shell of its own making.

Usually when people live in the city they are thinking of the country, and when in the country, of the city. The New Yorker dreams of Paris while the Parisian wonders about New York. And we go through life without definitely realizing any place. They all remain unreal to us. We speak of the sensation that our visit somewhere was like a dream. It happens sometimes, too, that the novelty of it is too sharp for our slow-moving senses, and when we recover from the shock, it is already time to go. It demands distance to see the thing as a whole.

June 18. Monday the 16th Mother signed a slip of paper, rose from her chair and said, "Je n'ai plus de maison!"[1]

[1] *"I no longer have a house."*

When the man who bought it left the house, she cried.

Soon it will be our turn. Life seems to have flowed swiftly these days, and the turn of events is going to leave a deep mark on us, and alter much. The plans to go to Paris have crystallized with unbelievable rapidity. Having sold her house under the pressure of countless obligations, Mother has turned to the considerations of Joaquin's career—and Paris. Hugh instantly pressed the bank to let him go to the Paris branch. Nothing is yet absolutely certain, and yet we know it *has* to be certain, and we will make it so.

Half the day we spend thinking of Paris, what we shall do there, how we shall live, the bad and the good of this change. The other half is spent regretting—Mother, her house and her disappointments and lost opportunities; I, the exquisite little home we have made of the bungalow, my desire to write for this country and, above all, Eugene and Johnnie, Richard Maynard and Frances. The uncertainty, the inexact imaginings as to when, how and why—these trouble us.

Just now for the first time I realize the wisdom of religion, which teaches us not to attach ourselves to our worldly goods, for they are perishable, to think only of life eternal and to love only God.

Everywhere I see the marks of my passionate interest in those worldly things, and now I wish I had loved them less, that I might leave them with a lighter heart. I have lavished so much time and care on our little home; I have thoughtfully selected and hung the curtains and the paintings and the tapestry which were among Mrs. Pausas's[1] belongings when she sold me her furniture. I cannot count the hours which I have spent in contemplation of each room, rising to change a mere detail which did not satisfy me, applying all my ingenuity to fabricate out of scant material what my imagination demanded. Only lately things began to please me. I had a feeling of space and harmony and coziness when I stepped into the parlor. The dark-green lacy curtains are long and clinging. Facing me is a tapestry of soft greens and browns that melt into the brown couch, whose lines are very simple, very straight, and the same harmony carries the brown into the soft and dark greens of the rug. The note spreads to the floor, which is beige, and rises to the beige-colored walls. And then the line breaks, and the rest are accents, bright-yellow glass bowls, lampshades verging more

---

[1] *The wife of Francisco Pausas, a Catalan painter.*

on orange, which also appears in the pillows on the couch. The fireplace, large and smoke-tinted, is of dull-red bricks, and on each side the bookcases occupy the same width as the fireplace. The frames around the paintings are dull gold; and there are two old chairs—one a black Queen Anne.

The dining room repeats the gold and turns to blue for a key-note. Here I played a trick on my family. I had an idea which even to me seemed rather extreme. In order to be able to carry it out, I attributed it to a more reliable source, mentioned books on interior decoration, etc., and having won half-hearted consent, I bought blue silk and tacked it behind the glass door and sides of the china closet, so that the plates, glasses, bric-a-brac, were no longer seen. The eye traveled with pleasure over the smooth blue and fixed itself on a lovely watercolor hung above, and rested on the blue bowl filled with fruit, the only ornament on the closet. My family surveyed the effect at first suspiciously and finally approvingly, but I did not disclose my secret. In this room there is no definite sensation, like the harmony of the parlor, unless it is the suggestion it gives of the possibilities of the poetic in a dining room.

The bedrom is more definite in mood. It is again the rose I mentioned in our little apartment, with walls of pale gray, soft-rose lampshades with gray tassels, a bedspread of creamy lace with rose silk lining. I painted Hugh's hairbrushes and handkerchief box gray, and I have only one picture in the room, a photograph of Mother in a black frame.

The next room is where I have let my fancies run free, where my imagination has taken riotous shapes. It is a queer room from the first glimpse you catch of the Moorish doorway, with a transparent curtain instead of a door. At the right of it hangs a little altar lamp of brass and colored stones. You lift the curtain, bow your head beneath the curving lines of the opening and face the Moorish windows with blue curtains. The walls are gray, the rug has blue in it. On one side there is a dressing table of Moorish design, with a long, narrow mirror hung above it. Before the window is a Moorish stool with a Moorish iron jar on it, whose curious lines are outlined clearly against the light. Between the window and the desk, I formed a couch with boxes, and it is ideal to sit there near the light and sunshine. The desk where I work also has a hint of the Moorish in its design. On the top of it I placed my journals between the bookholders, a red vase, a candle-stick. The light of the blue candle illuminates Beethoven's death mask, which hangs above it. Next to it there is a watercolor of Venice and a casting of a child's head. At night the room is bathed in green light diffused by a lantern, which gives the room a curious air of unreality, of the fantastic. And then there is the garden to which we also gave much of our time. Three mornings we were up at six o'clock to prepare the beds for the vegetable seeds. We planted a little elm tree at the front, now about a yard and a half tall, and three rhubarb bushes in the back. These are the cold facts. In later years they may help me to reconstruct a picture of our home.

It would be amusing if we did not go to Paris after all. I have been writing verses on a buried friend, and now the friend is not dead at all! That would be a queer sensation. If I were forced to live three years in the bungalow, I probably would not feel so sentimental about it.

I am teasing Mother with all sorts of questions: Shall we take the phonograph with us? Perhaps there aren't any in Paris. Do they have Pyrex dishes there? And Collie dogs?

The truth is that I do not want to admit to myself how deeply thrilled I am at the thought of going there—to the Paris of Balzac, Flaubert and Anatole France, to the Paris of the poets, of Dumas and Victor Hugo.

I once said I thought patriotism was a form of narrow mindedness, that there was no reason why we should love one country more than another. I exulted in my lack of it, for I was and am a girl without a country. I love with equal intensity, in different moods, Spain, France, Scotland, Italy and Belgium; and the realization of this country's youth, its struggles towards intellectual development, have nearly brought tears to my eyes at other times. In cool moments I look down upon them all critically, with the same sense of imperfection that human nature gives me, with the same desire to take the best of each and gather it in one perfect being, one perfect country. Yet all the while the name which made my heart leap with inexplicable emotion and curiosity was Paris.

June 19. I am an invalid.

"You are going to lie on that couch and not do a single thing," Mother said this morning with motherly firmness. To tell the truth, I have been sick a long time, visibly so during our vacation, acutely so since I came back, but I would not surrender. Last night we had Johnnie to dinner. Every time I stood up from my chair I wondered whether I was going to faint. During the evening Mother visited a little while. When she kissed me she said: "Why, this child has fever!" And tucked me into bed.

When I am sick and am forced to lie on a couch hour after hour, then I feel I have as much right to my diary as to medicines. It is the only time I am not ashamed to write indefinitely and uselessly. That is how I finished what I began to write yesterday, and I propose to continue.

Again life presents itself to me as a picture. Hugh in New York is bending over his desk. Here I sit on the couch, my head against the tapestries, my journal on my knees. Mother is bustling in the kitchen. When she is not cooking, she sits before me, knitting. The door is open, and through it enters the warm air and the sunshine.

Being sick is rather enjoyable; I think I was always fond of it, even as a child. To be left alone, in bed with books, always made me selfishly happy. It was in bed that I first developed my literary talents(!). Father[1] used to think I copied what I wrote, until one day, when I was nine years old, I wrote a description of Joaquin, which settled that matter. Yet as I grow older I cannot enjoy idleness as well. Today I abandoned you to mend stockings, and then, the sense of my obligations growing stronger, I began to do little things around the house, dragging myself on one foot, as it were, and finally, seeing I had a headache, realized I had better return to my writing. Nothing is better for headaches than to wear your eyes and your mind out writing.

What this proves is that I am growing into a better woman. I used to enjoy watching myself as one watches a curious insect, and I used to sit for hours recording all the queer little moods and thoughts of that insect, oblivious to the world, to the fact that there were more useful things to be done. I have apparently lost the gift. Though none the less egoistical and tremendously interested in every quiver and flutter of my inward mechanism, I realize that my egoism can become a monstrous defect. Therefore, I mend stockings.

Often I ask myself frankly why I do not spend the time studying others as closely as I study myself. Why, for instance, do I not tell you every act and every word Hugh lives and utters? I spend my life loving and admiring him, but I certainly do not

[1] *Joaquin Nin, composer and concert pianist.*

prove it in my writing. He says the same of me, and does the same in his journal.

Sometimes I think it is because I am afraid. How can I trust the delicacy of his thoughts to my writing, which is not trustworthy? I do not care at all, by contrast, whether my dull writing betrays a dull mind; I do not care if what I see through my moods reveals weakness, bitterness, envy, vanity, or discouragement. Here I stand and interpret myself; that interpretation itself may be a farce. Do I know the truth about myself? If one day I admire myself because I am loved, because my Love said I was beautiful, because I wrote something that pleased me, because I have just heard someone flatter me, and if I should write about that emotion, the one who reads it will turn away disgustedly and say: "How conceited!"

That is what journal writing is. What I write of Hugh is not Hugh himself. It is my interpretation of him. All I see in him now is because I love him, because he loves me. If he should do me a wrong, I would read a different meaning to his whole character.

Yet I keep remembering the childish descriptions I first made of him, for which I now blush. How little I knew him, I say to myself, when I read them over. On the other hand, when I read descriptions of myself, I do not blush. That is just how I was. So at the time, it was truthful writing.

One thing I cannot understand—my reaction to sensuality, to the depiction in literature of the lust of the flesh, such as Anatole France achieves in *The Red Lily*.

I read the book on my way from Woodstock and it revolted me. I said to Hugh: "I never knew such things had been written. They did not exist in English literature."

And then today I came across a book review which spoke of the refined sensuousness France developed as soon as he knew himself, which in later books became simple sensuality. It satisfied me to hear another say that, for I was troubled at my prudishness, as I have been troubled a million times through life. Now I do not mind seeing my nature recoil instinctively, to see the fine line it has itself created between the lust of the flesh and love. And after all, I am glad that English literature trained my spiritual nature and made it stronger; so that I might learn intelligence from the French, and love from Hugh, who read me poetry on our first night and who knelt at my knees and hid his face in his hands before turning off the light, the Hugh whose delicacy and sensitiveness every day keeps me from the things I had feared of life.

June 23. Health again, and with it work. Enric came to see us. His· eyes are more serious than they used to be, his mouth more determined. I noticed those things as he talked last night, while his thin, sensitive hand played about his dark suit. He talks well and impressively and enthusiastically, but does nothing. He seems to have no fixed purpose in mind, no definite desire. How much of the world's genius, I wonder, has dissolved into nothingness through sheer lack of initiative, of capability? Is not Eugene wasting the riches of his mind? And Richard Maynard? With this in mind I wrote the last a fanciful and lengthy letter.

I do not mean lack of initiative so much as lack of something I will name enthusiasm for want of a better word—lack of desire, lack of purpose. Is it the fact that I know so well what I want and want it so much that makes me, without talent, do more in fact than the others? I have so much *desire*, so fixed, so determined a plan. If my mind were for a moment suddenly revealed to Eugene, in one of the moments when it centers itself entirely upon the purpose of my life, he would be considerably perturbed. He may think me, judging with the older cautiousness of his mind, childish and mad, or shallow-hearted and vain. For I am preoccupied with success of the homeliest kind, success materially, Mother's comfort, Hugh's satisfaction and pleasure, Joaquin's future.

While I write? Oh, no. While I write I am the dreamer, intent only on achieving art. But those other things give me the impulse, as well as the secret and cherished desire, to write because I love writing; they make me begin and carry through a heavy task. It may be sheer animal activity. Only I would like to have the clear recipe to give Enric and Eugene. Or rather I wish that I could disappear and that these two should be reborn with their genius plus my volubility, activity, spirit, boldness and ambition. So with Eduardo and Richard Maynard.

The idea of thus vanishing appeals to me. Would there be anything else worth giving away before disappearing from the earth, except to make another responsible for the writing of this journal so I might leave with a clear conscience?

June 24. What, after all, is our American life—the life which we may soon abandon? Is there anything in it that is characteristic, which affects us fundamentally? Are we in any way different here in attitude of mind? Is the life itself detachable from individual character?

These questions I ask myself all day. I try to analyze our life, to see if it *is* a life, and fall again into the same old bottomless pits of futile reasoning. At first I succeed in following a certain logical analysis. But in this I cannot go very far without stumbling, for when I have compiled my observations I find that our life is not like our neighbor's, and therefore is not American. What then *is* the American life?

In a moment I can see the lady to my left, who washes her clothes, cleans her house, tends her children, who goes to church on Sunday. The husband goes away early in the morning and works in his garden in the evening. Again there is Mrs. Duble, who works like her husband. They have a maid and no children. They go to Europe every summer; they have a car and many friends. In Forest Hills there were many women who spent their afternoons at bridge parties, while the children went out with a nurse. Their husbands spent Saturday and Sunday at the club playing tennis or golf.

Then, after all, our life here is an empty house out of which we made a home, with a certain number of customs and commodities which we adapted to our character. We have done nothing that is expected of young couples. We have rigorously selected our friends, we have practically no social life in the worldly sense of the word. If we go out, it is to a concert. When Eugene comes we spend the evening philosophizing. Part of the day I am simply woman, working around the house.

Once in France, I shall know precisely what I will miss. But they will be externals—things like our bathroom, for instance. Soon we shall have another home, the same life, more friends, perhaps like Eugene. We carry our world within us. Is it not a pleasant thing?

We are enjoying our uncertain plans by planning everything with certainty. Mother is more or less happy. As soon as Hugh is gone and I have tidied my house, Mother and I go marketing together, up and down Jamaica Avenue. The elevated train rumbles over our heads, the shops are all lined up in a row on each side. The baker is German, the butcher is a Jew, the delicatessen man is an Alsatian, the vegetable man is a Russian Jew, the grocer is Irish, our upholsterer is Scottish. Not much American life there.

On our way home we meet some people coming out of a

church and the school children leaving for lunch. I have lunch at Mother's house, with Joaquin. The big old house is cool and empty. People drop in now and then to look at the piano and the furniture that is for sale. A Russian family still lives on the top floor of the house. They are aristocrats, but they have very large gas bills and leave their clothes hanging on the line on Sundays, so we are not exactly on friendly terms. While Mother was away, we had typical, melodramatic scenes on the days their rent was due. I was the villain in the play, the collector, but when I got out of breath Thorvald and Hugh took my part in turn. They, the Menkins, remind me of Mother's American life, which consisted mainly of a struggle for a living, which ended in a gigantic debt and memories of the life of a rooming-house executive. Fortunately, some of our boarders were our friends, more or less, like Elise Owen and her mother, the Norman family, including Frank, and Ruth Morgan, with whom I correspond now. I must not forget Enric and Mrs. Dempster, whom I visit now and then.

But I was describing an ordinary day in our life. In the afternoon Mother brings her knitting here while I iron or clean my house or mend stockings. Or else I take my sewing to her house if she has work to do. Usually we help each other. Towards five we separate. While my dinner cooks, I write letters or my journal. Richard M. is away, so I have to write to him.

When Hugh comes we take the little kitchen table out and have our supper in the garden, close to the left side of the house, where a wooden fence keeps the sight of our food from the neighbors. At dinner we wonder if we ought to read French books, so as not to be caught in ignorance of that culture, or whether it would be wiser to read American books, in case the French question us on that. It is quite a problem.

I wonder if I shall find nice diary books in Paris.

Experiment in Studies of a Husband by a Wife:

This morning I fell asleep again after we had said good morning to each other and he, instead of waking me, stole softly out of the room, dressed and cooked his own breakfast.

I wakened in time to scold him in an admiring tone and to see him off. He is always so neatly dressed in the morning. His face, just shaven, is fresh and soft, his eyes are clear and blue. He dresses slowly, too slowly for my temperament. Indeed, he is always late, except at his work, and I am always too early, so now the two extremes have formed a perfect combination. We are on time always everywhere.

I was saying he dressed slowly. He deliberates over his ties, he polishes his shoes with infinite patience, and I think he dreams, too. Often I catch him gazing absent-mindedly out of the window, holding a shoe in one hand, the shoehorn in the other. When I call him he suddenly looks at them, starts, remembers what he is supposed to be doing and begins to hurry.

He is in good humor always, and loving. We laugh much during breakfast, and afterwards I help him with the last details; I brush and tidy him.

"Now, Pussy (we call each other Pussy), you won't work hard today, promise?" he asks.

I always do, and afterwards . . . well, afterwards I do as I please. But anyway, he leaves in the morning with a fine feeling of lordliness and knowing he is obeyed. His step is light as he leaves the house. He smiles and he waves to me until the curve in the road swallows him. Each morning he leaves me the strong memory of his clear eyes, his smile, his warm, long kiss, his entreaties not to work hard, his promise to come home early.

In the evening towards half past six I begin to watch for him. He walks quickly homeward, he is happy to come home. Our reunion is a sweet one, although his eyes are dim, his face is tired and sometimes the peace and joy of the morning are gone out of him. His nervousness never escapes me. I spend the rest of the evening soothing him. But first, after refreshing his face with cold water, he sits down to his little dinner, which I cook with care and serve as daintily as I can. Then he talks to me and I tell him whatever will interest him.

Many long hours each day of his life I am deprived of him. I know what he does and feels and thinks from half past seven to half past six at night only through the hints he gives me. I often try to understand the occupation to which he must consecrate the best part of his day. If he is a half-hour late, I feel terribly cheated of a precious thing; I even sulk, I worry. Like tonight, for instance, when it is seven and he is not yet here.

Well, he cannot help being late any more than I can help doing my share of the work at home. So we scold each other in a special way; that is, lovingly and not unpleasantly.

He is always so very gentle, so patient, so loving, so eager always to please me, "to become better," as he puts it. He tries continually in those little things men so often neglect; he hangs up his clothes, he watches the ashes from his pipe.

Now when he comes I will probably abuse him: "Oh, Pussy, why do you come so late?"

He will just smile and beg forgiveness and humor me until I smile and probably draw from his pocket a book he has brought me—spoiling me like a child and again making me feel that he is so good I ought to be ashamed of myself.

July 5. I could not trust myself to write of Hugh for I am in the blackest of humors.

The scene takes place in Point Lookout, a continuation of Long Beach, where we came to spend the customarily hot days of July 4th weekend. We took rooms in Ghul's Hotel, renowned for its cleanliness and clam chowders. We planned to spend Thursday, Friday, Saturday and Sunday on the beach, to sleep well at night in the cool air of the bay and ocean. Thursday morning, Mother, Joaquin and I started off, loaded like camels, to be joined later by Hugh, in the same condition.

That first day on the beach Mother's bones ached from lying and sitting on the sand, and I got a sunburn which has kept me awake nights ever since. The lunch we brought was full of sand, the sea where we swam, full of weeds.

About eight o'clock Hugh arrived, his eyes full of hope for the joys that would be ours on the morrow. That night we lay down wearily on mattresses no more than one inch in thickness, and immediately a hoarse phonograph was turned on and dancing began so near us that we sometimes thought it was taking place in our very room. We were awake until eleven and the next morning awoke with aching bones.

We discovered that the two towels allowed us were expected to last us a week, that we were supposed to make our own beds and clean our room if we could not do without these luxuries. We had to empty the pails and fetch fresh water, and as none of us like chowder, we lived on fried fish three times a day. The menu is invariable: pie, fish, potatoes. Not so the weather, which has been so cold that we had to run about all day to keep from shivering. The only moment of pleasure we had was in the evening, when Hugh, Joaquin and I returned to the beach, lit a blazing fire and roasted marshmallows and our noses, and lay on a blanket watching the Long Beach fireworks and listening to the waves.

Hugh is in the city now. It rains spasmodically, and Joaquin and I are sitting at one of the restaurant tables, both of us giving vent to our emotions. Joaquin's writing is the result of propaganda and he has begun a journal. This does not thrill me as much as might be expected, seeing that it is perhaps the eleventh time he has done the same thing. This morning he seems to have taken to it more seriously, for he has begun with a laborious description of himself, which is the unmistakable sign of the true journalist.

Johnnie and Eugene are coming tomorrow, and if it were not for them, we had seriously considered abandoning the charming village.

How disappointing life is in small things like these, and I marvel at their power to darken my moods, but then I appeal to you to approve my state of mind. Here we are expecting to have found the one place on the Island where the intolerable July heat would not martyrize us, and it is cold!

Here is Joaquin who has proposed to become a finished pianist in the few weeks remaining before going to Paris, and he has missed a lesson and finds no piano in the place.

"Why don't you read?" asks the Worthwhile Person.

Ah, my dear, you are touching tragedy. Read, you say? What unfortunate spirit moved me to take Marcel Proust's *La Prisonnière* with me? The books, two volumes, revolted, baffled and bored me, although before reading them I almost wept when the bottle of grape juice spilled in the valise and tinted cover and pages with a most delicate shade of mauve. Meredith's *Adventures of Harry Richmond* escaped the dyeing, but I fear I could not have wept over the entire loss of it. For the first time I am not true to my admirable Meredith.

If I were a painter, of course, I would not be at loss for amusement. There are the rowboats and launches on the bay, the bobbed-hair girls in one-piece bathing suits, the sea, the ships on the horizon, the rough, tan fishermen, the lobster-colored city people, such as we are. But cold and dampness are fatal to intellectual pursuits.

Evening. We sit on a sand dune watching the sea between the tall blades of sage grass. I struggled the whole afternoon to interest myself in Meredith, who so fascinated me in *The Egoist* and in *Diana of the Crossways*. Beautiful writing, yes, impeccable, majestic, rich, colorful, with strong characterization. Hugh, to console me, brought Henry James's *The Ambassadors*, but became interested in it himself, and so I was left again to amuse myself and to write my own books.

I made a curious little study today, in love. Hugh took the 6:30 boat this morning. I walked with him to the landing and watched him step into the launch, which was quite full with commuters. While the pilot untied the ropes, I stood on the boardwalk and talked to Hugh in a low voice, making impersonal remarks. I thought he did not mind anyone hearing, for I knew his feelings on the subject. Before a crowd, I think, Hugh would hesitate to express anything, even if I lay dead at his feet. He answered me, as I thought, rather briefly, scarcely looking at me, and when the boat started he smiled weakly and did not wave back to me.

Baffled and dejected, I returned to the gloomy day I described. I wondered what he was thinking and whether he was displeased. I went over the three-quarters of an hour before his departure. Was he vexed because I had hurried him? But he almost missed his boat and I helped him not to. Because I wore my bathing suit and he wanted me to hide myself in a cape? He was jealous, did not want the other men to see me? I was sure he did not love me any more. I visualized him on the boat, his eyes fixed sadly on the water. He was disappointed in me; I was impatient, perhaps coquettish—for I wouldn't wear my cape. All day he would remember my voice urging him to hurry and my reproachful eyes when I had to return to the forgotten valise.

It was the end. I had lost him because he did not love me any more. I was so sure of it that all that morning I felt the pangs of our *separation*. I was alone again, I could not help doing those things which hurt him. Of course, I would not meet him on the landing in the afternoon, for I felt humiliated and would proudly and silently wait on the beach. I arranged that when he came I would not smile, but look distant and pale and mysteriously and inexplicably sad. And then we would see.

Mother, Joaquin and I were stretched on the sand. As the hours passed I grew restless. Finally I asked the time. It was quarter to three and the boat was probably just arriving. I decided I would walk casually towards the hotel, to get something in my room.

Thinking thus, I began to run and arrived breathless to see the crowd walking towards me, and Hugh with a light step, swinging a heavy valise and walking quickly to where I stood.

"Hello, little Pussy," he said with his usual wide smile, and very tenderly, "What has my little Pussy been doing today?"

Of course, once in our room I regained my dignity. I would not kiss him, accusing and reproaching him. "Why, little Pussy!" he almost cried with surprise, which was sufficient to relieve my doubts. "I never meant—I—you know how I feel in a crowd." He finished by taking me in his arms and kissing me. He was horrified at my story and was doubly tender, so I lost nothing by it—except that I felt our separation as completely as if he had left me, never to return. We had been, in all reality to me, separated from half past six this morning till ten minutes to three. I was alone those hours, I lost him, missed him. Such is the strength of the imagination and such is the power of the love to whose hands we deliver ourselves, body and soul. Since childhood I was awed by imagination and realized its tricks, its perversity, its fickleness, its wonders, its beauty. But it is only lately that I have asked myself: How far does imagination shape our life? *Is everything only imagination?* Is love a product of it, does it live within it, or spring *from* it? Does Hugh love me or does he fancy he does and I fancy I believe him? Why did I feel this morning that he did not love me? I felt it while he, in the city, was buying me a book and little things to please me and, as he told me later, thinking of me, wishing he could return to me early. He did love me and I could not feel it. I did not believe in it.

I just told Hugh about this. We got into such a deep and hopeless discussion that I became sleepy. Particularly after Hugh said that the fact that I did not believe he loved me did not mean anything, since he did, and consequently the *fact* of his love could exist independently from me.

July 11.

To "Dick" Maynard:

. . . I know you are particularly worried about Hugh, you think he will be expatriated (if we go to Paris). But as far as that goes, don't you believe we belong in certain countries more by temperament than by birth? Hugh is not in harmony with his present surroundings and the atmosphere of the bank. Often he comes to me in the evening with a feeling of revolt against the red-blooded, square-headed man of business you and I both know. In order to make his way among these men, he does much that is against his nature, he drives himself. And, mon ami, I do not want him to make money for me, I don't want it. I just want him to enjoy his youth and to have time to write, to read and rest, to live fully, in other words. He cannot do these things in this country without becoming instantly a failure. The square-headed man will step into his place and will look down on him. And even if I tell Hugh I think him successful because his intellect is developed, because of his culture, he will be bound at some time or another to measure himself by the standard of the others and condemn himself. In France that spirit does not exist . . . the standard of living and business are less tense and he will be happier in that atmosphere where ambition is of so different a character.

As to our "home," when I urged him to analyze exactly what it was that pleased him in this house, we found there was not one thing I could not duplicate for him in Paris, for the things he mentioned were those every woman can make with her hands, and I carry the power with me!

You asked me questions about Hugh's journal, and in a moment I realized that, naturally, Hugh's journal would be more interesting to you because it is the journal of a man and you may feel towards my "épanchements"[1] and womanly emotions pretty much as you feel towards Marie Bashkirtsev's rhapsodies. . . .

Hugh and I, compared with you, are a pair of Meredithian egoists, however, and I suppose that none of our methods would suit your nature. You have to work, as you say, in a roundabout way. You dread the "I." Perhaps it would be best, then, if you remained outside of your journal, so to speak. You have a genius for self-effacement which sorely troubles your friends! I, for instance, want *you* in your journal . . . but if you will not appear, then write as you say. Perhaps you could convince yourself you are writing another man's story; give him another name, if necessary, call him "he," and you will have a book like Henry James's *The Ambassadors*, which is as minute a study of a man's impressions as any journal could give, and beautiful.

July 12. We leave for Paris in December. The decision was made after far more hesitation than anyone would have expected from us, but lately we have become more practical. To leave New York for Paris seems, to a romantic, a prospect everyone would envy. But we spent days adding and subtracting figures, regardless of sentiment, probing opportunities, Hugh's future at the bank, chances for advancement. After painful deliberation—for sensibly and practically speaking, the advantages were on this side—we realized that theorizing was futile since we had to go anyway, for

[1] *Outpourings.*

Mother and Joaquin must go. So now, having settled the problem, we are free to romanticize. We have five months in which to appreciate American life and in which to imagine things about Paris which after a week of life there we will have to discard.

July 29. The preparations are exciting, and I am making mine to the tune of Henry James's *The Ambassadors*, which in some ways gives a deeper and clearer meaning to the step we are taking. It interprets Paris to an American, and after all, I must recognize that I am one of those Americans. I feel it when America is belittled, when American life is libeled. Shall I defend it to the French, I, the Frenchwoman by birth and by affection?

There is irony in the situation, for I love and sympathize with people whom my mind has condemned. I am like a mother with a bad child. I know my child's faults, but cannot endure others to criticize him. And America is a child, a child that you look down upon for its childishness, and yet whose very youth, efforts, enthusiasm, are the only things that interest us in life.

July 31. I had a shock last night, an impression which has left a deeper mark on me than seems reasonable. Hugh and I had a misunderstanding, no matter the cause. I did not want to speak to him, and so I left the bedroom, where he was preparing to go to bed, and lay on the couch in the parlor.

I understood perfectly the mood and spirit which had made him say things to Mother I had begged him not to say, and I knew he was right in saying them and only human in not being able to restrain himself from saying them; nevertheless I could not soften his attitude, one of belligerence, and its newness had shocked me, after years of such unbroken sweetness and patience as I had become accustomed to.

Lying there, in the very warm night, I believed he would not come to me, for I had hurt his pride. Yet he came and lay beside me and spoke softly and pleaded: "Talk to me, talk to me. This is foolish, it shouldn't happen between us, let us understand each other."

We did talk, and before his humility I softened and confessed and we were happy again and united. I asked him, wonderingly, how it was he had come to me. He confessed he had had a struggle with himself before coming, fighting down his pride.

"And yet you came, you were humble. . . ."

"I love you more than myself. And this love," he added, "is

what you have done to me, for before, I would not have come, I would have remained hard—for I felt hard inside."

I brooded on this and then the memory of "before," those other days, returned to me. "I have known the hard side of you long ago. But it was that which hurt me so tonight—your old expression, the hardness of your face." I searched his face, fearfully, but found no trace of the expression which sent me away from the room. He was gentle again and loving and humble.

We made a promise that, as he felt hard sometimes, and proud, and as I felt sometimes exactly the same, when we have a misunderstanding both must meet each other halfway; neither is to be expected to make the entire effort towards understanding. We promised, clinging to each other: "Dearest, we must not quarrel, oh, we must not lose each other."

I want particularly to remember my promise today, when it is so clear to me that I love him more than myself and that through pride or unreasonableness I must not lose him. So far, we have never, not once, been separated from each other for more than a moment—the time it takes to explain things to each other and to forgive each other. And that is because we love truly, love our love more than ourselves.

And yet, such is the retention of my feelings that last night's vision of Hugh, changed by a return of the old, combative spirit, the spirit which, as he tells me, made him speak up to each of his parent's interferences, has troubled me like the sudden apparition of an ugly picture found among many beautiful ones. Once my sight of him is blurred (and I will not look too long), that, to me, the wavering of the perfect thing, is the beginning of the end. No one can show himself in the guise I dislike, even for a moment, without leaving a painful impression, and no one can say to me: "Forgive and forget," for though I forgive, the disappointment is eternal, it has passed through my spirit, like a false note, and the echo of it never leaves me. Cruelly, it is reproduced, faintly perhaps, and I wait for a loud sounding of the true notes to drown it.

August 4. The cloud has passed, and today I blame myself, and only myself, for the black moment.

Strange days these. Mother sells the furniture I was so accustomed to think of in connection with the dear old house. Each piece, as it goes, brings memories. I have sat with Joaquin and Mother tearing up old papers and letters. From these, too, arise the strong smell of the past, yellow, acrid—unbelievably far away. Behind the person you look up to stands the other of long ago, one so different. So it was with Mother, even with Joaquin, in whom I vaguely sought the golden-curled little boy in the yellowed photographs, whom I wheeled in his baby carriage, whom I watched while he played in the park.

Father's love letters I saved from destruction and brought home in a curious state of excitement. I have never read them, but they are safe in my hands, *their* story—where *ours* began!

The piano is gone. Joaquin wrote a poem to it, resembling the farewell of an Arab to his horse. And slowly go this object and that. Mother and I, however, never sentimentalize, for money has become such an event to her, and on the amount of it will greatly depend the success of her life in Paris. It is strange how each piece of furniture enters a different home and changes its appearance. My dressing table, for instance, has a new air, for a rich lady has it. Yesterday I saw her reflected in the mirror which I so constantly questioned.

Strether, in *The Ambassadors*, did not know the experience of tearing himself away from his old life. The realization that he was torn from it came only later, but Mother, in her own way, and we in ours, all know what we are losing this very moment, and we hear every moment the sound of the tearing, the crackling and snapping of the life that is rending.

Am I thankful for the long period given us to realize? As ever, yes. If I were suddenly transplanted to the middle of Paris, I would still be partly here. No one can prevent me from *looking* back once in a while, as I know I will, but I shall be there whole and complete, more fitted for the new adventure.

August 11. A friend asks me: "You will, I suppose, be terribly contented in Paris?"

Indeed, no. I have reached the period when I feel dissatisfied with every country, while loving much in each. Paris will not satisfy me completely, any more than New York has.

But today I felt the first keen pang of regret, even though it is Mother and Joaquin who are leaving the 13th, not me; I regretted for *them* what they are going away from. I sat alone in the dining room, from where I could see the peaceful street through the French door, with the big old trees bowed; and also the empty parlor, with three half-closed trunks, the bare walls and mantelpiece, the bare foyer, the empty pantry closets; and I could hear the ticking of the clock in the kitchen, which would in time tick all the hours away between this moment and the day of Mother's departure.

The house has shown me its other face. It was different when I judged the large rooms merely as bread-winners, trying to rent them, trying to have other people see the trees outside, the fireplace, only to have them turn and ask: "Is it a warm room? Does the radiator work well? Is the house noisy?"

Is the room warm? Well, no, it really isn't, but then I had never thought of that. I used to go to bed early and read, or else I used to write by the fire. Couldn't you do that?

I talked almost like that to the stolid woman who was before me. But no, of course, she could not understand. And the room was cold and she did not stay, although Mother counted on her rent.

And was the house noisy? The children, little Joaquin among them, play outside, they laugh and shout, and how lovely it is to hear them. And Joaquin plays his piano, yes, quite loudly. He makes beautiful harmonies. They fill the house, fill the soul. No, I did not tell them this. But they heard and would not stay.

August 16. They are gone. The house is silent and so empty. That morning I went to see them off I think I shall never forget—not because of the pain of separation, for we shall be together again in four months, but more because of the strangeness of Mother's return to Europe exactly ten years after her arrival—the strangeness of seeing her precede us in the tasting of a new life, to which she goes with so different an outlook.

The next morning I cleaned the entire house, swept the dust for the last time. I purposely kept active so that I might not feel sad, for I see sadness in everything.

Everything is unreal. The thought of that ship crossing the ocean, bearing an exultant Joaquin and my emotional mother, the sight of the big house outwardly unchanged, with the sunshine and the trees and the peacefulness all about it—the thought that soon I will see my father, my ghostly, shadowy father, in shadowy Paris. Yes, unreal, because underneath these changes, these movements, these outward activities, there is a meaning, a something that moves invisibly, that we cannot understand.

The house, for instance, is still. Yet I look at it for a long while and it becomes ghostly—it seems about to speak, to move. The shadows of the branches play on the faded walls—I watch and listen, half afraid, feeling something is going to be explained. But no, it remains the same, so impenetrable. It is loved, it is abandoned, as we love and abandon human beings.

August 17. I sometimes envy the disposition of people who can sit and enjoy every enjoyable moment of life without concern for others or for the future or the past. Their minds *rest*, but mine never does. I am always grieving, hoping, pitying, wondering, reasoning, and there are moments when I feel so, so tired, like tonight. Everything around me is so peaceful. We are sitting on the porch, and Hugh reads while Laddie lies at our feet. The trees are fresh after an afternoon of rain, fresh and still. Sunday couples walk down the street, arm in arm, scarcely disturbing the silence with their whispering. The grasshoppers sing louder as the night comes.

I have not written enough lately, and therefore have been less calm and less reasonable. Even Hugh has felt my tenseness and chided me for being so defenseless. I must write more and regain the poise which my meditations here gave me, that softening of the sharp edges which lately I have felt so often.

There, already I feel peace. And while I feel this subtle change, I encourage R. Maynard to write his journal, "to develop his personality." This was not my idea—it is the conclusion he himself has reached while evolving all the things I had said about journal writing. Tired of explaining a thing I do not understand myself, I let him interpret it in his own way. If I examine his idea too closely, I realize that journal writing may develop not only personality but also egoism in its most perfect form. I find that it gives me intense relief as well as pain.

I write little Mother my first letter, although she is still at sea. While telling her of the many things I had done since last Wednesday, I suddenly realized how I had willfully evaded the company of my own thoughts by keeping inordinately busy. And only today did I begin to relax, soothed by a day of abundant light and softness and of absolute solitude. Though occupied, though hanging still on a kind of uncertainty, I am at peace again and happier. I have not the heart to say why my mother makes me unhappy, but it is so, and not to brood on the last days before her departure, I kept tensely at my work.

And now I rest today, dream of Paris, and merrily, almost, look down on my finished book, *Aline's Choice*, because I know now it is worth nothing and that it was but the first step.

People pause to read the "For Sale" sign on the window. They look at the patch of grass, the tall hedge, the flower boxes, the tiny porch, the little gabled red roof—they look lingeringly, counting their money, as it were, wondering if it could buy every bit of this dollhouse. Sometimes they come in. I show them with pride the fireplace and the built-in bookcases, the sunny bedroom and pretty kitchen and the other patch of grass in the back. Sometimes they are bold enough to criticize, and the blood rushes to my face. When they like the house, I become "gushing." But the cost of it always cools them down. They walk away, sometimes looking back once more, so cheerily beckoning are the red geraniums and the open door.

September 2. Worn out and dazed by a thousand occupations— selling furniture, having it moved, arranging and planning, spending days with Baby,[1] who is in the city, writing letters and accounts, plus housework and caring for Thorvald, who was sick for days, and cooking for occasional guests, plus the heat and the tension, until now unbroken, under which I have managed Mother's affairs—I finally spent three days in Boonton, N.J., with Tia Coco[2] and became calm, for the worst is over.

I write while waiting for a storm to break, hoping the rain will cool the burning air. In a little while my Love will come, and Thorvald, who is now staying with us.

Mother's first letters come slowly in, joyous and hopeful. Relieved of worries as she is, she now makes me realize how much she worries me. Hugh thinks I am far too responsible, that I treat my family as if they were helpless. He begs me to worry less, and I shall. Each year, I believe, I become more reasonable. Everything in me now points that way. I am only unreasonable in my devotions. Will that last? *Respect* has ceased.

And now, when I can't respect, as if I should atone in some way for the whims of my mind, I love all the more.

October 18. For days our little home had been at peace. Thorvald had gone, and Hugh and I, alone, tasted again the sweetness of walking together, of talking in soft whispers. Our evenings have been calm, filled entirely with a loving consciousness of each other, and only each other.

---

[1] *Antolina de Cárdenas, a cousin.*
[2] *A.N.'s Aunt Edelmira.*

"Mother is well," I told myself, "and soon I shall be there to watch tenderly over her happiness." And I let my heart and mind fill themselves with Hugh alone, and forget pain and the world.

And then today—a letter. A mere formality of giving Mother a copy of her divorce papers has thrown her into one of her characteristic and maddening states. Angry, offended, belligerent, she courts suffering again, of her own free will. Poor Joaquin writes according to her feverish dictation—a pitiful, childish letter. Oh, at first, pity was what I felt. But my pity has exhausted itself lately; Mother has too often taken advantage of it, so that after a moment I rebelled and angrily condemned her unreasonableness.

All day I abstained from writing, ashamed of the bitterness which filled me. But I have lost my endurance.

With what care I had been softening and molding Father's attitude until his letters overflowed with patience and devotion. With what infinite tenderness I explained things to him, won him, so that he stood ready to obey my every word. I begged him to be charitable and tolerant. It took months to reach a complete understanding, difficult letters to write, the subtlest things to be put into words. And in one hour Mother destroyed it all by an outburst of passion.

The worst of it, the thing which I find unendurable, is the thought of the suffering she inflicts upon herself. Every outburst cuts her more deeply than it does the one it is intended for, except me, I think. Pity for her makes me ashamed of every feeling of rebellion and despair I have. It prevents me from abandoning her, as Father abandoned her, and as Thorvald has in a spiritual way, and as Joaquin will. All her family has turned away from her. They have lost patience and refuse to bear up any longer with her. God, give me patience! In my thoughts I have turned away, too, when my strength has given way, when I actually felt broken by her belligerent spirit. And I am the only one, and I must, I must stay with her.

With what pain I contemplate my changed relation to her— I, the once submissive, sweet daughter, who saw nothing, realized nothing, felt nothing, but my vague, inward world. Heaven was merciful on me for that period of insensibility. And when I opened my eyes to everything, life in general, and to Mother, when I became an individual myself and found ideas which opposed hers, then the calvary began. And to save me from unendurable pain, heaven willed that I should marry and have the courage to leave her home, to build my own where I could run for shelter.

But such intense suffering could not last. Gradually I learned to reason about it—for Hugh's sake. He begged me to be stronger, not to be so open to pain, to learn to shut it off. At first I suffered because Mother suffered. And then I began to see that she courted suffering and was alone to be blamed for it. Then I worried less and brooded and wondered. Now I am becoming hardened. Perhaps in this state I may help Mother more, and with a clearer head find a way to keep her happy.

October 19. Sick in bed, and my poor Love is nurse and cook and entertainer, all in one. Too weak even to *worry*, I respond feebly and submissively to the sunshine and to Hugh's sallies as he meets one by one the problems of housekeeping; and I plan with childish faith the furnishing of our Paris home.

Even now I look forward to our trip as to a honeymoon, I dream about the new home to be created. And yet until now there is not one dream like this which has not been poisoned by some imperfection. And why should things be any different in Paris? Human nature in general, Mother, the business world, will bring the same problems and sorrows. No traveling can free us from these things. Why then look forward to the future with more pleasure than we take in looking at the present? I live for Hugh now; he has dreamed of living in Paris, and therefore I do, too.

He just came into the room, caught me gazing off into space and remarked: "You are never too sick to think, are you, Pussy?" And I let him believe it.

October 20. When I was a child, up to the age of sixteen, solitude had no terrors for me, and I sought it. At that time I thought only about books, about generalities, about dreams, about the sweetness of people and of nature. Now I have become so intensely human, so cruelly alive to everything, that solitude is agony. Alone now I seldom dream, and more earthly problems haunt me. Today, for example, after a day in bed, which always has the power to separate me from the world, I rose with that "distant" feeling. A letter from Mother, another from Father, a call from a creditor—and my fragile inner world retreated. I set about to remedy things, to write letters, to talk clearly to the angry man, to think practically, to act!

"Mother: I beg of you in the name of your religion, which indicates sweetness and resignation, in the name of your children, who love you, not to renew the eternal battle of the past, not to revive old stories, old misunderstandings, not to revive a drama long past that we have done so much to forget."

The habit of feeling and thinking in me is stronger than any other. I have often thought that I could escape by filling my hours. But I tried that in Cuba, and if I were busy a month and were given five minutes to myself, I would crowd into them an eternity of sensibilities. If I did not write, I would feel and think just the same, and perhaps more intensely, more cruelly. No, it is hopeless. I have ceased to struggle against my nature. What I must do is *face* the demons of my oversensitive imagination. Half are my own creations, and by reasoning I can dispel them. Others, like my feeling of absolute responsibility for Mother's happiness, I must control intelligently.

Now I have discovered a new one: I have made myself responsible for Father's happiness also. I must not have too many children; that I am beginning to realize—for I suppose I will worry about them even more, and I will become a ghost myself and useless to those I love, except as a lesson, which might thus be summarized: Don't take life too seriously.

My life with Hugh is a thing apart from this turmoil. It is the dream from which I never awake. For every beautiful thing I lose by my contact with the other world, in his I find a new one. Every minute that is mine I consecrate to the growth of our dream. We look upon our trip as a honeymoon, and with the vanity of a bride, I see pretty things that I may wear to please him.

Two interests I seldom mention and which, day by day, are developing more seriously are the Art of Cooking, and the Art of Interior Decoration. Often, if anyone should look over my shoulder, expecting me to be engaged with writing a novel, I can be found cutting out recipes and pasting pictures of interiors in my scrapbook. Every bit of this is imbued with a mysterious meaning —home, his home, his love which made it.

Instead of dreaming, now I love. And while loving, I create what I afterwards recognize as a dream. When I lose myself in despair, as I do sometimes in these pages, it is because he is not here. When he comes home and puts his arms around me, instantly I am soothed and strong again.

October 23. Gently, yet firmly, R. Maynard admitted the other day that his frank attitude towards journal writing is this: It is often done, and in his case copiously so, during one's youth. But it is always, or nearly always, *outgrown*. And I wondered.

For, he maintains, it is a waste of time, in the sense that it is done for none other than yourself and that while doing it you take time away from other things of greater value perhaps. Also, he says, when older, you express your ideas either in life or in some form of art or work. And at this point, the journal ceases to be of service.

Until I talked with him I never tried to analyze my journal writing. I can't do it even now. I spend an afternoon talking about it, and the moment he utters a reason, such as I have given, I am mute with astonishment and find no retort.

It is true that I write less in the journal. I am too busy living —more than I used to be. But it is also true that nothing I do, write, say or read can replace this particular and very unique form. And if I outgrow it, I will lose something beautiful which has so far sustained me. What that something is I am still incapable of telling Richard M. And he wants to know, so I should find it.

Speaking in utilitarian language: I do not become fully conscious of events and places and people until I have "phrased" them. This consciousness, sometimes so painful, is useful as a literary asset. It becomes a habit of observation which has this advantage: that it includes two processes generally separated and each demanding its own time. The moment I see a thing or feel it, I put it into a phrase, as I have to carry it to my journal in that form. I do it so swiftly now that it seems but one thing: *Seeing and feeling in phrases*.

Tried to escape from anxiety concerning Father and Mother by thinking of others, and invited Mrs. Dempster to lunch with me and spend the afternoon here. Her little boy played in our backyard while we sewed and chatted. It was a lesson to hear about her worries, to realize how few are free of trouble and how much more others are suffering.

The day was shorter and sweeter. How unbearable the hours can be sometimes. We have 53 more days to wait before sailing.

October 25. Every trouble in this peaceful and sunny hour has become smaller and I wonder how it is that I ever saw it as a giant thing. To normal persons, life must be so much simpler and happier. I cannot imagine what it must be to feel as I do today, every day. It must be comfortable, and it is no wonder that they can grow fat and smile at everything. But I would not like to be in their place. There is a certain "toughness" about these people and a coarseness of texture, so to speak, through which, if pain cannot pass, neither can the subtler joys and appreciations.

One of my neighbors is of this kind. You think of her as impenetrable in the sense that things cannot touch her, and in certain moments the sight of pain passing over that enduring surface, without leaving the faintest scratch, calls forth admiration.

And so for the thousandth time, I reach the same conclusion: that sensitiveness and consciousness, though painful, are gifts from the gods, and they are to be appreciated.

In my "studio" now there is a trunk, a hatbox and great disorder. The desk and all ornaments are gone. I sun there instead of writing, fill the drawers of the trunk with neatly folded clothes.

There is another trunk in the parlor, disguised as a bench. Outside, the sign "For Sale" is still tacked and brings no response. Thorvald is on his way to Mother, and she writes hopefully about his coming. All these are the visible events. I should tell perhaps that we are reading French books, thinking about Paris all the time. To say that we are restless is to say little, because now we are ready and the passing of time only brings us regrets for what we are going to leave.

I pose for Richard Maynard every week so that we may finish the painting; and we have long talks and read each other's writing. Last night we were invited to dinner, and to listen to their radio! Mrs. Maynard [Lorraine] was particularly charming, but I could not rid myself of the realization that I understand men better and that I can talk more easily to men and win their friendship. What makes matters worse is that Mrs. Maynard herself is restrained and shy, and when she was so sweet last night I was tempted to go up to her and kiss her and break the ice. But I am always afraid of such impulses and wonder how the other person will take it and whether perhaps there is nothing to be understood and nothing to be friendly about. I always imagine a little scene in which I want to show my sympathy and my friendliness and receive an answer somewhat like this: "How sweet of you! But you know, you *are* a good friend of mine. Why, I have told you more about myself than I have told anybody else. You know *everything*!"

Because, after all, the thing which startles me most about people is their limitations. You come to the *bottom* of them so quickly. And I have peculiar eyes. I am always led on by imaginary shadows in which I think I have divined another well. Hitting the bottom so often becomes painful after a while. So now I fear and wait and let people reveal themselves. I am not such an explorer now as before.

Among the people who came to see my furniture, which is also for sale, there was a woman who wanted a desk, and as it was still in the studio at the time, I took her there to see it. Showing her into the room, I said something or other about it being my brother's. She looked at the small bed, the closet filled with Thorvald's clothes, and suddenly her eyes alighted on the castings of Beethoven and the child's head hanging on the wall, and she burst out laughing. "Isn't it just like a boy," she exclaimed merrily, "to have such funny things in his room!" And I joined her in her laughter, but for another reason.

November 2. For practical reasons Richard Maynard thinks I should begin writing my journal in a loose-leaf book, and with the typewriter. He insinuates that my refusing to do so is a mark of my lack of progressiveness. Sadly I have turned over these pages and brooded. Handwriting has a homely flavor, human, alive and expressive in itself. It shows my calm moments and my nervousness. I don't need to mention whether I am in a hurry or whether I write on a train, on a boat, at my desk or on my knees. Besides its own expressiveness, there is the silence I love while I write. No click of machinery, no stamping letters, none of the signs of the "professional." Quiet, intimacy, where all unites to express what my machine cannot.

But then, later it must happen anyway, for we have promised to send each other pages from our diaries instead of conventional letters, and Richard M.'s plan will solve the problem of time, which is so real to us both. Meanwhile, through pure economy, such as is daily practiced in a Scottish household, I must finish this book first. And therein lies the secret joy.

November 3. Only yesterday I wrote that my handwriting showed my calm moments and my moments of nervousness, but today I will see to it that it is not so, for I have just come home to find another despairing letter from Father, for whose happiness I am struggling so fiercely now, and having answered, I lost control of my feelings and paced the house, sobbing. Then I sat down, facing my journal, and started to form the round, even letters you see now, and forming phrases, struggling desperately to control myself and trying to fix my mind on handwriting, on thoughts as remote from the scene of my real problem as I can possibly find.

It would be of little use to read Carlyle or Emerson, neither one of them ever being concerned with the happiness of others but with attaining peace for himself; and that is simple enough. But I would like to find a philosophy in the world which could remedy such a pain as mine.

Richard M.'s thoughtfulness, his talks, the interest I have in his work, the warmth and cheeriness of his studio, had sweetened the entire day, which began early this morning, and I dreaded to come home. It is now that I have come to understand the desire of unhappy people to go away, to change, to travel. They think they can escape the sorrow which haunts them, that they can leave it behind them, with the inanimate objects which formed their surroundings.

Hugh is coming home later than usual tonight, when I need him so much. But he shall come home now to a calm, smiling wife, and I will make him happy, for after all, sorrow and despair can wear themselves out too.

With childish thoughtlessness poor Joaquin paints for me delightful pictures of his life in Paris, and of the things we had dreamed of enjoying. And to my own surprise, I realize that we, both Hugh and I, have thought more about Paris than about New York. We should be taking our last look at people and things here. I do, when I can remember. I sit in the train, on my way to the city, staring around me piercingly.

People come less frequently now to see the house. The winter is upon us and most have found the homes they wanted. I left the flower boxes at their posts, keeping guard, and nearly freezing, in order to attract the eyes of the passers-by, but at night I stealthily bring them inside. There is something pathetic in the way I stand them there, like a fading flag soon to be taken down altogether and the castle surrendered.

November 6. Surprised at my own reasonableness, my good humor, my philosophical attitude in general, I wish among various things to pay tribute to Rafael Sabatini's genius for storytelling—we saw his *Sea Hawk* in the movies and were thrilled by it, in spite of the fact that Richard M. assures me the ship, supposedly worked with oars, left the telltale dancing trail of the steam engine. Historical inaccuracy or anachronism did not bother us, and me in particular, the uneducated one.

Lest I spoil my beautiful smoothness I must not write too much here, although I may say that in these cool moments I can do more for my dear, poor mother than during my fevers. I spend whatever moments escape my careful watch (to eliminate idleness completely) making plans and seeking to find a solution, a way out of our entanglements. Is this not more useful than my former lamentations?

November 7. There is nothing beautiful about housework, and I can understand the restlessness and the dissatisfaction so many women feel now after having once tasted that independent work which freed them from drudgery. They were happier in business and in art than in the kitchen. To the woman with the least intelligence, there must come, at some time or other, the realization that housework is animal work and that there are other occupations in the world a thousand times more refined, more enriching, for which she is also suited and to which she has a right.

Such discontent took hold of me today. I told myself I would prefer to be posing so I could pay a servant to do the rough labor I was doing. I long to be a lady, not fitfully, not for a few hours when I pose for Richard M. or for a weekend, but every minute of the day. I try eagerly to glorify my work, to think that I am creating as much as if I were writing—that I am homemaking.

But the smell of dishwater, the stained fingers and the violence of scrubbing, are strong realities, and I cannot ignore them. Sometimes I wonder, when I hear all that men say about woman's lack of logic, of intellect, of balance, whether God did not mean that we should be stupid so that we might, without a murmur, desire nothing better on earth than to bear children and do low, menial work. And the few of us who revolt, who aspire to be more than beasts of burden, are punished by the futility of our longing for emancipation. The very spiritual in us returns to us as punishment, because we want love and a home as ardently as the unawakened woman, and to have it we must work.

Of course, gold can save this problem. But gold never comes to the dreamers—except in dreams.

November 10. But then housework has its charms. Richard M. happened to come Saturday afternoon, bringing some friends to see our house, and he exclaimed enthusiastically over the neat appearance of it, the good taste even, the prettiness. And for a moment I forgot my discouragement and was proud of my humble work.

In this case it is a question of overlooking the means and keeping the end in view—the end which is poetic enough and artistic enough to satisfy the most exacting.

Sunday our house was like a museum, and quite a crowd came to look it over. We had the fire burning all day, partly to keep us warm, partly for effect, and between visitors I wrote and Hugh read the papers. The domestic situation was peaceful—not so the foreign. Our correspondence has dwindled to cables, for I cannot trust myself to write Mother, and they will not give me any definite news, which convinces me that they have something of which they are secretly ashamed.

Meanwhile, Father wins my respect by his reasonableness and his restraint and his patience; and I will compensate him.

November 12. Was startled to find that the lady who felt things so little cried with me today over a story we saw together in the movies. All women, apparently, have that susceptibility in common—the pain it causes them to think of the possible loss of their husbands. The lady in the story lost hers, but won him again and forgave him. Sniffling, we both agreed that we could not do as much and that it would break our hearts. And sniffling, we went home, thoroughly in sympathy and quite moved by the thought. Our husbands will probably both receive an unusually warm homecoming kiss tonight.

About husbands, then, all women are sentimental and all women are fools, as far as I can see. But it has troubled me sorely to see my theories so shaken up by the mere sight of someone else's husband gone astray. Oh, dear, how commonplace wives are, how monstrously alike!

In me there is a kind of fatalistic preparedness—so that if my husband should go astray, I would expect it, but could not, nevertheless, receive it with any more poise than if it came as a surprise. I do not mistrust Hugh. I mistrust life in general, human nature, myself—fate perhaps—I do not know. Beautiful things are fragile. Perfect things, in the same way, are fleeting. Nothing seems to have substance, endurance, constancy, except the tougher things of life—the prose. Poetry is evanescent.

November 14. Heard a very amusing criticism of my first book (for I have started a second) by Frank Monteiro, an artist-photographer. He thought it resembled the first painting of a student, which the master, with a few strokes of his own, could pull together. My book needed to be pulled together. Monteiro was charitable enough to leave Aline alone. He stressed the fact that the book made him feel young, that it made him feel again the ambitions, the ideals and the energy of his youth; that the philosophy of the book was sound. In short, he augured that in ten years or so I would write pretty good stuff.

The truth is that today no one on earth knows better than I do the faults of the book. I could write a criticism of it which would satisfy the exacting critics of the *Literary Review* or the *Post*, for example. I could ridicule the novel with more vigor than Shaw himself could display, in the face of a schoolgirl's outpourings, such as he would meet in *Aline's Choice*.

And yet, a warm feeling takes hold of me when others give it a little credit. After all, I put so much into Aline's life, and it is not my fault that she is so young, for the author was young.

The second, *The Blunderer* it is called, will be better, I believe, and also I feel that it will not take me ten years to become mature and professional, as Frank Monteiro thinks.

Very cold-bloodedly, I add on my fingers the qualities I am told I possess, to be balanced against my faults. And the faults seem to be of the acquired type—the virtues are inborn, and therefore there is hope.

And here I might say that it is to my husband that I owe the best of my training, in taste, in finesse, in whatever it is that lifts writing out of the commonplace—writing, I say, not ideas, for they are my own; and to Richard M. I owe whatever I am learning of technique and the professional.

How can I put in so many words what I owe to Hugh? If my taste was for the finest and the most beautiful when I met him, he has at least deepened it, adding to it a partiality for the intelligent and the reasonable, which as a dreaming girl I but barely perceived.

Eugene, and also Erskine, helped Hugh in ridding me of an inclination for the sentimental, which I gained from a branch of English literature.

I have learned so much from all of them because I respect them. That is the reason why I left high school—because I could not look up to my teachers and instinctively rebelled at their oppression of the individual.

Richard M. says that now, unfortunately, I have the faults that go with extreme individuality: the lack of discipline and training, the lack of the gift to learn. But I wonder if I am entirely lacking in these things—for surely I have learned from Hugh, from Eugene and from Richard M. himself. I think my noisy and productive spirit troubles him. He would like to quiet me down and set me going again with the regularity and the servility of a clock. He is shocked that I should write so much while knowing so little about the traffic regulations. His sense of orderliness and of the safety of laws makes him tremble when I let my ideas loose and do not even attempt to steer them.

November 19. I have to write in the kitchen to keep warm and, oh, it is so bitterly cold outside. How I long for the day of our departure—when the house problem will be settled, when I shall be nearer to fulfillment of a too-long-expected plan of life; and for less cold, for cold has the power to make me deeply miserable; and then for the rest and comfort on board ship.

Of course, I don't need to mention Mother and Father. It would be sad to dwell on my impatience to see them and on the troubled feelings they both give me. Richard M. says that I am a strong character. Will I be able to steer Mother, to control Father?

The other night I realized acutely how I have changed in the last year. It was while we were sitting around the fire. We were talking spasmodically, as people do under the fascination of the fire, and were more inclined to meditate. Every now and then I rose to rearrange the wood, to extinguish a spark fallen on the rug. I was the only one attentive to the practical needs of the fireside. Hugh was too deep in his dreams, and the others were in a kind of drowsiness.

The scene brought me back to other days, in Mother's house, when Enric, Eduardo, Mother, Joaquin, Thorvald and I used to sit around the fire. In those days I used to give myself entirely to my feelings and my thoughts, watching the fire drowsily. But it was Mother who stirred it with the poker, and it was Thorvald who would take care of the wood. And today it is I who tend the fire while the others dream.

Then, what is it that has happened to me? And what does it mean? And will I cease dreaming altogether soon?

December 8. 102 West 75th Street. Our adventure *really* began on November 29th when we left the bungalow and took this room, which now contains all our worldly belongings, a trunk full of clothes, a lavender-lined hatbox, a typewriter, a guitar. . . .

Through an immense window I have a most characteristic view of the city—so typical that if I drew it, it would be called trite. We eat out, we travel around the city in the bus. And as Paris looms nearer, our regrets grow, subtly, for things we had never noticed until these last few days . . . New York's peculiar attractions. There is the park, Riverside Drive, gorgeous Fifth Avenue, with window displays that are each one a gem.

The crowds pour in and out of subways, in and out of universities, in and out of concert halls, with equal energy and enthusiasm. They stand for hours before the paintings at the Exhibition of the National Academy. They support French, Italian, Swedish and chop suey restaurants, and they support the best European artists.

So versatile a book should satisfy us all. But the artistic, the intellectual, the cultural ones turn to Europe for the things they cannot find here. They pack up and sail, under the pretense of business.

We, who have sighed for Europe, are the Impatient Ones—those who cannot wait for the art that is just born here. The pioneers remain, and what a gigantic undertaking, theirs!

But we, in a few years, surfeited with Europe's beauty and Europe's art, bored perhaps by Europe's perfection, by the sight of things so eternally accomplished, so hopelessly finished, we, I believe, will return to the half-modeled clay, to the unfinished work.

December 9. The wisdom of those who have lived longer than I, though I never recognize it at the moment, is afterwards nearly always justified.

Only a few weeks ago R. Maynard asked me whether I feared that someone might read my secrets in my journal. I smiled and boasted that I had no such fear, and wondered why he should have it. Only a few weeks ago! Since then the full meaning of his fears has been revealed to me. I discovered that I had not been writing because I did have secrets—secrets I could not trust my journal with.

Several weeks ago I had a disappointment, and I flew to my

journal. I sat down eagerly with my heart so full . . . and I did not write.

Days later I said to myself: "I was foolish to be sad over that, yet it exists. But I must not write of it, as it would do more harm than good." I missed the consolation of confiding in you, although it would have been nothing but an act of pure selfishness.

Then it happened again and later a third time. And today my mind was full of these thoughts I had not written, and they weighed on me. Then I remembered R.M.'s remark and I realized that I was growing older and that my experiences, from now on, will often be secrets from the world, from my Love and from my friends.

It was so simple, before, to be open and confiding. Everybody was more or less nice. I did not find anything to be sad about, except in my own imaginary and inward life. The angers of my girlhood were mild and mostly self-reproachful. I evaded criticism, I evaded *facing* things, I evaded *thinking* of wrong things, and therefore, how simply I opened my heart, how harmless my confidences.

Now that I am older, strange, inconsistent things happen to me, things I am ashamed of—a *good*, noble-natured man *bores* me, my loved ones have *faults*, strangers try in every way to cheat me of my money—and my faith.

The whole face of the world has changed. I am not sad now because the leaves have withered, or because Hypatia[1] died, but because Mother is perhaps blundering, or because someone unexpectedly proves himself stupid, or another selfish.

And I suffer in silence. To satisfy my habit of communion, I would have to bring upon the heads of people I either love or pity weighty accusations that I have not the heart to utter.

From now on, what stand shall I take? Not to tell all—to select, perhaps. It would be better not to see, not to feel the things I am ashamed to write, but that I cannot do.

I must not forget to tell you, when I have time, about the second difficult moment in our marriage, and how we came out of it.

We had a delightful lunch with Dr. Erskine. He told us the story of the book he is writing now and was, generally speaking, and above everything else, terribly *clever* and terribly *human*.

Why must one, at such times, talk in order to be talked to by

[1] *The heroine of* Hypatia, *by Charles Kingsley.*

a man like that? Or else, why can one not become equally clever at times? His was a mere soliloquy, and Hugh and I, although of course we talked, were the awed spectators. For a moment I felt like saying to Dr. Erskine: "Dr. Erskine, I am frightened to death of speaking to you. Will you please talk to me on and on. . . . I can *understand*, at least, oh, *so much!*"

Hugh, at the first lunch, with the enthusiasm of a lover, filled Erskine's ears with talk about my book. I let him, then. Erskine smiled at him, listened to him, exhibiting a polite interest. But I felt, oh, so keenly, that Hugh had unconsciously been foolish. This time he wanted me to bring quotations from my book, or from my journal—anything, something. He begged and entreated me, but I held firm. The result was that Erskine talked of his work, which was certainly the work of a genius, and talked warmly and sincerely.

There is no one on earth *truthfully* interested in others' work if he is himself a creator—no one. I am more interested in my own writing than in other people's. R. Maynard, who deceives himself and really believes he is interested in my writing, never exhibits certain facial expressions except when he is telling me about one of his own stories. And he perhaps is the most unselfish man I have ever met.

Thank heaven, egotism is also our salvation. Without the desire for self-improvement, self-achievement, what would we do? R. Maynard would spend his life distracted by my lack of technique, and I would be in a perpetual state of despair concerning his slowness. Erskine would spend his days correcting his pupils' verses instead of writing poetry himself.

Yet while admiring Erskine I did discover his weak point. He lacks the genius that Mlle. de Lespinasse[1] had, of bringing out the best in other people. He perpetually drops others' ideas to follow another of his own. He failed to bring out the best in Hugh and the best in R. Maynard, to whom we introduced him after the lunch. In fact, he has a gift for belittling people. Now that is all very well as long as what Erskine brings out of himself is by far cleverer than what he might bring out in others. Looking at it philosophically he makes a choice whose wisdom is unquestionable.

Nevertheless, I question the results of such an attitude. His writing must suffer by it. He misses deep experiences. He entirely

---

[1] *Julie Jeanne Éléanore de Lespinasse (1732–76), author of* Lettres de Mlle. de Lespinasse.

missed the beauty of Eugene's mind, Hugh tells me. And only last night Eugene sat with us, for our last evening together, and opened his heart to us and told us about his sufferings and of how he seems not to be able to adjust himself to the world, of how things shock and disappoint and hurt him to a degree often unendurable.

That evening sealed a bond of sympathy between Eugene and me which will never be altered. He suffers continuously that nameless thing I suffer but now and then. I understood him, and his confidence troubled and moved me very deeply.

Hugh and I did try to help Eugene. We searched our memory for the day on which our readjustment to things had begun, and we tried to describe what had helped us. We are at peace with the world now, comparatively speaking, because we have followed Carlyle's advice in his "The Everlasting Yea." Eugene is still in The Everlasting Nay.

We found our peace in domestic life, in work, in love; and I, particularly in writing. My imagination still has hold over me. I think it has over Hugh, too, but fitfully, with periods of rest and normal dullness in between. We at least no longer feel the terrible isolation Eugene feels. Even our nightmares are shared, and they do not seem like madness any more. Oh, I remember the old crises, the same blackness Eugene describes, the same sense of something giant and crushing and horrible and distorted. But more often now I see the madness of these moods. And I must find the exact cause of them for Eugene.

The trunk is nearly packed again. We leave Tuesday, and tomorrow is our last day in New York. We have spent most of the last days saying good-bye to people rather than to ideas and to things. That shows how much our life has changed. We have joined the crowd a little, and like others we have friends and obligations and conventional ties, such as Eugene would never endure. It is part of our normal life. No one knows what it costs us, sometimes, to pay some of these visits, to act like social animals. We are still too much the "sauvages"[1] and the dreamers to be always in the mood for conventional sociability, but we do it.

One lady, the one of the tough texture, takes me on a shopping tour when I would prefer to be writing. Someone else invites us to hear a radio when we desired to go to a true concert. Are Hugh and I cowards to compromise thus with the world?

That is part of our readjustment. We have ceased to be re-

[1] *Unsociable ones.*

bellious, antagonistic. We are mildly critical and secretly furiously individualistic, but to the world, a not unpleasant young couple who do not fit badly at a tea and are on the whole quite harmless.

We begin to see that bad things are not so bad, but ignorant, and that ignorance half the time has good intentions. We find things trivial and stupid rather than horrifying or monstrous. Ugly things as well as beautiful things lose much by actual contact. Eugene, through his imagination, exalts and distorts them both into what they are really not. He wonders that people around him seem to notice nothing wrong. It is partly stupidity, toughness of texture, but it is also a matter of habit, and because their imagination has little to feed on.

Solitude, criticalness, antagonism, these give the imagination the sting which poisons and exaggerates what it touches. The realization that things are in reality small, trivial, ridiculous and weak comes when one accepts, by the act of turning to something worthwhile. The energy spent in *suffering* could be spent in the only thing which can serve to destroy the causes of such suffering —self-perfection, creation.

It is really I who am preaching thus today when only a few years ago my world could be made black by the most childish disappointment.

I write while Hugh meets his mother, somewhere uptown, a meeting I arranged myself for their sake—for my Love, above all.

Soon it will be two hours that they have spent together. Who is this mother I have never known and who lost her son when he married me? I have such tenderness for her because she must have been so unhappy, and she is *his* mother.

Suddenly this last month our life has really become more breathless and interesting. I am a lady all day now, not just occasionally for a few hours in Richard M.'s studio. And soon we will be in Paris!

December 18. On board "La France"—the second day. Except for the rumble of machinery, I would not realize that every minute we are taken farther away from New York—the sea is so smooth and I have hardly noticed it, being so wrapped up in the interior, luxurious life of the ship. But nothing yet has consoled me for the sadness I felt in leaving.

Hugh's family came, all but his father, who had not received the letter he expected from Hugh. His mother and I kissed and wept together—how sweet she is, and how she has suffered! The reconciliation so long expected and for which not one of us dared take the first step is now fulfilled through my letter, and what a joy it was to see Hugh's happiness.

We parted from Eugene—Hugh broke down, but Eugene held his feelings back and walked away with his head bowed. And then from George Gillette, and this was, as things usually are with him, a rather light ceremony.

"The lady of the tough texture" came, and we parted easily from her.

Then there was Frank Monteiro, Ruth Morgan and Richard M. I did not break down until, hanging over the rail, from where we could see the people who stood at the end of the pier, I caught sight of Richard M.'s face, he who stayed the longest and for whom I realized keenly I felt the strongest affection.

Hugh wanted to stay on deck and watch N.Y. disappear.

"No," I said, "I couldn't stand it. I want to forget all about it. Let us go down and look at the presents." But before going down we looked around us and found that the sun had broken through the misty day, and it shone just for a moment.

Looking at the presents did not cheer us, however. I cried more when I saw how thoughtful Richard M. had been, giving me paper book binders, carbon paper, typewriter pads—all I need for my writing—and a rod fan I had expressed a liking for.

Everything disappoints me. I had dreamed of this trip and have found many things that are beautiful about it, but today, the *social* side of it palled on me. I have shut myself up in the cabin, feeling utterly wretched, while Hugh is taking tea with Count Guicciardi, of whom I shall say more later.

I had resolved to take part in the social life, but at the first taste of it I felt alone again, and unhappy. I should rather say that I disappoint *myself* in everything—that is more exact. I am too capricious, too different, I don't know what, but I tire quickly of insipid talk, or of a lot of talk. I cannot be idle. Oh, to think I have not yet conquered that, at my age!

In every other way the trip is so beautiful. The sea is smooth, our cabin is pretty and comfortable, the salons are luxurious, the food exquisite. There is no flaw anywhere, only in my own moods.

I have brought you down to the salon, where we shall hear music by and by. The sadness has passed, with the glow and formality of the dinner shared with Hugh alone. And also because of the flattering glances I received as I came down the stairs with Hugh and made my way to our table. That is the only thing that reconciles me to society, and what reconciled me to the social life in Havana—flattery. In the luxury of the turquoise-and-red salon I laugh at myself.

We spent part of the afternoon writing letters. That made me realize that we had left our friends irrevocably. All through dinner I watched the French people around us with a mixture of antagonism and curiosity. I say "antagonism" because the moment I came face to face with them, with their different voices, gestures, dress even, I felt something of their foreignness.

Hugh laughs at me and asks me what I am. Not American, that is certain, not French, not Spanish.

That fits my philosophy to perfection—the fact that neither in reality nor in feeling do I belong to any nation.

Fourth day. We spent one day in our cabin, while the boat rolled violently, but we finally grew accustomed to the strenuous movement and have ever since taken part in the normal routine of ship life with the other hardy sailors. We sit on deck chatting with Count Guicciardi, we have our meals with two actors from the company of the Odéon, we experiment with liqueurs and even with dice, and by the time we reach Le Havre we shall even be so completely educated as to be able to walk like this / or like this \ without awkwardness.

The French, seeing Hugh the American tagging after me, do not receive me entirely into their confidence. They don't know exactly what to make of me. Do they know, I wonder, that I cannot make *them* out? I feel safe only with Guicciardi, with Hugh and with my journal.

It is so strange to find myself with people whose thoughts I do not know and cannot guess. I used to guess correctly at what Americans thought. Already, meeting the purser in one of our walks on deck, I expected one remark from him and got another. He might have said: "Lovely day, isn't it?" but he said instead, "C'est ça, continuez a marcher. C'est un très bon apéritif."[1]

"He was thinking of his food," remarked Hugh, justly.

When I come down the stairs for dinner at night, and coming

[1] "*That's it, keep walking. It's very good for the appetite.*"

down those stairs in evening dress is the only dramatic moment in the day, I wonder what the ladies who stare at me so are thinking. It is safe to suggest that the American might either find me "cute" or "too skinny," but the French look is more critical. I feel that my expression is studied, as well as my features.

With men it is always easier. I am, generally, more at home with them on every occasion. They all have one weakness in common—you are pretty or nothing. Prettiness, with all men, will help you across the difficult moment. It is the women that bother me—perhaps I bother them.

Americans, just at this time, would find me in a most sympathetic mood, for already I look at them with misty eyes, like something dear and lost. If I were not married already, I could easily accept any one of them today and return with him to New York on the same boat.

Guicciardi has talked to us so much about women, about his ideas on marriage, about life in general, that I feel older already. But that is while he is talking. The moment I open my mouth to say something equally clever, equally ambiguous, equally experienced, then I feel like a fool, and a young one at that.

The reading of Anne Douglas Sedgwick's *Little French Girl* has deepened my experience (even though I could not forgive her for writing a book exactly as Henry James would have written it, only less well) with this added phenomenon—that I neither took the side of the French nor of the English, but was constantly passing from one to the other.

The young, blue-eyed, long-haired man who sits at my right at the table turns out to be a painter, besides being an actor at the Odéon. We had quite a little talk while Hugh, who was hesitating whether to feel sick or not, finally went to sit on deck.

Every now and then my eloquence is cut short by the table rolling from under me, or by my chair taking me to another part of the deck, in front of somebody else's half-finished letter. Sometimes, too, I have to walk a mile to find my ink bottle and crawl under the couch in the Salon Louis XIV.

And then, just as I am about to reveal a secret of the greatest importance, Guicciardi will come, always in search of consolation, as he has left a sweetheart in America.

The musicians wait for the passengers that were to listen to their concert, but the salon remains quite empty. And I wait for the musicians.

December 24. Paris struck my ears first of all with a sound like that of trumpets at carnival time. I was informed that those were the taxicabs. Then, after that, there was the grayness of the buildings and the shabbiness of the passers-by.

"But Paris is so dingy!" I exclaimed.

"No, Paris is ancient," Hugh corrected me, this being his second visit here.

After these things I noticed nothing else but Mother and Thorvald and Joaquin—Joaquin, my little loved one, who has tuberculosis. We must send him away, to the mountains. He must get well, but he will never be a pianist. What a pathetic little figure he is, sitting up in bed, with his books or writing. He can go out only in taxis, and even then not too often.

We found them all in a true French garret, with its casement windows and sloping ceiling. It was cold and uncomfortable, and at that moment, however artistic the atmosphere, both Hugh and I felt keenly why Thorvald is completely unnerved. If Mother goes away with Joaquin, he will return to Havana where he can work in more congenial surroundings. And Hugh and I will be left in Paris, which I do not love yet—which I hate, perhaps, tonight, with an English soul. For Paris has been revealed to me in two persons, both individually important enough to count: Father and Guicciardi.

Both, in different ways, are men of the world, supremely educated, with a degree of culture never even imagined by our best Americans—but how cold-blooded, how cynical, how utterly devoid of illusions, of delicacy, of purity, each is in his own way!

I understood my father in a flash. He met me with tears, to which I could not sincerely respond; he talked to me with a show of emotions I could not feel; he told me things which a year ago would have killed me with unreasonable horror and disgust. But yesterday I listened calmly, finding no answer to his irreproachable and vicious logic—in fact, I logically approved him, although I forgave, consoled and deceived him for the most illogical of causes—pity!—the heartrending pity I feel now for what I once hated.

Yes, he was Paris—intelligent, insidious, cultured Paris. Yet he did not get the best of me in this encounter, for I understood him better than he understood me. And the advantages were on my side, even though he is the one who knows so well, so beautifully, what to say and how to say it. But I, being his daughter, can also act when necessary, and I did act, by my silences, by my weighing of his phrases, by my poise—when, really, inwardly I was all cries of surprise, all doubts, all fears.

This stranger, my father, whom I have to reckon with and handle, has made me old overnight. Before, I lost so much time when things befell me in crying out, in childish surprise, while now I meet and face them.

Then, too, I have Thorvald's help. Thorvald has grown, too, even if in so different a manner. We had such a sound talk about Father, who would not have believed his ears if he had heard us, for it turns out that both his children are better actors than he is, for we saw through him. It remains to be seen if he has seen through us.

The problem is this: He is divorced from Mother and about to marry an heiress. It would appear that he should have no need of us, but instead of that he seeks eagerly to win our affection and our occasional companionship. We have reason to believe that his interest is not fatherly love. Then why does he want us? His protestations of devotion, his tears, his dramatic gestures, have all struck us falsely. I am going to find him out.

Thorvald believes that he has the following to gain by our allegiance: Social standing, which he needs as an artist much in the public eye (if we refused to see him, people would know it and conclude the fault was his); and the power to humiliate Mother, who had humiliated him.

I asked Thorvald if he ever considered that Father might believe his own lies. He had not, he admitted. Such complexities are not part of his nature. However, Thorvald, who admits of no compromise, has made his choice and refuses to see him any more. He only sees things in black and white. I am not like that.

December 28. Things became clearer in our minds when Hugh and I took a peaceful walk together on Christmas morning through the Tuileries, passing the Louvre to the Church of St. Germain-l'Auxerrois. It was a day of weak sunshine, so rare in Paris during the winter, but enough to dispel the mist that hangs continuously over the city, and for the first time we were conscious of the pleasure of being in Paris.

We watched the bird-charmer feeding his pets from a park bench, we hung over the parapet and blinked at the river, we paused at the bookstalls on the quay, thinking all the while: Paris is sweet this morning, Paris is sweet.

The first things I had noticed were the flower stands, the

women jostling by with their long, thin loaves of bread hugged close, the blue-frocked soldiers and the muddy cobblestone streets. I was still dazzled by the splendor, the newness and greatness of New York. Paris's old charm was slow to reach me. I was unaccustomed to appreciating the history of a house rather than its cleanliness, efficiency, appearance. The mists of Paris pierced my slippers before they reached my head and soul. I think the bookstalls have wakened the poet, and I see Paris as it should be.

I dined with my distinguished father and met the little lady he is about to marry. She is sweet and very true, and whether she is under his spell or whether she sees him as he really is and still loves him I have yet to discover. The most important fact is that he is at his best with her, and it was when I saw them together that I liked him best.

𝒦 1 9 2 5 𝒦

January 2. Tonight I hate Paris. The wind is blowing heavy raindrops about; the streets are wet and muddy; the automobile horns, more discordant and insistent than ever. Mother in her garret must be poking the insipid little stove so that it might come to life, while the cold wind rushes in through the slits in the windows. And then we are two steps away from the Rue du Bac, which Anatole France mentions in his *La Rôtisserie de la Reine Pédauque,* and the book is horrible, and it is Paris. Guicciardi liked it. Its virtue is its cleverness. I must learn the meaning of that word. Money has different values, and probably words have, too. You get more francs here in exchange for a solid-looking dollar. You get more complexities, more elasticity, for one compact, unswerving English word. "Moral," for instance, has been stretched here, whereas it is England's most stolid word.

Is it fair to Paris to judge it on a rainy day and while reading Anatole France? Any more than judging the French people's honesty by their taxi drivers?

We spent New Year's Eve walking up and down the boulevards, Thorvald, Hugh and I. At midnight, as is my custom, I neither felt nor thought anything with any particular sincerity. The world-wide ceremony acts on me like the fixed hour of religious emotion set by our church. Being in Paris did not thrill me, and for a moment I even wondered whether I had lost my youth, at twenty-one, because I have lost my sense of adventure. What am I, now that I can look so much more critically at things? Even as Hugh does?

Soon I shall have become so stable, so restrained, so worldly wise, that I will be able to write a book without the youthful "gushing" of my *Aline*. But may I keep the sense of beauty, the sense of poetry.

I find that life, day by day, is composed of at least one joy, one problem and one sorrow. Then there are the smaller ingredients: you always *learn* something, whether useful or harmful—that is difficult to analyze until later; you always *give* something; you always *grow* a little in one direction or another.

My problem just now, which will spread out over a number of days, is Father—Father in relation to Mother rather than to me. Logical and illogical situations are involved. So far, I control the affair. Mother is not hurt. Father is satisfied. Thorvald has been considerably broadened and molded in the process. But one false step, and everything will go wrong. Even gossip and things beyond my own control can destroy my work.

Hugh helps me by understanding everything. We have learned toleration together, and it is out of our common hardships that our philosophy has sprung. It is sweet, indeed, to have someone to grow with, to find that our marriage, instead of bringing a clash between two set characters, has been from the very beginning a melting into one another. And with a happy coincidence we always manage to change together, so that there is no time for even a temporary discord.

January 3. Today we move into a "pension"—which means boardinghouse, and yet doesn't, really sounding better and more refined. Simultaneously we will begin to live the true French life, as this hotel is full of Americans and the sound of our familiar tongue made us forget sometimes that we were in Paris. I rather liked this more gentle transplanting—a sudden plunge into a crowd of French people would have chilled me.

My ridiculous attitude towards Paris shows that I love with my intellect, not with my instincts and my emotions. My intellect was bred in English letters, and no instinct of race or birth can influence me. This dullness of the heart, this lack of responsiveness, shock me and please me at the same time. The humorous side of it is that the French would be the first to understand and to approve of me. The English would, by contrast, urge me to love my native city without reasoning about it. Through recognition of the supremacy of the intelligence, I belong, then, to Paris. Yet I kneel here, humbly sentimentalizing about the English. What inconsistencies! I shall truly end by being spiritually repudiated by all nations.

The Problem showed me a new face when Thorvald swung to the other extreme and chose to forget and forgive. I am still among the shadows and wondering how on earth Thorvald can take such uncompromising attitudes and make of the most difficult situations a simple one. Now he will see Father and meet the Little Lady.

"What of Mother now?" I ask him. "She must not be hurt."

"She must not know, that's all."

That's all! And that, with all aspects of the deception, keeps me awake nights! It is fortunate that Thorvald is going away. Alone I can pull my little cobweb so as not to break any of the threads.

January 4. 60 Rue d'Assas, Room No. 27. This morning, after Hugh left for the bank and I had stayed for an hour in bed, hesitating to wake thoroughly to a day of dissatisfaction, I finally rose and dragged myself lazily to the window and drew the curtains aside.

The sun was shining! Blinking at it with inexpressible joy, I dressed hurriedly and walked out. Paris on a sunny day is such a different thing!

The women were marketing, the children sauntering to school. Men were crying out their wares in the streets, boys were delivering the long loaves of bread in long, narrow baskets. In the mild air, the sounds of small, bustling lives rose in a kind of cheerful dissonance. I walked along with the rest, down a narrow street on a sidewalk a yard wide, and up the Boulevard Raspail, which is wide and has two rows of trees, to Mother's garret.

The shadow was lifted, for I had been terribly discouraged these last days. Paris was gloomy, Mother downhearted, the pension impossible, and on Saturday night when we went to bed between two damp sheets, after turning off a glaring electric light and seeing for the last time a wallpaper that is bad enough to drive us insane—to say nothing of the furniture—I wished that we had never come.

What it amounts to is that Paris must be seen romantically, that in every other respect, materially, practically, it is a dismal failure. And Hugh and I are not bohemians, although we thought we were. Life in New York has cured that if we ever had it.

Still dazed sometimes by the change, I have stood at the window studying the houses across the street, the passers-by. In rooms like ours and sometimes in rooms less habitable than ours have lived great writers, great musicians, sculptors, the best poets. They have worked at the side of a little coal stove, such as Mother has, and sometimes without stove at all, and they have done wonderful things. They have gone out under the rain and returned to musty and damp rooms and seen such furniture as we have seen, and even similar wallpaper, without losing their cheerfulness and their wits.

Then why cannot we do the same?

Of course, they had never known anything else, as we have. It is the tasting of many things which finally makes the connoisseur and the crank. We have known the art of practical life, known it to perfection. That is why our spoiled natures refuse so obstinately to adapt themselves to an almost primitive rudeness, so inexplicable in a city that is hailed as an intellectual center, because intelligence should spread itself into every art—and the "Art of Living" is certainly not the meanest of them.

If I give this weakness an undeserved importance, it is because I am above all preoccupied with the making of a home. That is my first responsibility. And it is in this capacity that I resent the difficulties I have met with. Afterwards my mind may find complete satisfaction here, but I cannot concern myself with that before the other. I am already impatient to sip Paris's honey and then depart—and its honey, because of the uncomfortable positions one must endure while tasting it, must be sipped hurriedly.

January 6. Last night we went to a concert with Count Guicciardi, and although the music was not so very good, I felt again that it had the power both to intensify and to harmonize experience.

The spirituality of things returned to me—the sense of nobility, of understanding, of charity and resignation. The petty discontent, the petty faultfinding egoism, left me. Music makes me good, as I would like to make people good by my writing. Then, for a moment, too, I thought that I had caught the purpose of things, that which makes the pains of our daily lives small and trivial by comparison—but then, it again escapes me, and one light note reminded me of the Demoniac Spirit, which I fear to discover at every turn of the road.

Through a curious perversity of mind, my absence from New York, my separation from such kinds of intellect as I have found in Eugene, in George Nolte,[1] in Richard M., I am drawn more closely to them, to English letters. The certainty that it is English I want to write and English-speaking people I want to be read by has existed only since I heard French and lived with the French. This separation has served to strengthen a once unconscious relationship, brought me a beautiful assurance, crystallized my vaguest dreams into a definite choice.

Whatever I had hoped to find here, what I criticized America for not having, what thousands of Americans are seeking here in Paris, is an intangible thing that I find complete only when the Americans come in possession of it; esprit, wisdom, culture, refinement—these shine in the French like precious pearls in a decaying oyster. By an extremity of intelligence, in many ways unbalanced, the French have reached an unhealthy, coarse kind of fatalism which is equal to the torpor of ignorant people, and their lives are not any more beautiful. This at least I gather from more reading of Anatole France, who is such a Frenchman and so beloved by the people he has expressed.

January 7. I have received such a beautiful letter from Richard M., written in the form of a journal, a delicious note of intimate confidence, of thoughtful communion, as if indeed he had written it for himself alone. I had the feeling that I was reading over his shoulder while he was writing his impressions on the day of our departure. And what I read was somehow so much more of himself than he ever showed in his formal letters—and it was this which gave me the greatest pleasure, the feeling of freedom and spontaneity.

But now I am distressed. He has started our journal correspondence with a boom, so to speak, and I wonder if I can live up to it.

Richard M. half feared, I know, that I should fit in so well into the life in Paris that my English would suffer. I had that fear myself in New York when I dreamed of Paris and, as Emerson puts it, when I hungered to be on the ship that sailed the other

[1] *An associate of Hugh's at National City Bank in New York.*

way from mine; but when I was on it I was not satisfied and looked for another sail. I had to be transplanted to know where I belonged, but now I know it, irrevocably.

Mother took me to visit two old French spinsters, and we talked with them in a little musty salon about sickness and religion and the cost of living. When they asked me with the most delicious politeness and concern "si je ne me plaisais pas à Paris,"[1] I was at a loss to analyze my true feelings and answered with a commonplace, thinking to myself that this unfriendliness of mine was probably due to a simple attack of homesickness. By night I was convinced, when Mother, Thorvald, Hugh and I visited Mr. and Mrs. Armando Godoy, Cubans, friends of Father and Mother, but at different periods. Mr. Godoy's celebrated library is the most wonderful I have ever seen; he has manuscripts of Hugo, Baudelaire, Anatole France, original editions of all kinds, beautifully bound copies of everything—but little in English. He loves Baudelaire and Flaubert particularly. In his possession are some letters of Juliette Drouet to Victor Hugo, and some of her household accounts, in which she makes entries like the following:

De la bourse de mon petit Toto	50Fr
Gagné par mon adoré	60Fr
Reçu de mon cher petit mari	100Fr
Gagné par mon chéri	50Fr[2]

I imagined Eugene in that library. Thinking of Eugene reminded me of my homesickness, which I had forgotten. From this I drew the conclusion that perhaps, after all, the place did not matter so much . . . but the books, the people. . . .

January 9. I have mentioned only the little sadnesses, but tonight I had to face the things that hurt me most after I bid Mother and Joaquin good-bye[3] and saw Thorvald off this morning.[4] Again

[1] *"If I were not enjoying Paris."*
[2] *From my little Toto's purse . . .*
Earned by my adored one . . .
Received from my dear little husband . . .
Earned by my darling . . .
[3] *They went first to Salies de Béarn and then Hendaye, in southwest France, for Joaquin's health.*
[4] *Thorvald went to Havana to live with his Aunt Antolina and cousin Charlie (Carlos de Cárdenas).*

the whole family is separated and unhappy. In this past day I have reached a decision about my father which no logic could have forced on me. Above all things I must not hurt Mother.

January 11. The stoic can love Paris. He can stand the cold, the rain, the dirt, anything. So can the artist love Paris; while he discourses with other artists, studies and lives his artistic life as he could live it nowhere else, he too forgets about other things. But today I, who am neither of those, loved Paris. By the gray light that fell through the big windows of the Louvre, we saw Murillo's and Greuze's work and Boticelli's, distinguished them from among a thousand others, and walked out of the gloomy palace filled with a sense of beauty, of color, of harmony. And then we stood again at the bookstalls, enveloped by the mists that were rising from the Seine, shivering but ecstatic, turning the pages of loved and coveted books.

And then I sat here, in the violently ugly room of the pension, still shivering, and yet felt ashamed of my first materialistic revulsions, and dreamed again of Murillo's Immaculate Conception and of the books and of the Seine and the mist-covered city.

Hugh has settled down to the reading of *La Rôtisserie de la Reine Pédauque,* after a heated discussion in which, with the most unselfish spirit, we both proposed to sacrifice the one pen we own to each other. He hypocritically flattered me and my journal, and then, when he saw me resign myself to writing, sank back with a sigh of contentment to his lazy enjoyment of somebody else's work. And so I am left to write a book while he reads another, and so it will be forever, I fear—that in quarreling over pen and ink he will be the first to yield, with customary gentleness.

I forgot to mention that, interwoven with more spiritual things, we were invited to a tea today. The apartment was warm; the lady, French and charming, married to a stupid American. There were others there, two mixed couples—Frenchwomen married, inexplicably, to Americans—and one thoroughly French couple. We chatted about how the French storekeepers and bus conductors were all so anxious to cheat in giving change, wherewith I exclaimed that it was done particularly to Americans, but the French hostess did not agree with me and advised me with a sympathetic smile to learn to count my change. I liked her, not because of this, but because her face was bright and her manner vivacious; and also because her flabby, dull husband suited her so badly. I waited hopefully for them to talk about art, and finally it came, in this form:

"Did you hear how Antoine is painting now?" said one lady.

"Why no!" exclaimed a second.

"Who is he?" asked another.

The lady explained that Antoine was her dentist, and that he had suddenly taken to painting wild, modern things.

"What a shame! What are they like?"

"Red and blue and green, all mixed up, with a tree in the middle going through a wall."

"That reminds me," said one of the ladies, "I'm having a dress made out of the prettiest blue stuff you ever saw."

"Really? Who sews for you?"

And we got talking about dresses.

Disappointed, I turned to the right, where Hugh was engaged in serious talk with one of the Americans.

"Well," he was saying, with the well-known wrinkles in his forehead that indicate deep concentration, "of course, business opportunities . . ."

It was not *his* fault. The other man was a *commerçant*.[1]

January 12. I tired myself out writing letters and seek peace from too much effusion. I was sadly meditating, besides, about my sudden and intense materialism. I think it is born of physical suffering. But then, as a young girl, I used to pride myself that the physical did not affect my thoughts or feelings, and I believed that I could conquer hunger, cold and weariness. Whence this change, this lack of stoicism?

How well I understand Eugene tonight—Eugene whose physical ailments have injured his spiritual life, have prevented him from creating, have kept him from the most ordinary form of literary activities. Yes, pain is useful. To understand Eugene, I have had to know, too, this phase of human suffering. But I must soon pass out of it, into another.

Today, in the dense fog, I saw Paris like a magic city. The shadowy people, the muffled sounds, the fantastic air that hung over the most common voitures-à-bras,[2] over the vague and featureless heads of the vendors. The Seine has completely disappeared. I walked over a bridge that spanned two clouds.

[1] *Businessman.*
[2] *Handcarts.*

At noon the fog was dispelled, and in the clearer light the city rose again, old, dead, to a progressing present, while only a moment ago it was alive with a rich and tremendous past. The softness under our feet, which had been like a Persian rug of enchantment, turned to plebeian grass, brilliantly green with humidity. The bridge at each end was firmly bound to solid earth.

I have gathered that the French do not live in nature as much as I am accustomed to. For one thing, they never talk about the weather.

It is a question of giving up some things for the sake of others. Surely, there is nothing in New York equal to the sweetness of awakening, as one does here, to the cry of "Mimosa! Mimosa!" which an old man sells in the streets—the delicate, fragrant, yellow flowers from the south of France. Paris is rich in flowers, and none of its gardens are quite withered, thanks to the gray mist upon which I brooded so disconsolately at first. I will live in the flowers instead of in Paris's wintry grayness.

Paris at night is deliciously quiet. The gas street lamps leave everything in a state of shadowiness, and the darkness is the more impressive because the houses are so firmly and completely shut down—the huge, massive portals are barred, the shutters drawn tight, the shopwindows covered with iron sheets or panel doors. To walk home late at night down the narrow sidewalks is to think of all the old romances one has read.

January 14. I had the most extraordinary experience. Working on my old journals, I felt that the reading of them made me *good*; I felt that I had no right to disappoint that "me" of sixteen who believed so sweetly in all beautiful things, that I should do nothing today to hurt the strange being who exists in those pages. I would be ashamed to disappoint her when I see so clearly there the ideals in her own girlish words. I have actually created a being of long-lost sweetness and faith, of whom I stand in awe and whom I revere. I may laugh at her youth, but not very long, for her sincerity silences me. Beautiful words written in the first flush of ardent aspirations, enthusiasms. They will guide me. If I can grow old while believing in them I will be able to stand before the Girl unashamed.

January 15. Still affected by the spirit of my old journals, and the Self I found in them, I walked out this morning and saw Paris in a more gentle and sympathetic way. It is true that the sun was shining and that it was less cold, but I have known other mild days here, and none were as sweet as today. I realized that what I was losing was sweetness—that things now tasted bitter when I applied my new-found wisdom to them. How wrong I was!

I will see the Problem on Saturday, and I know that I am going to feel old and motherly and that it will be difficult for me to tell the Problem about my decisions. Thorvald is happily far away from all this, and I almost envy him.

I exhaust myself writing daily letters to Mother and Joaquín, occasional ones to Johnnie, Ruth, Richard M., Frances, my aunts and cousins, so that I come to my poor journal with weary eyes and cramped fingers and write stupidly of complex things. If Hugh would only help me. But in the cleverest ways he evades writing his journal. To punish him, I paste all his notes to me here in my journal, where he cannot touch them and where I can read them over.

January 16. We had lunch with the Countess G.[1] With childish romanticism I had expected her to be a very stately and gracious-minded person who would receive us with much dignity and with whom we would converse about refined and delicate subjects. When we entered the large apartment and her son took us to his room, I thought to myself: "She will wait for us in the salon."

But no. A bustling little lady of substantial proportions fell on us with a shower of greetings and apologies, rushed us into the dining room, explained that, one of the maids having gone, the cook had to do everything, and what a pity she had forgotten the glasses—and those were the wrong ones (to the son who was helping)—and would we forgive her for the way she was obliged to receive us, etc., etc. (I promised myself that I would never apologize for my dinners.)

Later, the lady, with motherly concern, told me where I should do my marketing (we are moving near them), questioned me about this and that, satisfied herself that I knew enough about housekeeping, advised me about my husband, my mother and father, my dresses, the maid problem, etc., and religion, and impressed me with her common sense, her capability to save money and to run a household, her domesticity and her piety.

Once or twice she was called away to the telephone, and I was left to my meditations and the fifth French salon I have seen, with

[1] *Horace Guicciardi's mother.*

the usual marble-top fireplace, two symmetrical ornaments on it—
this time the traditional clock was absent. But elsewhere there was
the traditional Louis XVI green-and-gold upholstery, the artificial
flowers, lace doilies on the countless little tables. The piano had
turned its back to the audience, and over it hung a shawl and on
top of that was bric-a-brac and as many photographs as there was
room for. The walls and ceiling were carved. Portraits of ancestors
hung around the room. And amidst all this the capable home-
maker sat and said to me: "En Amérique, il n'y a pas de traditions, et moi, j'adore les traditions."[1]

"Mais oui," I said.

I have been writing. I have worked on my second book, on a play,
and planned for a book on "Journals and Journal Writing," which
I have a strong desire to write.

January 19. My Love and I have passed through the first crisis of
our marriage—passed triumphantly. But forever after I shall
never be at rest—the fear has come too close to me, and I am a
fatalist. I trust him, I believe him, but I mistrust and dread influences beyond him, the world. The very beginning of it (I
promised then to write of it) was in New York. Hugh was invited
out, for the first time without me, by S. from the bank, to a party
of men. It was when we were in the rented room on 75th Street.
I was, in reality as well as mentally, completely alone that night.
I went to bed and tried to read. The minutes were maddeningly
long. At eight o'clock I noted that he would be sitting down to the
dinner. At nine o'clock, that he must be finished. . . . Then my
agony began, for I did not know what he was to do afterwards, and
I was fearful and horribly jealous, jealous of those men, whom I
knew to be so inferior to Hugh, so unlike him, so hateful, jealous
of what they might teach him, what they might show him—
fearful that he would return to me sullied, changed, even if
vaguely, by an experience I had no share in. My imagination was
working with all its usual fire and wildness. I cried bitterly, I
paced the room, I wrote about other things, those furthest from
my thoughts. Twice during the evening the telephone rang, but
I was too terrified by my physical loneliness to answer it. At ten
o'clock he came. He was more loving than he had ever been. He
told me he had missed me, that he had not enjoyed himself at all,

---

[1] *"In America, there are no traditions, and I, I adore traditions."*

and had telephoned me twice. Finally, it seemed that he had even left them to do whatever they pleased, to come back to me. I was happy. I loved him more. I almost forgot all about the incident and our love continued untroubled by doubt and fear.

But now in Paris, I have to face a stranger thing. Hugh's work entails more sociability, and C., one of the men with whom it is important to maintain friendliness, is among the most detestable I have met in that respect. He invites Hugh to extravagant lunches, urges him to belong to clubs, and finally, on Sunday, he invited us both to a tea to meet his wife.

The tea took place in a luxurious hotel. Besides his wife, a small, pretty woman, we met a painter and his wife—a most curious combination of Breton and Hindu, who entertained us continuously with her untiring egoism, so that by the end of the afternoon I knew her life, her feelings, her soul, her ambitions— everything. During the one moment that she left us, to call up a friend, C.'s wife turned to me and we had a curious talk. Her husband never comes home to lunch and seldom to dinner. He is out continuously without her.

"And what do you do meanwhile?" I asked, profoundly troubled.

"I go out, too," she answered me, without the least satisfaction; rather, I thought, very sadly. This, with a few lingering, reproachful glances at her husband, who was talking with the painter, showed me her unhappiness. She asked me about Hugh and was surprised when I told her how seldom he stayed away for lunch—and the two times he did were because of her husband. Instantly she feared for my happiness. She warned me unselfishly not to let C. put ideas into Hugh's head, not to let Hugh fall into a terrible habit. While we were talking, the painter was inviting C. and Hugh to come and visit his studio. Hugh naïvely never doubted that I was included, but I, with premonition, managed to whisper to him: "Dear, I do not think he means me to come."

The surprise on Hugh's face made my heart leap. He turned to C. and asked him jokingly if "the wives are in on this." C. seriously said, "No, indeed, there I draw the line."

I shivered with a new feeling of iciness, as if I had received a mortal wound. The tea was over. Hugh and I went out into the fog and jumped on a shadowy bus, and we talked. He did not realize that the apparently meaningless invitation called for an important decision. I did, with a surer instinct than his. I told him that, if he accepted this, he would accept everything. C. would see that Hugh was willing to go out without me, and before he realized it, he would be floating down the selfsame stream.

I was fighting, like the most primitive woman, for the life of our love, for his purity, for our ideals of unity and loyalty, fighting to keep him from everything that a man like C. stands for, and I fought with every wile and trick and arm in my possession. I triumphed. I kept him—but I lost peace and security. I am tormented now by new fears, alarmed by new dangers. There is not a moment that I do not think: He is mine today, but tomorrow? . . . I want to grow accustomed to the thought of losing him someday, because I am too fatalistic to believe that we can always be as happy together as we are now. I want to face the very worst ways of losing him—to men, to their coarser companionship, to drink or to another woman. How horrible these things sound, how monstrous—how unlike Hugh, with his clear eyes, the goodness and kindness which emanates from him, Hugh with his loyal smile, his deep love.

My love for him is tyrannical because it is ideal, because I love his soul, his thoughts, because I could no more bear the sullying of his body than of his mind. I want not only his love but his ideal self preserved, stainless.

It is with the same puritanical soul that I look on my father as egotistical, untrue to the very core. He lies to me so much, in order to create a certain effect on me, in order to be for me something which he is not in reality, that I cannot love him. He is at heart cold and moved only by what affects him directly—his happiness and his comfort. I fear for the happiness of the Little Lady—she must be selfless and wonderfully devoted. Of course, she is his disciple, in piano as well as in life, and believes all he is. And yet, she is so true herself.

I wait for circumstances to separate us. I am cowardly in front of him. I do not want to hurt him, and yet all I can say to him, if I ever do say it, is: "I do not want to see you anymore because I do not love you and I am not interested in you."

Hugh, who is so good, cannot understand that I detest in Father things which I have spent my life destroying in myself. He cannot see that Father's traits were in my blood, that I knew them deeply, that I willfully and consciously crushed them out of my character. And what a struggle I endured.

Now when I see him, the embodiment of falsity, of selfishness, the depths of which I have sounded, I see him more clearly than anyone else could. He poses, he affects weariness, affection, he lies whenever he can glorify himself, he boasts of his charity; with false modesty he pretends to look down on his work. With him I am unhappy. The atmosphere is false, vicious and, in a subtle way, degrading. He is everything I struggled not to be. I feel him laughing at Hugh's candor. I know what he would think of Richard M., of Johnnie, of Eugene, even. In some way he would not respect the *sacredness* of my life—and there are many things which, with all his intelligence, he will never understand.

I think Mother was right when she begged us, illogically enough, not to see Father.

"You are too *good*, too *good*, Thorvald, Hugh and you, to *understand why!*" She was explaining with her *feelings*, her *instincts*, and at the time Thorvald, Hugh and I were not impressed because we wanted a logical explanation. But I think I realize now what she felt—the abyss between his ideals and ours—the bottomless abyss which it is useless to try and span.

It is with a mother's illogical relief that I saw Thorvald go away. I felt that away from Father he was secure. I am glad that I am left alone with the Problem. Alone, yes, because not even Hugh can understand my instinctive dislike, and I would not want him to understand.

January 22. In the morning, being deprived of the responsibility of breakfast, which the "chasseur"[1] brings us on a tray, I sleep late in the hope of gaining plumpness. I awake at 8:30 just enough to kiss Hugh good-bye and then fall asleep again until ten o'clock. By that time the city is wide awake and bustling, and I find some excuse or other, some errand to do, to be able to go out. In spite of my efforts, I react with the exactitude of a barometer to the atmosphere, and either rush back with quick shivery little steps to the more clement room or linger dreamily, with my nose flattened against the windows of the antique shops, or with my eyes glued on the lemon-colored, paper-covered books, tantalizingly uncut—or else I stand, open-mouthed, before the studio windows, which attract me now with a special meaning. All the while I am conscious of people swarming about me—the "ménagère"[2] with her market bag, children in their "bérets," with school bags under their arms, the students, the priests, the shopgirls, a Breton maid in her wooden shoes, the old man who sells mimosa, with his long,

[1] *Bellboy.*
[2] *Housewife.*

gray beard and black hat, the soldiers, the little stray dogs, the gendarme on the corner. The big bus can hardly move through the narrow street, and when it passes, one trips cleverly from the narrow sidewalk to the street and from the street to the sidewalk again. A baby carriage causes a congestion; everybody has to stand still, which is pleasant because it gives one a chance to look at the baby. I am speaking of a side street of course, Rue Vavin, which leads to the spacious Boulevards du Montparnasse and Raspail—and it is the little streets I like best.

Last night we had a moment of infinite sweetness—when both of us divined the jealousy in each other's heart and mingled kisses with the most ardent promises, with arguments, assurances. . . . We fell asleep holding each other tightly, murmuring: "I love you so, I love you so."

For Hugh is as jealous as I am, as sensitive, as fearful. Someone with a sharp sense of humor might find it in his heart to laugh at us both, and I would not blame him. I haven't laughed yet, but today, thinking of it all, I sang.

January 23. I have been making such an effort to grow old that my last attempt nearly resulted in white hair. I read Edith Wharton's *The Glimpses of the Moon,* and this most extraordinary book taught me more, in maturity, at least, than anything I have ever read. Above all, I think it appealed to me because it is written exactly as I would like to write, and this philosophical novel was, besides, written by a woman, in the manner of a clever woman.

The reason, I suppose, my hair did not turn white is because I made the fatal, young mistake of being *surprised* by it. Even gentle, uncomplaining Hugh said to me the other night that I would never be mature in my writing or in my character (the same thing) until I stopped being surprised by evil. No one had put it in quite that way before, but I was accused of youthfulness by Eugene, Richard M., Frank Monteiro, Mother and (for different reasons) by my Aunt Antolina.

I had hoped that Paris would cure me. It is amusing that it should be Edith Wharton who should begin. Anatole France I did not *believe,* while *I believe* Edith Wharton. And that is a very important distinction.

Reading *Glimpses of the Moon*—and I read it between 2 o'clock and 4:30, without stopping because I could not stop—

made me mortally ashamed of *Aline's Choice*. I don't think a more stupid book was ever written.

I sometimes marvel at the sweetness and patience Hugh, Eugene and Richard M. have for my writing. And especially when I took criticism so badly, cried in Hugh's arms and argued with Richard M. until I tired him out. I tormented Hugh with scenes in which I reproached him that he did not love me, that he did not understand, that *nobody* understood, and threatened never to write again, to destroy the book, my journal, myself, anything.

Hugh would cuddle and appease me, reason and entreat and finally, by his angelic attitude, earn the right to change one word, perhaps. But woe to him if time proved him in the wrong! Woe to him if by accident Eugene criticized the phrase he had inserted in place of my own! This fiendish delight in proving him wrong he also took angelically and good-humoredly, so I exhausted my ingenuity and tried poor Richard M. With him I argued exasperatingly and met nothing but patience and sweetness too, so after a year or so of this almost prearranged method, I submitted and am spending the rest of my days melted by gratitude as a punishment.

Once trained to docility, I seem to be able to learn from everybody and everything. Humility has replaced the stinging pain of criticism, which I felt to the point of despair. Ambitious but incapable of materializing my fantastic dreams, I suffered bitterly when I was shown how I had failed. Hugh, Richard M. and Eugene seemed united in a conspiracy to teach me the discipline of writing, and while I wrote with the ease of a fountain, they brought me typewriters, dictionaries, the Technique of Columbia, the Point of View of Henry James, the Restraint and Compactness of Eugene Graves—endless rules and traffic regulations, sermons on the Concrete, the Pictorial, Maturity—all of which, in a fit of rage, I metaphorically kicked into the river.

Instead of pulling my ears, they all three stood and waited. My better sentiments, touched by their gentleness, moved me to go to the river, fish out each and every one of the proffered idols, dry them and place them in a row before me, on my writing table, where they have stayed ever since.

And now I add to the collection myself, and with a gesture of deference place *Glimpses of the Moon* next to my *Antonyms and Synonyms*.

January 30. 15, Avenue Hoche.[1] We have left the flowery paper, the daily cabbage and beans and potatoes, the mustiness, the peculiar boardinghouse atmosphere of the pension, far behind. The two-room apartment, with its two French windows overlooking a court (serving more as ornaments than as givers of light) is somewhat more like a home, particularly after I had taken down 52 pictures of horses and nude women, changed all the furniture around, taken out of our trunk the familiar books, the familiar blue pottery, the familiar copper candlesticks—and given Hugh a breakfast exactly like the breakfast in the little bungalow. The breakfast convinced him that this *was* home, which proves how materialistic men are.

On Monday I sent for Mother because her letters were sad and lonely, so we have spent the week trying to cheer her up and have succeeded. We had an afternoon of beautiful understanding, when she talked to me dispassionately about everything, and I realize the immense difference between her and the Problem. Mother is good, almost childish in her trust of the world, and I found myself teaching her, making her calm and reasonable. But I know that her goodness is worth more than anything.

The Fear has visited me again. It was the second crisis of our marriage, more serious this time, for Hugh was angry and I wept. C., the evil genius, was again the cause of it, with an invitation to dinner in which I was included. Hoping to get out of it, Hugh pretended I couldn't come, thinking this cause enough for his not going, but C. insisted on having him. Hugh hesitated at the thought of offending him, and finally decided that he would go alone. He would not take me because "I suffer to see you among those common people." I realized that however idealistic his reason, he was shutting me out of his life. The results were identical. I struggled against this. He ended by deciding he would not go rather than go with me. But although we were reconciled, and cried together, I felt that something intangible was crumbling, that which is irrevocably changed by words hastily said in the moment of anger or hurt. We are losing something—I am changing. I sought peace in marriage, and there is none.

January 31. Hugh took Mother and me to the theatre. The comedy made us laugh—it *was* funny, even though they respected nothing,

[1] *The apartment of a bachelor friend of Hugh's.*

and the "polissonnerie"[1] was contagious, but I was happy that Hugh did not understand the coarse jokes and I did not try to explain them to him. Afterwards, I could not explain my reaction which followed the laughter—I was unhappy, disgusted, tormented by the carelessness with which the most horrible vices are exposed and used as a subject for wit. I tried in vain to enter into the spirit of the French, feeling vaguely that it was entering into me, and that, however ardently I rejected it, there are things I know now that I can never unlearn. The "sacredness" of things in Paris is constantly undermined by wit, by intelligence, by culture, and one remains appalled before the ruins, almost tempted to laugh at one's own "niaiserie,"[2] because the French laugh at it.

Letter to Ruth [Morgan]:

. . . and besides, in Paris it is good to write often, as every letter may be your testament. Why? Because crossing the streets here is purely a matter of luck.

Seeing this, I decided to stay home and write—I nearly wrote another book while we stayed in the boardinghouse, but don't be afraid, poor child, you won't have to read it! If you want to laugh, ask Mr. Maynard his opinion of my hero. It is the only time I have seen him honestly and eloquently disgusted.

Yes, I read *The Little French Girl* coming over. I do think the contrasts are well drawn and very true—so true that some of the problems they had, I have already met with here I mean problems of morals. I am having quite a ridiculous time about them because by education, by inclination, I am somewhat a puritan—or English, you might say. But I have been accustomed to the Latin mentality and therefore I see their side, too. . . . I suppose your sympathies were all for Giles—so were mine. I married a Giles—I mean, that kind, but then in my own family I have people like the mother in *The Little French Girl*, and I can't hate them either. Knowing all this, I realized the book was wonderfully true. Only, the authoress took much of her style and many of her ideas from a far more wonderful author and book—Henry James's *Ambassadors*.

February [1?]. Through seeing a simple movie story of Paris, well produced, I realized that what we should do once in a while is

[1] *Ribaldry.*
[2] *Foolishness.*

get a sweeping sight of the whole, instead of parts of life. It is only by flight that we can sublime. Daily life sometimes becomes a series of small, ugly, petty little slaveries which prevent us from feeling the heights; the beauty of the whole is lost in the sourness of the details. We saw Notre-Dame on a muddy day when wet shoes and shivering bodies prevented us from really seeing it. We see only parts of Paris at a time. I am imprisoned now in a dark little apartment in which I feel cramped and lonely and unhealthy. From here I go to the market in a narrow street. Then I come home again and wonder why I sit and cannot write. Spiritually I should be able to detach myself and to judge the whole. And then I would feel as I felt when the movies showed me, interwoven through the story, misty pictures of Paris taken from the heights, which made beauty stand out.

Woman is more in danger than man of becoming cramped and warped. Washing dishes, peeling vegetables, quarreling with crooked market vendors, sweeping dust and scrubbing stones, washing clothes and mending socks—all the countless ugly little demons that pursue us every day, haunting our womanly possessions with the fear of coarse hands, of grimy faces, of dusty hair, of frown-ridden brows, of wasted eyes—oh, these make us small and shut us off from the hilltop of existence, and it is a struggle of our minds to continually steal away and strive to reach the top, if only for a moment.

On the whole, we do all those countless, ugly, little things for the large, vague Love. But what gifts could we offer Love if we lived permanently in a rarefied atmosphere? And when Love turns and wounds, how can we not see the sourness in the little demons?

February 3. The crisis passed. Hugh was surprised by what he describes as my too active imagination. He persisted in asking me: "Do you feel that anything has changed between us?" until I admitted I thought something had changed. Finally I had to confess that I no longer found peace in our love. "Then you have lost faith in me," he said sorrowfully.

I had not lost it, but my faith was shaken by his hesitations and the struggle. He could not understand this and finally I had to resort to the usual wiles of woman and make-believe to make him happy. I wonder if my imagination does exaggerate the meaning of things. How sweet it would be if I could see things the size others see them.

. . .

Mother left last night, and I miss her terribly. I never understood or loved her as well as I have this week, and it gave me such infinite satisfaction to see that I made her happy. She left us smiling, feeling better in health and spirits; and today I missed our talks, our outings, her teachings about cooking, and I wish she were here again, reading or knitting by my side.

How sweet those days were, when we did the housekeeping together, went out to the "marché,"[1] downtown on errands, window-shopping, once to the movies and once to the theatre— and on Sunday we took a carriage ride through the ·Bois in the sunshine. After I saw Mother off at the Gare Quai d'Orsay, Hugh and I had dinner together and spent the rest of the evening in a secondhand bookstore, picking up two books out of fifty we desired.

Now that Mother is gone, I have nothing to do but house- keeping and seeing friends occasionally. Hugh wonders why I should feel lonely, when that was a feeling absolutely strange to me before. It must be that I have become more human and that my inward life has weakened, or perhaps it has grown merely sadder and I feel the need of hushing it now and then in a normal activity. And there are normal things which I love, I must confess, things like pretty clothes and fashions, an occasional whiff of social life for the sake of its visible beauty, meeting people with whom I can talk about intangible things. I am not altogether a hermit, or altogether a woman, but a little of both, and there are moments in this brown salon, with its gray windows, its old furni- ture, when writing and reading cannot comfort me entirely, and I miss the cheerfulness of the bungalow, the posing for Richard M., the walks with Laddie, Eugene's visits in the evening and our long talks by the fire, Johnnie's occasional visit, with his buoyancy and freshness, the daily marketing with Mother, the Sunday movies, Thorvald's jests and teasing, and even the phonograph I used to turn on when it grew dark.

February 4. We were so happy last night. After a cozy little home dinner in the salon and an hour of talk, sitting close together on the sofa, while Hugh sipped a liqueur and smoked his pipe, we went to bed and he took me in his arms and said: "How happy we are together, my darling, what a perfect marriage!" And he re- peated once or twice that our marriage was without a flaw. And I

[1] *Market.*

believe him. In the morning the air which came in through the open window seemed softer to us.

"It feels like spring!" Hugh said, but I teased him and told him I thought it was just we who felt like spring. Yet he was right. When I went out to market, I felt the air become softer and Paris seemed less somber. Walking through the crowded streets which lead to the market, I felt that I no longer minded the ugly, little things and that I loved Hugh dearly and that when the real spring came, I would learn to love and understand Paris. Feeling virtuous, I spent the most domestic day, doing all kinds of things I usually hate to do, like mending socks, for instance, which gives me freedom to think and after a while an intolerable desire to write. For reward, I wrote a long letter to Richard M., and now I am writing for Hugh as I used to in the bungalow, with the same calm.

February 5. I am convinced that I would love Paris better if I knew more history. In Paris one must live in the glory of the past. The sense of poetry is not sufficient—one needs learning. Mere instinctive feeling cannot be applied to every form of beauty.

Eugene, through his knowledge, can appreciate books which mean little or nothing to me. Can it be that I have relied too much on the woman's instinct and that now what I thought I could appreciate through my poetic sense, my untutored imagination, my eyes, my ears, I need erudition to grasp entirely?

An example of my weakness is the way I understand music. I have accurate ears, I recognize and remember perfectly the most difficult pieces if I find them beautiful. I am profoundly moved by certain music. But I can never tell one composer from another, I never remember a title, I have never learned to distinguish between styles and epochs. I have a *feeling* for music, but I am simply *ignorant* of music as an art.

The nearer I come to the end of this book, the less inclined I feel to continue typing my journal, as Richard M. and Hugh advise me to do. I like the little books, I like to write by hand, I like the appearance and character of handwriting, I like not being able to change the pages, to alter what I have already written. It is in every way more *authentic*, more original, more expressive. Am I like the French, attached to habit, to sentiment, to the love of preservation; incapable of changing or of progressing?

February 6. I think Hugh and I are happy because we live so wisely. At least we find joy in rising early, in working, in eating moderately, in walking, in going to bed early. Neither of us is in all-enduring health. If we lived as carelessly and as strenuously as other people, we would be wrecked. A small amount of social activity, a great deal of calm, that is what we grow best with, because both Hugh and I are blessed or cursed with a never ceasing mental activity—a mental energy which holds in itself *all* the energy in the united lives of those around us.

February 9. I spent Saturday morning in bed with a cold, crying over the heartbreaking story of *Corinne* by Madame de Staël. To calm my indignation for the detestable and weak Scotsman as well as my admiration of Corinne, I had to read the preface over, and in spite of that I could not convince myself that the book was a story. The impression does not leave me. I quote passages over and over in my memory—the differences between Corinne and Oswald, in character, in their appreciation of art, of religion, of morals; the marvelous chapter on the difference between Italian and English poetry; all of it written in such pure and scholarly French, with so much erudition, so much wisdom.

Sunday, with Hugh, I visited the part of the Louvre consecrated to modern sculpture. I found a bust of Corinne there, by Gois. After reading the book and being so moved by the portrait of the woman, I found the marble expressionless and unintelligent. How could anyone miss her fire, her eloquence, her vivacity, her depth of emotion, her nobility!

Sappho, by James Pradier, sits pensively and gracefully with her head bowed. The gesture alone is interesting.

The little head of Louise Brongniart, by Houdon, so dainty and childish and light, seems so young among Richard Furieux, Atlas, François Arago, that one cannot forget it. I am afraid I cannot appreciate gigantic sculpturing, I who like little, fragile things so much. They strike me as so much physique, so much flesh. I never think of Greek gods as terribly tall.

Hugh, of course, is very tall, but he is so slender and his neck and hands are so fine. I wonder if some day I myself could render in marble the mingling of perfect physique and spirit, which Hugh is, which could satisfy at once the artist in love with illness and the poet in search of a soul.

February 10. Letter writing, which is taking so large a part of my time, is doing my other writing harm. After dispatching a six-page letter to Richard M., I feel as if I had written enough for the day, or at least as if I had written *something*, and I feel quite tired and satisfied. And now Frank G. Monteiro writes me a very long and very beautiful letter, which means the beginning of another correspondence. He is the artist-photographer whose name I have sometimes mentioned, but of whom I have never made a sketch.

Monteiro is a bachelor, gray-haired, and a Portuguese. He does photography in Forest Hills to earn his living, but he has the soul of a painter. He talks deliciously, humorously, lengthily, and writes the same way. He reads fine books, judges people acutely, is isolated by his work and appreciates any friendliness shown to him. Hugh and Johnnie always liked and appreciated him. When we married, Hugh having told me about him, I suggested having him to dinner. As I grew to like him, too, we had him occasionally to Sunday supper or tea. He entertained us with long-drawn-out stories of his life. Like all bachelors, he stayed late, and we did not invite him too often on account of that. But he was so grateful for our companionship, and I am glad we are not going to lose track of him.

February 12. Hugh and I have accepted taking "tea with the world" now and then, as I said to Eugene, in trying to explain to him why we submitted to several of life's conventions, why we accepted friendships he would not understand. But out of these compromises arise sometimes the most unexpected and rare experiences.

We were invited to have dinner with Mr. R. of the bank. A taxi drove us through the Bois to Saint-Cloud and deposited us in front of an iron gate. A high stone wall prevented us from seeing the "alentours"[1] of the house, and when the gate was opened we walked into a blinding alley of light which fell from the door of the house. I felt that there was a garden around us, but I did not look, as I expected at every moment to find our hostess waiting for us on the doorsteps. But no one came to meet us. A shy maid took our coats, and the host showed us into the salon. I always shiver on entering French salons, not only because they are actually cold, but because the light-toned furniture, the glaring display of lamps over my head, the multitude of ornaments, pictures and bric-a-brac wound my love of harmony.

While Hugh and Mr. R. and Mr. M. talked, I tried to form a

[1] *Surroundings.*

picture of what the hostess might be like. Knowing that the host was twice as rich as we were (!), I wondered if I were well enough dressed. It seemed to me that the fact that she was not yet ready showed she was careful of the details of her personal appearance. I imagined her giving herself a last touch of powder, straightening a wisp of hair, turning before her mirror—everything that I do myself before I feel quite ready to meet anyone.

Finally the host made inquiries while he prepared an apéritif, to which I had to submit. It seemed that the lady was putting the babies to bed, and I expressed an impulsive desire to see them, so we all marched upstairs. We saw the babies but not the mother. She came finally when we were about to go downstairs again, and I was the first to see her. She was tall and squarely built, with light-brown hair brushed back into a simple chignon, large blue eyes, and square features, and wearing the plainest dress I have ever seen on a woman of her station. She greeted us a little awkwardly, seemed afraid of us and astonishingly humble. We finally found ourselves seated around a table set with exaggerated perfection.

The hostess followed with anxiety each move of the flustered servant, and I noticed that her hands, as they moved here and there, straightening and rearranging, were plump and square and slightly red. She being preoccupied with service and her husband with the opening of a bottle of wine, Mr. M. knowing little or no French (the hostess did not know English), and Hugh shy about the French he knows, no one talked. I was discountenanced by the simplicity of the hostess, who looked at us very seriously, and I was afraid to speak, afraid of my gestures, embarrassed by my well-curled hair, my powder, my red shawl, my black short dress, my flesh-colored stockings and satin shoes. And the faint wave of perfume which my dress exhaled worried me. But how could I have guessed? Hugh had said: "He makes four or five times what I make, he has a house in St.-Cloud," and I had imagined everything so different.

Feeling it unsafe for me to talk, I tried to make Mrs. R. talk, but she seemed eager to efface herself, to let others talk. Her husband, having opened the bottle, took up my remarks feebly, and she encouraged us with a wide, childish smile. At this, I grew more courageous. Besides, the entrance of an enormous and polished "langouste" had created a topic of conversation, not very intellectual but safe enough—and so the ball of conversation started rolling. Fat Mr. M. laughed at everything, and although

I could not make out what he was laughing at, I was grateful to him. By the time the second course and the red wine arrived, we were all animated—all, except Mrs. R., who seemed determined to contribute only the material necessities of the evening—the salt, a second helping of sauce, more bread, another pear, perhaps —and who watched like a mother over our welfare.

After dinner she swallowed smoothly a liqueur of which the very taste burned my lips, and she smoked without any grace at all—more as a matter of necessity. She seemed to have no vanity, no artistry, no desire to shine.

Then we went to the salon, but Mrs. R., under the pretext of entertaining me with the Victrola, took me to the dining room again, where we sat to listen to the records she chose. Then it developed that she loved music. The plain, unpainted face was illumined by an unexpected beauty. She talked to me about her children, about marriage, of how she loved the piano and loved reading, but found little time for it on account of the housekeeping and the babies. I asked her what kind of books she liked. She was at a loss to explain that she liked deep things. Perhaps, seeing my clothes, my powdered face, she felt she could not talk about deep things, just as I, seeing her plainness, felt I should talk very simply. Finally we both forgot each other's exterior.

Under her influence, my love of color, of form—the clothes and fashions I always justify by my sense of artistry—suddenly seemed petty and wrong. Meanwhile, I am not sure of what she felt, except that, holding my eyes with hers, she seemed inclined to speak with all the fervor and eloquence she obstinately withheld at the table in the presence of men.

We all walked to the station. The men took long steps and went so far ahead that we could barely see them. The street was like a path along the side of a mountain. On the left, the hill descended abruptly and seemed to flow into a lake of lights— Paris was at our feet, seen now through an iron grille between the branches of low trees. And once, silhouetted against the sky, we saw a small château, all dark and half-hidden by several old trees.

Mrs. R. seemed conscious of all this beauty, as well as of the delicious coolness of the wind which struck our faces as we walked. With exquisite thoughtfulness and humility, she helped me over the muddy spots, guiding me as if I were a child. But I do not know which one of us really felt more humble, for I was awed by the clear radiance of her face and her unaffected silences and short phrases—phrases entirely deprived of superfluous ornaments, spoken only because she thought them, not once descending to the varnished small talk of which I myself make use so often for the people who "live" small talk—for there is a life just like the talk, created to express it.

February 14. I think I was the more impressed by Mrs. R. because I had just finished reading another book by Edith Wharton,[1] and I had felt such sympathies for poor Lily Bart, who lived only for the very things Mrs. R. ignores. My admiration was stronger than my sadness when I read Edith Wharton's masterly descriptions of society and what in it appealed to Lily's love of beauty. In so weak a fashion I tried to say the same thing in *Aline's Choice.*

Deceived again by a story into believing I was seeing life, I exclaimed towards the end of the book: How I wish I could tell Lily Bart what I have discovered! It is true that I miss the beauty of luxurious surroundings, that I sometimes dream of Havana and of the life I might have had there—idle hands, perpetual gliding over lacy, carpeted, flower-strewn ways—that I miss it all, as Aline's mother missed it, that I murmur sometimes against the ugliness of the backstage life, that I sometimes wish I were on the stage itself. Oh, it is all true. But when Hugh holds me in his arms; when he thanks me for the little dinners I prepare, his face alight with the pleasure of finding what he likes; when he comes home at night and rests his head on my breast and tells me about his work, which was all for me; when on Sundays I put on the dress I have remade for the third time and the hat I have trimmed for the fifth time, and we go out together, walking arm in arm, and he smiles happily, tenderly, proudly—then, and at many other times, I know that this marriage, with all its little sacrifices, is the most beautiful thing that life can give one.

I went down to the bank to call for Hugh and we went out together to have lunch. We were hesitating as to what we wanted to do most after that: I wanted to visit the interior of the Madeleine and Hugh wanted to do something frivolous—when the rain settled the question, and we walked home along the Boulevard Haussmann under an umbrella. Such a familiar walk now, because we

---

[1] *The House of Mirth.*

take it every day after lunch. We take it lingeringly, stopping before the windows of the shops, which are lined up all the way to the bank.

It is like a glimpse into the life of Paris: the French are writing this, painting that, wearing such and such a thing. If it truly means anything, we are learning a great deal by walking up and down Boulevard Haussmann.

If only the sun would show itself oftener. It has come out these days, almost brilliantly, holding forth a promise of clear days, and I have felt my step growing lighter, my soul expanding. But the moment one speaks of it, like a shy or rebellious child, it disappears. It cannot bear to be looked at. And yet how beautiful Paris is in the sunshine! The stones, so gray, so faded, so dead with age and rain, turn gold. The Etoile at one moment seemed really to be radiating glory.

February 18. Three happy days during which I have worked assiduously on my second book. The first day I wrote 1,500 words, the second 1,800 and today 2,400! I do not know what to make of what I am writing. It seems to come out in spite of me, like chattering, and I write very fluently and steadily. I feel a sort of power and assurance, while at the same time, when I have finished writing, I am struck with fear at what I have done. I read a lot to Hugh, who was tired and half asleep. He seemed pleased enough, only I am afraid it was because he hardly knew what I was reading him.

When I say I write steadily and fluently, I do not mean without a struggle. I slip constantly into the old faults—moralizing, superfluous explanations. Also, I am so impatient that often I am obliged to return to fill my poor skeleton with flesh. The story runs away with me, in order to get to my climaxes quickly. Whether for good or for bad, I have become more of a storyteller than a philosopher—though ideas are the things which lead me constantly.

Sunday we had a tea to celebrate Hugh's birthday. Guicciardi came and Mr. M., who was with us that night of R.'s dinner. There was also an American art student, a friend of George Gillette's, whom I had expected to like immensely, having heard that he was shy and a puritan. I had been waiting to see such a person, as a reaction to French life—and not having seen one since the 16th of December. But when I came face to face with him, I shrank back. Guicciardi was exceedingly amusing and interesting, at the expense, of course, of more or less sacred subjects. He left first, and we commented on his eloquence and amusing ideas. D.F., in a tone which left no doubt of his meaning, said: "But of course, he has received a very different education from ours." The prudishness, the coldness of the distinction, its narrowness, displeased me, and I wondered why.

February 20. On the eve of my birthday and bowing to tradition, I try to consider thoughtfully the significance of this venerable day—in vain. Dates never agree with my transformations. My real birthday this year was when I read Edith Wharton's books. My New Year began when I succeeded in having my story run smoothly, when I found a renewed interest in my second book. My holidays are many—every time I go downtown with Hugh, when the agitation of the city, like the quick rhythm of some Spanish danza, makes my heart beat faster. My religious festivals fall on whatever day the sun shines—those are my Mass-going days, when I can pray.

Reading my old journals does me more good than listening to sermons. Thus I grow old, I start new years, I enjoy things, I pray—all at different times than the rest of the world.

I was never so careful of words, of superfluous exclamation marks, of dashes—and all because my book is coming to a close, and I cannot resign myself to the use of a typewriter and large pages. I have asked Eugene his opinion—I wait to see if he will understand what I feel. But I may have to decide before his answer arrives, as he is so lazy in matters of letter writing. I might have asked Eduardo, but Eduardo is my disciple and he will feel the way I do. Hugh, being a banker, appreciates the efficiency and utility of typing. There is no room for sentiment now, except in the moving pictures.

Hugh is a perfect lover in the most beautiful sense of the word. I never imagined any man so thoughtful, so delicate, so subtle, so appreciative. He expresses himself like an artist—he mingles beauty of soul and body. His love also takes expression in little things, in common, everyday-life things. We come down then to details which love makes ineffably sweet. He has a cold, and I take pleasure in jumping out of bed very early to bring him breakfast. He comes home late, knowing that my dinner has been kept waiting, and so he brings me a book to make up for it. If I am tired some morning, he makes his own breakfast and dresses as quickly as possible. If I am ill, he watches over me all night. He listens to whatever I write during the day, even if he is sleepy and tired. I listen to his talks about the bank, even if I am bored. I mend his clothes; he spends the money he has been saving so carefully on perfume for me. To please me, he hangs his clothes up neatly every day; and so that he might sleep a moment more in the mornings, I clean his big shoes the day before. At night, if he is wakeful and feels lonely and begins to think of things that worry him, he calls me and we talk for a little while, and I caress him until he is soothed and can sleep again. If I am cold, I call him and he picks up the blankets that have fallen and holds me close until I get warm again.

I have given up luxury. I work, keeping house for him and attending to his comfort. But he works for me, depriving himself of things; he dresses less well than he did as a bachelor; he no longer takes singing lessons or guitar lessons or buys whatever he fancies. He gave up his tennis so as not to leave me alone. That is marriage, giving and taking. But both of us think our marriage so very beautiful.

February 22. There is a kind of luminousness in frivolity, even if it is artificial. And it is that we found in the "thé dansant"[1] we went to yesterday with Mr. and Mrs. Duble. Dressing for it was such a pleasure—discarding the apron, the sensible dress, drawing out of the closet the frail chiffon dress, the satin shoes, the silk stockings. And then the gay music, the vivacious coloring of everything, the reflections of color in the mirrors. The people were disappointing—idle, bored women; small, weak men; languid, fierce-looking South Americans; inane, ridiculous American flappers. The people are always disappointing, but the scene, the form, the movement, the coloring—those are always enchanting.

I had a moment of rebellion when I came back to face my rusty little gas stove, potatoes to be peeled, dishes to be washed. I covered the chiffon dress with an apron, but I could not cover the flurry and heightening which accompany the fact that for two hours I had been a lady, dancing and receiving compliments. But after a while Hugh and I kissed each other, and felt peaceful again. Reading more of my book before we went to sleep sobered

[1] *Tea dance.*

us completely. And today he writes letters while I chatter here, both quite "bourgeois" again.

It is amusing to observe how differently we feel towards the acquaintances who drop in on us now and then from New York— people we were not too anxious to cultivate, for fear of being drawn too deeply into their lives, which did not satisfy us. But when they are transients—having just come from New York and about to leave Paris for St. Moritz or Rome—how interesting they seem. We are sincerely glad to see them—they have become significant links to the chain that binds us to New York; they are sentimentally representative of a people we have idealized by remaining away from them. We forget their faults, we see only that for the moment they are very charming and alone here in Paris, where we, too, are alone. They leave us so soon, with just enough time to have created an agreeable impression.

February 23. Nearly a year is encompassed by this small book. At one time, I could fill one in a month—with enthusiasm, with vague dreams, with exclamations of surprise. Now, though I live so much more deeply, my writing is compact and subdued, and I am busier and cannot indulge in contemplation. I must catch things swiftly, with fewer strokes. And the amusing part is that I wrote more bulkily when I was too shy and too awkward to *talk*. Oh, I remember the moments, in the face of strangers, when my hands would become cold, my body tremble with the effort to master my desire to run away and hide. And now, though I still have the impulse and though it is always with an effort that I rise to meet social occasions, I do not betray myself, and I can talk, quite passably, and I *write* less! All of which proves nothing. One thing never changes—my ideals. I still reach out for the same things—goodness, beauty, intelligence, creation.

February 27. Whatever it may augur for the future, I have chosen, by the fact that I am writing by hand in a book instead of using my typewriter, to follow my impulses and my instincts rather than the advice of others.

I felt so sure of myself today, walking up a boulevard towards the Madeleine in the face of a strong, steady wind—the kind that strikes your face, flings your hair back, away from your eyes, and sends your scarf flying behind you. I liked the sensation of throwing myself against it, to master it by an unwavering walk, going full pace, against the invigorating impact. In this mood I entered the Printemps[1] and chose my book. It was not until I came out again, and blinked as I looked at the sun on the street, that I realized the wind had filled my eyes with dust. . . .

March 1. Yesterday afternoon we caught the Bois in one of its most unusual aspects. Just as we passed the gate, leaden clouds gathered over our heads and poured rain and hail on the startled promenaders. Mothers, children, nurses, lovers, old men and women, students and dogs, all suddenly disappeared. Automobiles rushed homeward and carriage drivers opened their umbrellas. Hugh and I did same.

"I'm Scottish," said Hugh. "I love to walk in the rain."

"So do I."

"Well then, let's go."

Suddenly the rain and hail stopped short, and a gray-and-purple mist fell all around us and over the surface of the lake. We rented a boat, and Hugh rowed us to a little island, where we walked up a gravel hill to a chalet and sat on the porch before a white-top table and ordered chocolate and cakes. Behind us were a pair of lovers discreetly kissing. Before us stretched brilliant wet grass and mist-enveloped trees, from which came the cooing and twittering of birds. Beyond, the hill descended into the lake, and beyond the lake a few cars and carriages passed by. Without these we would have thought ourselves miles away from Paris. We dreamed together on that quiet and soft afternoon, sipping chocolate and nibbling cakes and turning now and then to look at our little white boat rocking on its chain. When Hugh rowed us homeward, the rain started again. The leaden sky turned the lake's water black, and on this deep, black, undulating surface, swans languidly floated.

March 4. Last night we celebrated the second anniversary of our marriage, but we thought about it from the moment we opened our eyes. Hugh insisted on giving me my breakfast in bed. At lunchtime I walked down to the bank with him, as usual, but if such a thing were possible, he was even tenderer in his looks and words. We wanted to give each other presents; he insisted it was he who should give me something, as he was eternally indebted

[1] *A department store.*

for what I had given him two years ago. But I argued that he had given me his love and so much happiness. We ended by postponing all presents by reason of the state of our finances! But in the evening I prepared my little dinner more carefully than usual, and he came home at 7 o'clock instead of at 8, as he has been doing. We had a reminiscent and tender evening, like the most sentimental of couples. Finally, we went to bed with our books and our journals. Hugh stopped in the middle of Joyce's *Ulysses* to write a poem. But in the wonder of d'Annunzio's prose in *L'Enfant de la Volupté*, I forgot to write. What Hugh wrote was very beautiful—the loveliest gift he could ever make me, I told him.

Will the third year be as sweet?

March 7. It rains. Paris is silvery and leaden. The apartment is of a deeper brown, a listless, worn brown, which in the corners does not even detach itself from the purple shadows.

According to my moods, I work on the second book, on the play or on the journal. But this morning I, too, sank back among the shadows and felt the physical *moldiness* of the French creeping over me. No wonder that I warm my spirit over the leaping flames of d'Annunzio's prose.

I met d'Annunzio when I was ten years old, when Father and Mother gave a concert of old Italian music, at Arcachon, and he came to congratulate Mother on her beautiful diction and interpretation. He seemed very ugly to me, small, with a pointed beard, searching eyes and a huge forehead. Joaquin attracted his attention by his eyes. D'Annunzio said to him: "You have the eyes of a passionate one. Beware of women."[1] And that was all I remembered.

March 8. Hugh reads now, and the sight of this calm life makes my heart swell with contentment. We seem to be drinking every moment, absorbing rich experiences, instead of spending ourselves. We feel young and strong and happy and free. I am thankful for the prolongation of this period of our marriage. Afterwards it will bring children and responsibility and seriousness, but now it is the mere companionship of lovers who work only for each other, who take their pleasures together.

[1] *See* The Diary of Anaïs Nin, *Vol. I, p. 193 for a different version of this incident.*

March 9. A letter from Eduardo brought with it fragrant associations and ideas. He is to me the embodiment of the Poetic Ideal into which I breathed life one day, in Lake Placid, by talking about books and writing. Since then my creation has lived. It changes, and I change too, but the varied-colored flowers are always from the same seed. I love in him the poetry and the love of beauty, the youthfulness and the sensitiveness which I saw first, even though today they are grown larger and deeper and are less intimately known. To see Paris with him would be like seeing it with Loti, with Rostand, with Shelley, Keats or d'Annunzio. He is to me so perfectly "lyrical," physically and spiritually. Now and then I miss the dilated eyes, the spontaneous gestures, the dreamful phrases, the rich tones and fabulous imaginings, the curiosity and the surprise. I would like to hear him rhapsodize over Florence and Venice. He is the true Donatello, as the young Italian appears in the first part of the *Marble Faun*—Donatello who has not suffered, Donatello who is so exultant, so joyful, Donatello with blond hair and sea-green eyes.

How contrasting Eugene, Eduardo and Hugh are! Hugh is the only one whom I can love wholly—the only one who can be everything to me, every day. Still, I am made of so many parts that I am capable of loving other things in other people.

But today, on a spring morning of pale sunshine, I paused in the midst of the colorful agitation of the city, on those little cement islands which lie in the streets of Paris, between two rivers of dense traffic, and I tore open Eduardo's letter with impatient joy and wished he were here with me.

March 11. How undefinable is the change Paris makes in one. I only realized it while reading in my journal of the shivers with which I read my first book by Anatole France. Since then, an understanding of his genius has flowed noisily into me. I read his other books calmly; his sensual expressions rise to my lips as naturally as the expressions of surprise did before. Not that I accept sensuality. My dislike for it is too deep, too complete for that. It never touches me. It is a thing I feel with my mind just long enough to understand the presence of it in other people. Nevertheless, I am not shocked by it. In a few weeks I have accepted it unwaveringly, as part of life. I love purity, but I can understand the impure. I am still startled when I hear unfamiliar phrases on Hugh's lips. He asked me today if Anatole France was a man "who had had many affairs with women." I looked at him before answering.

Why, of course—a natural question, here in Paris. A mild phrase compared with France's own phrases, with d'Annunzio's phrases. But we never spoke, or read, or thought them in New York.

Spiritually, I hate Paris for the importance of sensuality in its literary and human life. Intellectually, I am glad to learn, to understand everything. It hurts me that Hugh should pass through the Cavern. But why should I wish his growth to stop while mine continues? I do not want to live in lies, but I await anxiously for the day when, knowing everything, we shall choose the True and the Good and the Beautiful as realities.

It was only last night that I said to Hugh: "Anatole France *troubles* me. He writes and says so many things which sound logical and sensible, but which I cannot believe, which disturb me. To argue with him, I could not use logic. My arguments against his ideas come from sources which he does not consider—almost mystical sources."

"You would have to use superlogic," said Hugh, for that is what he calls those intangible beliefs we have: superlogic.

Hugh and I have battles of interests. His work has never occupied him so much—it is more important now, and he never ceases thinking of it. In the evening he talks about it to me, tells me everything which puzzles and annoys him. We discuss the problems, and now and then I can help him by applying to the business tangles simple reasoning on character. I sit on a pillow at his feet with my head on his knees while he smokes and talks to me. The frowns are deep on his forehead. When he has told me all, he asks me to help him forget it. Then I tell him about the books I have read. I am his book reviewer, as he says. Or sometimes I read him what I have written. The frowns disappear, his thoughts relax, and I feel him resting from the strain of his day's work.

The apartment does not seem so brown when he is home. I forget the rain and the day's gloom. I rest, too, because during the day I write enormously, and do little things that I dislike about the house. I have finished the play.

March 13. So much reading confuses me. It makes me wonder what it is I want to write, and how. It makes me think intensely, about *everything*, and it gives me a fever which day by day burns me more violently. It is the fever of life, the consuming desire to live intensely, to create something strong and great, to understand all things, to possess every knowledge and every experience, to *do* and to be giant. I want to be everywhere at once. I want to read more, to see more people, to be more alone with nature, to write more. In the middle of a small task, I rebel—the fever takes hold of me and I am blinded by illimitable visions of greater things to be done. I want to be at the heights of life every moment, to penetrate the past and to divine the future. Every extreme fires me to volcanic anger—the unhealthy physical apathy of the French, the inhibitions of the puritan, the magnificent animal energy of the Americans, the aberrations of the Italians—I see all the weaknesses, the incompletenesses, the holes, the exaggerations. I want to waken the French with Emerson and Carlyle, subdue and refine the Americans with French finesse and subtleties, to temper the Italians with English wisdom, to free the puritans with a plunge into the lawlessness of d'Annunzio.

The Frenchman, by nature, is sensuous and sensitive. He has intelligence, which makes him tired of life sooner than other kinds of men. He is not athletic; he sees the futility of the pursuit of fame; the climate at times depresses him, though he may not know it. He turns, then, for refuge from wearisome intelligence and bleeding sensitiveness, self-consciousness, self-ridicule, to the sensuous enjoyment of woman, which gives him momentary life, a semblance of activity, even of creation, a moment of self-forgetfulness. As woman is the only dispensary of sensuous joy, she rules France. France is woman, says Romain Rolland. Men, fashioned by women, become more sensitive and effeminate. By this need of her, the Frenchman, whose obsession with woman can be seen in his writing, in his everyday life, in his gallantry, places an illimitable power in woman's hands. And woman rules, occupies an inordinate place in France.

In Spain the men are also "apasionados,"[1] but it is a whole-bodied subjugation to woman, without the submission of the intelligence. The men's brutal power at once obtains what it desires from woman and keeps her at home, subjugated. The French lack the physical dominance to do this. With woman they become soft and pliant. It is the obeisance of the tired thinker, of the tired cynic. In Spain the men think less and act grandiloquently. They

[1] *Passionate.*

appear to their women as heroes. The French are content to display culture. They leave the display of muscle to the American, whom they vaguely consider barbaric. It is the American woman alone who has tamed the brute proportions and molded them to her selfish service, perhaps because the American man is *good* and generous and mingles the English respect of woman with the gallantry of the French and the heroic offerings of the Spanish—asking nothing in return. His weakness is not knowing how to offer himself as gracefully, as beautifully, as the French would offer a cigarette. His power, with a little art, would knock all other races senseless.

This is one of my "clear" days when I am obliged to leave the things I am doing to pursue an idea which tantalizes me. The whole world seems illumined and I see everything at once. On other days, I go about with a candle, seeing only a circle at a time and blackness beyond the candle glow. And last night I was left even without a candle. I tossed in bed, unable to sleep, impatient for I knew not what, anxious for the days that are passing, eager to live, fearful of wasting time backstage. Anatole France's discouragement and sense of futility gave only a keener edge to my convictions. I believe more in my play than in his sorrowful lassitude. In my play, David, the old man who recovers his sight after long being blind, "builds a garden where there was none." It may be the eternal conceit of youth. It may be that a spirit of contradiction, and nothing more exalted than that, urges me to combat the senility of the French. Or it may be that the sun is shining and spring is floating around me. Whatever the cause, I am astounded and amused by the numerous things I believe in, the numerous desires which urge me to action. I wave Carlyle and Emerson over my head, like torches or firearms, over the peaceful, pleasure-loving French. They will look up at me from their meditations, their delicate dinners and their love affairs and think they are hearing the battle cry of the red Indians who live over the Ocean, the ferocious Indians, tattooed with dollars all over their body, who eat "pâté" and think it is pie and who imagine Paris to be a sort of Luna Park.[1]

The fever calms down when I cook my dinner. Instead of continuing my divagations, I wrote dutiful letters to various people. And now it is almost time for Hugh to come home—Hugh whom

[1] *An amusement park.*

I saw today in the bank, busy over some banking affair, and whose new aspect gave me quite a shock. He was talking very earnestly, very definitely, with much dignity and seriousness. His eyes were sharp and friendly, but not soft. There was something about his whole attitude that was extremely responsible and determined. I could not find the boy who teases me, the ardent young lover who tries to please me, the "pussy" with soft manners who purrs in the evenings, with his pipe, his liqueur, and his hand in mine. I wondered what would happen if I called out "Pussy" to him at that moment. The thought of it struck me humorously—it fitted him so badly, that name, for the big, wise man of mine. But then "Pussy" would not fit me either when I am writing with pressed lips and serious eyes and strained mind. If he called me, as he might, "Pussywillow" in the middle of what I was writing, it would instantly demolish my dignity. Yes, I think it was his dignity which amused me so preposterously. I am married to a banker, a clever, capable, efficient man, whom other men look up to, for whom other men work. He reigns in the bank with superiorities of which I seldom get a glimpse. I reign at home, and he abandons the scepter when he inserts his large key in the resounding keyhole, and I run forward with a happy: "Hello, my dearest Pussy!"

It was the realization of his talents which made me say to him the other night, at a concert, that I admired him for the work he was doing as much as if he had written a book or composed a sonata. He had looked sadly at me when I applauded the pianist—until I said this.

"Do you really mean that?" he asked, pressing my arm with delight.

"I do—because you are doing something you did not want to do. You would have preferred artistic creation, but you forced yourself into business for the sake of our marriage and our children. And you not only made yourself do it, but you made yourself do it *well*, as well as any artist ever executed himself in his favorite occupation."

This gave Hugh a new élan. It was only fair that I should recognize his merit, but he did not seem to expect me to recognize it. He thought that my admiration would go most naturally to the accomplished musician or talented writer. But I knew better, even though his dignity does amuse me, and even though I have baptized him "my humorous banker."

The backstage life sometimes is more beautiful than the play.

Perhaps, after all, I don't want anything else—if Hugh remains as he is, an intelligent Pussy.

March 14. Hugh, or Sir Hugh, as Richard M. calls him quite appropriately, observed that my contact with the French is making me think far more than I did in New York—which is true. It is so simple to slide back into unchanging thoughts. Once you have described the scenery, the people, the daily actions, they remain more or less stable. The only things that change are the ideas and the attitudes, but I had less time for the considerations of these things in New York than I have here. Most of my visiting is done by letters, which are quicker than conversation and admit no back talk. With more time, new and exciting scenery, new people, new literature, new atmospheres, it is not strange that I should think more. I think all day with a beelike continuity.

The new people, particularly, act like wind on my sails. We know a South American child prodigy, Antonio Valencia, who was sent by his native country to study piano here. He is about twenty now, olive-skinned, black-eyed, small of stature, and extremely gifted. He has gentle, unassuming manners, an unusual share of modesty and simplicity and much goodness. He is Joaquin's best friend at the moment, and has an admirable influence over him, musically and literarily. Then there is Donald Fletcher, the puritan, older, and a student of piano and architecture. He is all inhibitions and shyness, throwing off occasional opinions with nervous eagerness.

Guicciardi is unique. It is impossible to generalize him, or to condense him. He is full of contradictions, of complexities, of franknesses and self-revelations, of inexplicable sadnesses and inexplicable pleasures, of intelligent freedom and old wisdom. He seems to evaporate himself in talk until you are certain there is nothing left inside of him which you do not know, but suddenly, by a word, he betrays another full and confused roomful. He has an air, uses impulsive gestures like Eduardo, with superlatives and exclamations, and has countless other characteristics. I couldn't paint him in one sitting, nor, perhaps, in ten. He reads [James Branch] Cabell and Dante, and loves America and Italy. But that does not explain him.

Then there are the men in the bank and their wives, whom we visit occasionally. Except Mrs. R., none are out of the ordinary range.

And the transients: Louise Midelfahrt, the red-haired Norwegian pianist who once stayed at Mother's house in Kew; and J. Salter Hansen, from whom we rented the apartment, a political adventurer, a genius at giant national undertakings, with a wide circle of acquaintances, from Jack London to Secretary Hughes[1] and Rothschild, a gourmet and, in his youth, a writer of psychology à la Freud; he thought us "a very refreshing couple."

Whether through these meetings or through the books I have read, I have acquired a vision of ideas which are separating me from people like Richard M. I begin to feel the things that *he could not understand*. With a tightening of the heart, I realize his limitations, as I have realized before the limitations of many others. I respect other people's ideas too much to ever say the ridiculous phrase: I feel myself growing up and above them. No, but I am growing *away* from their ideas, away from closed doors and barriers. In Richard M.'s world there are too many closed doors.

March 18. Days of glamour—beginning with Saturday afternoon when Guicciardi took us to the Musée Carnavalet, above the home of Mme. de Sévigné. He chose that rainy afternoon to lead us through narrow streets and into the courtyards of the old hotels and to the Place des Vosges. "It's on a day like this one must see Paris," he said, as we followed him over the slippery cobblestone streets, listening to his imaginative explanations. Then in the evening, to please Hugh, who thought it necessary, we went to a dance given by the bank, but did not stay very long, and ended in the cabaret Coq en Pâte, where we danced until three o'clock with Americans, Russians, French flappers and vampires, sipping champagne between dances. The characters amused me—the cynical, languid women with heavy strings of pearls and painted eyes, the brilliant Russian women whose cavaliers kissed their hands when they met and when they separated—brilliant in clothes and figures, but with tired eyes and sullen mouths; the French vampire in black, with flat, soiled hair and half-smiles, who tried her charm on a young, awkward boy who did not even possess an evening suit, so young was he; the loud-laughing, witty Frenchwoman with three coarse companions, drunken Americans. . . .

The entertainment consisted of Russian songs with guitar accompaniment and French songs I scarcely understood. During

[1] *Secretary of State Charles Evans Hughes.*

one of the plaintive Russian songs, I felt as if my soul were floating home, and looking down at my red velvet dress, my red fan, the glass of champagne before me, I wondered why I was there that night, and why I felt like staying. Not one moment do I feel close to the others, and not one moment do I feel that our desires are the same. We do not seek the same pleasures when we sit in the same way, brightly dressed before the bright champagne.

Then last night we attended Father's concert, and the struggle, which I had forgotten while he was ill and I did not have to see him, returned to torment me even more intensely. The glamour faded then, and even the Spanish music did not have the power to revive it. Today I brood like an owl and cannot find peace anywhere. I sink back into the brown shadows while the red fan lies hidden in tissue paper.

Pierre Loti leaves me a sweet, sorrowful and dreamful impression. Reading *Le Livre de la Pitié et de la Mort* filled me with a ghostly emotion, with an even deeper pity than I feel already for everything and everybody and with a softness and weakness that I have always struggled against. I float on languid dreams which rest me from the fever. In reality, the moment I spend dreaming after closing a book lasts only a minute. Soon I am up again, turning over the leaves of my play or my second novel with ridiculous earnestness.

It is so much more difficult to interest a European than an American—not physically, of course. In this respect, the Frenchman is the weakest victim; but whereas the Frenchman will grant me an admiring glance when I walk down the street, his mind, I know, would be difficult to capture, while the American either would not notice me at all or would surrender entirely. Guicciardi, who is the most cultured European I have met so far, gave me a glance of superficial approval when I first met him, but in other respects he entirely ignored me. It is only now that he is beginning to see that I have ideas and that besides being looked at, I like to be talked to intelligently. Even now he only considers me as a type. He likes too many things, sees too many things, to be satisfied with talking to me. He likes one girl because she is the kind he would enjoy making love to as a game, regardless of brains; another, because she has ideas, but she would not do on frivolous evenings; another, because she is Russian and attractive, and doubly so because she is married; another, because of her innocence, of which he tires; just as he tires of one who is all complications. Still another is too thin for more than temporary admiration; another has a "cute" walk and can entrance him for a day on board ship until he discovers that she is affected in other ways too. What can you do with a man like that? Who can *fix* him? He is as elusive and fluid and evanescent as a rainbow—and as colorful. His whims amuse me because he is not my husband, but heaven help his wife, unless she is equally changing and spread out into numberless souls.

I, who am accustomed to the steadfastness of my beloved puritan, who, even at my side, has eyes only for me, let Guicciardi discuss with me the charms and faults of the women around us. But once home, I gave Hugh an extra tender kiss, and I loved him more. He has never asked me why. He must know there are too many reasons and that some of them, like the last I mentioned, are too childish to be told. But not for my journal.

That steadfastness is part of the American simplicity of soul. The French have a multitude of souls, both through temperament and through culture. Temperament gives them a greater range of sensibilities and emotions; culture, a knowledge of more sides to people and ideas. They are full of interesting complexities, which, after a while, tire you. American simplicity is restful but uninspiring.

The cosmopolitan crowd we saw the other night at the Coq en Pâte was as impossible to penetrate as an oyster hidden under a thousand layers of shell. By contrast, the same type of pleasure-loving people in New York would be as easily deciphered as a first reader in a kindergarten.

March 19. Today Sir Hugh has a half-holiday for Mi-Carême.[1] I have put my black dress on, with my red shawl, and I am going to call for him at the bank. How much sweeter the days would be if he were always home! But then neither of us would work. The days would be spent in ramblings, in dreaming, in reading and love-making. We would, like Shelley, lie at the bottom of a boat and watch the sky. At times I think it is wrong that we should spend the best years of our life separated from each other, and working.

[1] *Mid-Lent.*

And yet, perhaps these chains are molding our characters, and it is the discipline which fortifies our spirits. Hugh would be weak without the severe demands of his work, and so would I if I had him at my side all day. But I cannot help dreaming and watching the clock impatiently for the beginning of our afternoon together.

March 20. Having worked on my booklet on journal writing, I have reached a degree of exaltation on the subject which makes me feel and act like a madwoman. I had to cease writing in order to sing and dance, as I felt as if I were bursting. Then, regardless of the high ideals I have been setting forth on the subject, I started to work off my excitement here, with my Bible right before my eyes—or rather, my Commandments.

Here they are in their first impulsive form:

"I understand by the writing of a journal the absolute truthfulness and freedom of a soul communing with itself, the exclamations of pain, of joy, the dreaming, and the criticism of life. It must be a free running of the tired or compressed faculties, a restful abandonment, a strengthening reiteration, a satisfying outflow of emotions, self-confession, self-criticism, self-blame, a retention of beautiful things, of inspiring things and of knowledge, a following and unveiling of ideas, a development of philosophies, an exhortation to the fulfillment of individual perfection, a reminder of the clearer and higher moments in the intellectual life and of the kinder, nobler moments of the human life."

March 21. Yesterday was the happiest day in the life of my writing. I discovered, with ecstasy, a form in which I was utterly free. It was my own, and I abandoned myself to the power of it without restraint. Under this joyous power the booklet on journal writing grew to surprising size and character. Novel writing seemed to me at that moment something to which I could not conform. *This* was what I wanted to do, what I am fit to do! *This*: the subject of journal writing approached from whatever aspect my mood urged. No traffic regulations, no pattern to imitate, no restrictions of tradition or taste evolved by others, no strict standards. I could stop where I wanted, follow my moods and thoughts in utter freedom.

Richard M. would be chagrined if he could see how I escape sometimes from the correct forms he has taught me. In this escape

I am myself. It may be a very grave blunder to follow this naturalness. The booklet will prove whether it is or not. In it, as in the play, I will roam freely.

Now I am sick of the second novel. It seems compressed and airless and stilted. What will become of it, I hardly know.

To Eduardo for his birthday:

Because I am living in Paris and so far away from you is no reason why I should forget the letter you have always received for your birthday since we have known each other.

Since we have known each other! What a torrent of recollections falls from these words. Since the days of fragrant and dreamful Lake Placid, followed by your first timid letter to your shell-enclosed cousin—wonderful letter! Written in so magical a way that it did not frighten me, and brought not only an answer but the opening of a secret door that was never to be closed between us.

Do you remember afterwards the days you spent in our big, old house, the walks on those misty evenings, the constant dreaming, the endless flaming talks which fed our ideals and our aspirations, the harmony meetings by the fireside? We used to think then that the house was enchanted. One Easter vacation you and Miguel Jorrín[1] tried to analyze the charm. We were sitting together after a delicious, exuberant talk.

"What is the inexplicable charm of this house in which one does nothing and is never bored, in which we can speak of all the things one loves?"

"It is the people in it," I said.

"It is *you*, Mimi," said mon cher cousin.

No, it was none of that. The beauty came from our enthusiasm, from the fullness of our mental life, the gorgeous coloring of our visions.

If, since those days, maturity has subdued these, if experience has toned down the naïveté of our desires; if knowledge has changed the course of our enthusiasms, nevertheless we know the house in which we were happy. We can return to the pure source of our beautiful joys and wash away the taste of ashes in our mouths. We may, and we must, pass through other houses, but we must not lose the key to the first.

[1] *A brother of A.N.'s Aunt Julia.*

In memory of those beautiful days I will think of you on your birthday—in Paris, in the spring!

March 23. The little crises multiply themselves, and we steer the course of our marriage with nothing but a deep love. There was the night when Hugh realized, not without bitterness, that he was becoming the typical "businessman" we both hate. The work being more difficult and Hugh feeling many more responsibilities, he has given not only his time to it, but his soul. He came home late, bringing work to do for the rest of the evening, and when not working he talked to me incessantly about it in a way which clearly showed how obsessed he was. Nothing could turn his mind away from it, not the mention of books, the sight of the literary review or my writing. He listened to me with an absent smile, only to return again with more intensity to the problem that worried him.

I did not blame him. I understood that we were passing through an unusual period. We agreed that we must make sacrifices now for the sake of the future. Sometimes at night, after a lonely day of writing and housekeeping, with the repressed desire to show him my creations, I would turn away from his tired embrace and brood sorrowfully on the wasting of our youth. But I said nothing and watched the work gain a stronger and stronger hold on him. The preoccupied expression was on his face oftener than the smile of relaxation. I saw him becoming more and more like the other men, the men whose sole thought and feeling is business. The specter of what he was becoming terrified me. I could no longer consent to its realization for the sake of what we might possess some day, materially. What was more precious than his youth, his strength, these days of our love?

"It is not worth it," I said one night. "Come back to our books, for my sake, don't waste your youth like this, and mine."

He was struck by the fear that I did not believe in his soul any more, that I had ceased to look on him as a companion. It was true that he was no longer my companion, that he was becoming like a providing machine. . . . But it was not too late to come back to our ideal. He is coming back slowly.

Today he had, however, a full day. He left me early, before 8 o'clock. He came at half past twelve and had a hurried lunch. He did not stay up to sip his liqueur or smoke his pipe. I walked down with him with a tightening heart and came back unwillingly to the brown apartment, to a writing nobody is going to read or care about, to a reading which fills me with an excitement that it hurts me to suppress. I am alone in my spiritual life, fermenting with youthful expression to which no one responds. And poor Hugh, tied to the bank, is filled, body and soul, with his work.

He will come home as usual, tired, obsessed by the bank, asking me from habit rather than from interest: "What have you done today, little Pussywillow?" and without waiting for an answer he will tell me about the success of his last suggestion to the management about the carelessness of one of the stenographers, about the resignation of a man in his department, about the lost folder and the interesting talk with a French business genius.

I understand now the spirit that pushes some married women to embrace an inane social life, to spend their afternoons in a club playing bridge, to "go around" with other men. They are accused of selfishness because meanwhile the poor husbands are killing themselves with work. They have no right to kill themselves with work. By doing that they kill all the living beauty of marriage— the companionship, the united enjoyments, the united growth.

Only the love of writing and reading keeps me home, but even then I feel the longing for companionship. Twice a day, once before my mirror and once before my desk, I ask myself, "What is the use?" It is in vain that I seek a more exalted "raison d'être." All humanity, fame, cannot replace the insatiate desire of a woman in love with her young, ideal and chosen companion. He is trying to come back. I am waiting.

March 24. Today my writing is the result of a promise made to my darling. We had such a sweet evening together, talking in the way we used to, forgetting the bank for a while and reading together. He criticized my writing, gave me a few suggestions and some encouragement. Conscience-stricken by his sweetness, I confessed having written the preceding pages, and he forced me to read them to him. They affected him deeply, so that I felt very selfish and mean to have had such thoughts. But anyway, they brought him back entirely, and as usual with us, after many confidences and confessions, we felt closer than ever and happier than before.

"It is all over now," we said together.

I promised not to look for another companion, which was the chief cause of his worry! As if I wanted to!

The chief result of all this is that he promised to take an extra day off in addition to the Easter holidays so that we may go to Hendaye to visit Mother, which will also rest him.

In announcing the visit to Mother, I mentioned a mythical young couple instead of ourselves, and she will be surprised!

March 25. The tea I gave for Louise Midelfahrt on Sunday only served to bring out the superiority of Antonio Valencia. He had mature and balanced ideas on music, on literature, on racial differences, on sculpture and painting and the first hopeful understanding we have of the French we have seen so far. Hugh was delighted with him, and we will see him again.

Today I am invited to the studio of the painter friend Louise brought with her to tea. It is raining and I feel "sauvage" and wish I might stay home. But then there is nothing strange about this. It always costs me an effort to meet people, but afterwards I am glad. My first instinct is one of distaste and reluctance. Why can't I cure myself of this?

Beginning to read Renan's *Dialogues philosophiques*. I have gone no further by reading Renan than by following my tormented thoughts two years ago, alone. Except that I have learned that revolt is a crime, leading only to destruction.

Why do I want to be good? I know it will bring me nothing. But so few are good, and goodness does make other people happy, and as long as there is so little happiness, I want to help in the making of some. I feel so much pity, so much tenderness. That is my principal gesture—stretching out hands to sufferers, mentally, physically. It is the gesture I chose unquestioningly, as the only reality.

Guicciardi argues with me about the stupidity sometimes of this gesture. He claims I use no foresight, no ultimate intelligence. I felt sorry one night for a pedantic speaker whose discourse seemed unending. I listened quietly and suffered. But others, more sincere than me, began to clap impatiently.

"They are really doing more good than you are by feeling sorry for this *one* man," Guicciardi said. "Their frankness will prevent him from ever delivering a long speech again and tormenting another big audience. Thousands of people will be helped by an act which seems unkind to you at this moment."

He is right. My pity must not be a momentary emotion; it must be an intelligent perception, an act of the intellect.

March 26. We had two sweet evenings. Tuesday, after dinner, my Love and I walked down the spacious Champs-Elysées, his arm in mine, talking about the first days of our meeting. He told me how on the night of the dance on March 12, 1921, when we first saw each other, he promised himself to become my friend when his family left for Europe. Three months passed during which my deliberate, slow Scotsman contented himself with dreams of me. Then his family left and he came to stay with his uncle, our neighbor. The next time he saw me I was standing before our house with Miguel Jorrín, Orces[1] and his friend. Partly through shyness, partly through the fact that he was annoyed at seeing me in the company of such youthful boys, he did not cross the street to speak to me. I neither saw nor felt him. He passed again, on purpose, watching for me, but I did not notice him. After that he came home every day by Audley Street, hoping to see me. Then came the day when we smiled at each other, he from the sidewalk and I from our porch, and the day when Mother invited him in. And the beginning of everything!

Last night we passed from the romantic to the philosophical. I read him my summary of Renan's first dialogue, and we walked down Boulevard Haussmann discussing philosophical problems without dignity or gravity. The air was too soft for that, and our walk together in rhythm too exhilarating.

As to the tea yesterday afternoon in the studio of Miss Samson and Miss King, top floor of a house in Montmartre, it was not unusual but agreeable. I was too full of Renan to appreciate the conventional talk about art, the hackneyed phrases about painting, the French, and other subjects. It was nobody's fault that I craved a talk with some very old, wise, erudite and intellectual person about abstract ideas, and about Renan particularly. I felt solemn and ashamed of my solemnity.

March 27. It is when I want to put the secret of our activity in so many words that I find that there are no logical causes. I was trying to give Frances the recipe. She wrote me about her misery, her lack of interest in life, her drifting. I tried to argue with her and logically take her out of this inertia and unhappiness. But the more I wrote, the hollower the words sounded. Why should the things that make me happy make her happy? How can I urge her to do things when I do not really know a sensible cause for all this

[1] *Herbert Orces, one of A.N.'s admirers.*

"doing"? Do I really know why she should write? Do I know what makes me write?

In face of this lack of energy I am at a loss. I do not know what to say to Eugene, or to Frances. One is a revolté and the other an indifférent. Why should I exert myself to breathe peace and life into both? I have always done that. I have not been content to feel myself burn; I had to try to set Eduardo aflame, Enric, Miguel, the artists I worked with, Frank Monteiro, Eugene and Frances and Richard M. and Ruth. Some flared up, like Eduardo; others burned for a moment and then died down, like Enric. Ruth responds mildly. Richard M. "gets tired of thinking" with me. Eugene responds theoretically, but not otherwise. Frances burns spasmodically. Reading my letters overworks the miracle, she told me once.

And I, with a faith beyond explanation, a faith I cannot see, write her vaguely, to spur her on, of *certainties* which I cannot express as flowingly as I feel them. But she will feel the spirit. I wish she would come so that we might work together. My best answer to these troublesome questions that are put to me is: "Come and watch me work. Don't ask me to explain everything, for I cannot do it. But don't you feel how consuming it is, this work, how beautiful, how powerful, how invisible and nameless, is the force that drives me on?"

I feel like some of those simple, pious souls, who are angered and worried by the logical attacks on their faith, which they do not have the talent to defend on the same grounds. My work is my illogical, my beautiful, my inexplicable religion.

March 30. Gone is our peace! We have to move again on the fifteenth of April and continue our wanderings through inhospitable Paris. Looking for apartments or pensions or hotels and planning for our moving and our trip to Hendaye will keep me from writing.

There are so many things I hate in myself—the apathetic moods which follow a long and tense period of activity. Today I could not write, I could not read with pleasure, because there were so many practical little things I should have been doing instead. Ugly weakness which attacks the imagination and the will. All afternoon, after walking down with my Love and visiting some hotel rooms, I sat in the apartment, sluggishly appalled and oppressed by the darkness of it, the moldiness of it, and by the darkness within me. As Christopher Morley says in one of his wonderful articles for the Literary Review, ". . . to readers who have never been held and sickened by the whirling emptiness of an artistic problem, who have never carried in their hearts the dead faggots of a dream that could not be ignited . . ."

An accidental glance over the book reviews gave me the first feeling; an effort to rouse myself by handling my work gave me the second feeling. And now it is too late. My Love is about to come home, and I have nothing to show out of this long day, nothing sparkling to offer him with my homecoming kiss.

All days, I suppose, cannot be rich and beautiful. You cannot make a habit of creation. But surely, one should be *alive* every day, at least alive, if not productive. I am puritanically ashamed of laziness, and I sometimes wish I had never acquired this conscience, for I could then enjoy idleness as a natural state of the soul.

March 31. The first sweet, warm day of spring, warm enough to be spent outdoors, and I sit in the Parc Monceau, before the Corinthian colonnade, which is reflected in the small lake. Ivy has crept from the feet of the columns and covered their tops, overhanging, and also tremblingly mirrors itself in the water with the floating leaves and flowers.

For the first time today I remembered how I *never* could work in the early spring. My soul dilates and I cannot draw it together so that its strength may flow.

The hours pass. I dread the return to the autumnal rooms, the climb up the obscure and moldy stairs, the preparation of the dinner. When it is dark, I tell myself, I will go home. Moments of inaction, of pale and selfish dreams. But the most severe utilitarian will admit that once a week, at least, one must go to church and pray. And this is my day of worship: I worship beauty with my silences, with my dreams, my contemplations.

How wicked I would be if Hugh were rich. How wicked I am already in my thoughts. Today, returning from the park I felt a wave of rebellion against all my little duties; I wished I had no dinner to cook, no dishes to wash afterwards, none of that eternal, vicious circle of housework. How weak I am, how lazy at heart! I feel it in the languor that comes over me when I sit on a pillow before the gas stove, to feel the heat I love so much. I am bad when I lie in bed in the morning, hesitating to get up because the making of breakfast awaits me. I am bad when I enjoy the luxury exposed in the shop windows, when I feel intolerable desires for a new hat or a new dress; all my enjoyments are bad—my love of luxury, my desire to be served, my love of visible beauty, my moments of languid dreams, my preference for meditation, for reading and writing, my idle love of nature, of brooding over bookstands and in antique shops.

It may be just the softness outside which accentuates my weaknesses, for usually I have had a firm enough control over them, since that day long ago, at sixteen, when I realized my selfishness.

Yet not even that hateful epithet, "selfish," can awaken me—contact with beauty disarms my will and dissolves my conscience.

April 2. More soft, sunny days, and I am unable to pull myself together. I do the most necessary duties in the apartment and eagerly seek an excuse to go out. Towards eleven I set out to the bank, where I have an appointment with Hugh at twelve, but it really takes me only twenty minutes to walk down to 41 Boulevard Haussmann; I try to make it last an hour.

We took a light lunch and went to visit several furnished apartments, which we did not like, and ended by sitting in the Café du Dôme in Montparnasse, the artists' quarter, where we rested and satisfied our thirst. At four I was home, but only to change into a warmer coat and run hatless to the park. And now I sit here, without thoughts, reading uncritically, paralyzed by the depth of my sensations.

Poor Stendhal. It is not fair to read him on a day like this. His *Le Rouge et le Noir*, the muddy, stilted old story springing like some old witch on a day of festival, when I find life so entrancing, irritates me. I am entirely out of tune with its worthy and probably reformative realism. Critics should have no moods in order to judge fairly.

April 3. Return to thought, to profundities—through seeing Pirandello's moving play *Henri IV*. Old ideas which Ibsen had first awakened haunted me again. But though I felt the meaning in the play so keenly, I do not think I am capable yet of transcribing it. One idea, only, seemed very clear and utterable to me—the same which haunted me when I wrote in *Aline*: "You know, it is always so. Every man thinks the other mad because he does not seek or believe what the other seeks or believes."

And also the idea about what we *really* are, what we *seem* to be to others—the mystery of personality and of our understanding of each other. I have always occupied myself with this idea, and that is why I can write of it. But the others, the awesome, disturbing clarities of Henri's so-called madness, those are strange to me, and I am afraid to touch them with words.

Cold and rain also seem to bring back reflection to me. Can it be possible that mental energy could depend on so scientific a cause as climate? Is it true, as they say, that Spain has produced more romancers, playwrights, poets, than philosophers and scientists? Would I think less if we lived in Italy, and more if we lived in Ibsen's Norway?

And yet what greater depth of imagery-thought than in Pirandello? How keenly, how painfully, he brought out the mysteries of self, of the imagination.

Hugh was pleased because we had such identical feelings about the play. Behind us an English couple sustained the most stupid conversation about people they knew, about other plays, about marriage and politics and diversions. The play seemed but an interruption to their vanities. I was boiling with suppressed indignation. After a scene which exalted me, to hear their monotonous small talk, as if nothing had happened between one remark and the other, made me so unhappy that I almost cried out.

By contrast, Hugh, who understood, who felt, who not once uttered a discordant phrase, grew more and more wonderful in my eyes.

Yet not long ago, when I was going to the theatre with men and boys, I had to submit to their small talk between acts and force myself to hush my serious reactions in order not to startle or displease them. All of them, if I had told them my real thoughts, would have thought me mad and never invited me again.

The memory of these things made me say to Hugh: "Darling, it is with you alone in the whole world that I am *entirely myself*." And we came home on a cloud of a love.

Before falling asleep, another idea disturbed me. Hugh had made me feel his understanding, but I could not remember that he had expressed it. The more I thought of it, the clearer it seemed that it was I who had talked about the play and phrased our opinion and our emotions. A fear troubled me. Was I developing spiritually at his expense? His work keeps him from following ideas as I do, but why does he let me express everything?

I asked him.

He said that it was all as it should be. He had no time for spiritual life. When he had a little time, like last night, he was too tired; he was happier in letting me *express him*. He felt that he was living it just as completely in this manner, but I insisted that he was missing the habit of self-expression, that he was sinking into acquiescence.

Sometimes I wonder, even if Hugh had time, whether he would still be in a state of acquiescence. He never seems to feel as keenly as I do the *pain of letting others speak for me*. I felt such an unworthy pain when I read Amiel, when I read Ibsen, when I read Renan, Edith Wharton, and finally, last night, when I saw the play. I can never resign myself to be the *audience*. I am immediately made desperately restless, with envy or desire, to emulate the *creator*. I cannot listen patiently or watch passively. I have to *give* the spectacle. Only twice have I heard Hugh say regretfully: "I wish I had written that book!"

Oh, but some day he will be free, and I will know, for I do not want him to be tied like an ordinary man—he, the most unusual and the most delicate of men. And meanwhile, it is with religious constancy that I keep him from sinking back completely. For the moment, I can help to fill him with every thought and every spiritual experience. His being will be rich with absorbed knowledge, and he will be the more ready for the period of creation.

I am worried about this "pain of letting others speak for me." What if, instead of proving me a creator, it proved to be merely an immense and horrible vanity? Why should I be sad when another has expressed some illuminating idea? Because I should have wanted to express it myself? But I should not care *who* expressed it, I should be glad only that it has been expressed, well expressed. I must sound this. If it is vanity, I must struggle against it.

There are so many things I am at war with in myself. Another one of them is irritability. I do not know if it is the French who irritate me with their contempt of Americans, their petty thefts, their petty business manners, or whether I am growing more irritable as I grow older. In New York, general good humor and placidity of character saved me from such a state. Here, I cannot stand the mockery, the staring, the stupid curiosity, the national narrowness. It is just that I cannot see the French sentimentally. I judge them as a foreigner, and to the foreign eyes, at moments, they are insufferable. I quiver to see honest and straight Hugh among them, when, with their eyes, they laugh at his accent, when they cheat him because he is an American, when, as a result of disagreement, a bus conductor, makes insulting allusions to America. I long to put them all in some insane asylum, tied, until they calm down.

Oh, I cry sometimes for less culture and less intelligence but more health, more stability. The sight of a pink-faced, square-shouldered, unintelligent-looking American in the streets of Paris, at irritating moments, is so refreshing and soothing. I want to unite in myself depths of culture with an equable temper, for I love both in others. I will take Hugh as an example.

April 4. Awoke to this inspiring thought of Renan: that all the struggle and the efforts of the world should tend to an hour of perfect thought in a genius—a moment of vision which will bring *material for more thinking*—thought that forever enlarges itself, deepens itself, which never ends in itself but to which each genius in consecutive centuries brings the essence of the century's apparently purposeless and cruel struggle; for each great thinker will be a new consummation of nature. As soon as this consummation is achieved, the world returns to its labor, to bring forth, out of a million mediocre and inferior beings, one Galileo or one Newton, a Descartes or a Renan!

Then the world has a purpose, a purpose which entrances me. Whatever thoughts Hugh and I can bring to our love, transmit to our children, will pass from them into others, and from among all these will gather in *one* clear and superior mind the essence of a multitude of thoughts become *one* thought.

That is the only immortality. That is a worthy cause for our suffering, our efforts, our struggle for individual perfection. To such a creation Hugh and I must bring the very highest and noblest in ourselves.

April 8. 22 Rue Pauquet, near the Etoile.

First Scene.

(In a large, sunny room, with two windows that open on the street. A couch with a little table next to it, loaded with our books. Bed and night table and armoire in old ivory. A fireplace to the right, with the traditional clock, which looks with a quizzical round face at my two candlesticks and their blue-and-orange candles. Next to the fireplace a little writing table with a green blotter, my fat account book, a little chubby lamp and another traveler like the candlesticks, the inevitable and worn, familiar-faced ink bottle. At this writing table sits a young lady in a green dress. While she writes she occasionally looks at the clock, as it will soon be six o'clock.)

Young lady: "Well, I don't think I can write any more today. Hugh is coming in a little while and I must see that the valises are packed before our light supper—or else we will never catch that 7:15 train to Hendaye!"

Second Scene.

(In Hendaye. A cheerful bungalow facing the sea and Spain. The whole act is accompanied by the sound of the waves and of the piano, the last played by Joaquin, at present the chief character in the scene. Joaquin keeps a journal on the pattern of his sister, A., and between these two there is now a close spiritual and intellectual link, which the difference in age makes only more interesting. A. is at present the Influence and Joaquin the Disciple, but the development, the surprises, the mental births, the youthfulness, of the Disciple are a constant inspiration to the older Influence, who feels at times as if she were reborn in the youth's period of thought.)

April 15. At the beach in the afternoon.

The newness and the charm of our first days in Hendaye were effaced in my mind by the intolerable pain of Hugh's return to Paris alone—our first separation. The moment I saw him carried away in the train, I lost interest in everything; I felt soulless and lifeless. My first night without him since our marriage was spent in restless turning and pain; above all, I could not face my journal, and I read as much as possible instead.

He left at five o'clock on Monday, and it was not until today that I felt a little happier—thinking that tomorrow is my last day here and that Friday night I shall be at the pension. And I who love my little mother so much!—what a powerful chain binds husband and wife together when, in two years, it can grow stronger than love between mother and daughter. At least I made her happy by staying, and but for that tightness of the heart, I gave her all I had in me to give—to the sweetest and most unselfish of mothers.

Sitting here in the sand in the first pale sunshine we have had since we came here, I can look back more peacefully and almost contentedly to those other days—from the very first day, when we took a carriage to Mother's yellow-and-green bungalow, which stands almost at the end of the town, and found no one home, to the last day, when I watched Hugh's train shrink away. That first morning Mother and Joaquin had gone to church after being told the train was an hour late, and they came back at last to find Hugh starting a fire in the old-fashioned coal stove and me unpacking our valises. The surprise was complete. We laughed and talked about it the rest of the day. After lunch Hugh went to sleep, as we had spent an unforgettable night in our second-class wagon, a night of aching bones and revolted senses and soured humor. A description of our fellow travelers would read like a page of Joyce, and I do not think that in this clean air I could faithfully recall the nauseating smells and sights.

The next day was Holy Friday. We planned to see a procession in Fuenterrabia, the Spanish town which we can see on the other side of the Bidassoa, the river which separates France and Spain. We went in a tourist car, and at the frontier, at Irún, Hugh was turned back because of some irregularity in his passport—a visa necessary for Spain in the case of Americans. We walked back to Hendaye crestfallen and discoursing on the inanities of the laws. At the corner of a narrow little street which descends abruptly to the river, quite near Loti's house, a boatman stopped us, and we told him our story. He promised he could get us into Fuenterrabia, and we followed him down the street to a stone quay and into his little boat. He rowed us across with smooth movement and strength. A Spanish guard questioned him leniently, smiled at me and let us pass. We were standing then at the feet of the little city, which is built on a hill. The church towered high above us. The boatman led us through the city's gate of arched stone, and we mingled with the crowd in time to see the end of the procession, which tells the story of the crucifixion. The statues of the Virgin, of the saints and of Christ towered over the heads of the crowd. A respectful silence accompanied the passing of each statue, but in between, the swellings of the Spanish tongue filled the air. English and American travelers gazed with curiosity and without understanding at this barbaric expression of a faith whose beauty the Spanish race loves to see in visible symbols. The crowd bowed their heads while the last symbol passed—the Christ entombed, carried by four Roman guards. The procession closed with sad, expressive music, which rose like a plaintive chant between the walls of the old city.

Though this was a reenactment of the saddest days in Catholic church history, the crowd was irrepressibly joyous and exuberant.

Religion to the Latin is not the severe and gloomy tyranny that it is to the Protestant, that it was to the Puritan. I invited Hugh to discourse on the contrast, but he was too busy noting the names of the streets in Basque, for Eugene.

The next day, by crossing over in a little boat again to Fuenterrabia and taking a bus to Irún and then a special trolley, we visited the luxurious summer resort of San Sebastian, with its ancient churches, the palace of the King of Spain and the casino. We were in Spain and yet I could not believe it. Childhood memories of Barcelona, of Málaga and Valencia, were confused with my impressions of that day. I could not feel that it was *new* to me, or even strange. As a child I had seen Spanish soldiers, and women carrying bundles and jars on their heads, and men with those peculiar brilliant smiles; I had heard such accents; and I had been in those magnificent old Spanish churches. So I merely remembered and lived in a dream rather than in a fresh experience. The sight particularly of balconies reminded me of my childish meditations. I used to like sitting out alone on our balcony in Barcelona, thinking about things, and writing already, soliloquizing. It was while those same Spanish mountains grew smaller before my eyes, while I stood on the ship that was to take me to New York, that I began my journal.

That Saturday in San Sebastian, in the semidarkness of Santa Maria I was moved intensely, painfully, by a vague restlessness about things not yet expressed. I have been inarticulate in front of many things these last days, from the bronzed faces of the sailors who rowed us across the Bidassoa to the four rows of carved saints that rose from the altar of the Church of St. Jean Baptiste at St.-Jean-de-Luz. The history, the color, the soul, of the Pays Basque have stirred me into speechlessness. It is just as if I were still very young and did not know the name or the meaning of everything, while aspiring to name and to understand with such violence as to break through the shell that encloses me.

Why should things appear to me in such a complex and subtle way? Later, later I will read Loti, or someone else, who will tell me quite clearly everything which I madly pursued. And then I will cry, because I wanted to write it! Possibly this Pays Basque, which fascinates me so, whose strangeness I want to penetrate, whose soul I want to possess, has already been piously or impiously dissected.

I am too impatient. I should let the simple things, the daily scenes, take possession of my mind instead of trying to possess them. I should let memory mix my colors so that I can paint my subject in unity. I should like Hugh to peacefully take down the names of the streets and the villas in Basque, peacefully inquire of the bookseller in town whether there is any Basque literature, order the one newspaper which he said existed in that tongue, which is destined to die away, and peacefully turn homeward with a volume of Loti's *Ramuntcho* in one pocket and a package of post cards in the other.

April 18. Home again in Paris in the ivory-colored room, sobered by a return to wifely duties and equally dutiful letters and yet at the same time stirred by Hugh's augmented fervor and devotion. But as he says, we did not need to be separated to be certain of what we mean to each other. He did confess that he was distressed by his unmended socks, and that he could not find his pipe or his slippers or his cuff links, and that a wife, from a practical point of view, was a very necessary object.

April 21. Finished Renan's *Dialogues philosophiques* and found him a little tiresome towards the end, particularly after he rates woman as incapable of the exercise of thought.

Nor did I enjoy his prophecies about beauty and the arts. . . . Of course, I was partly peeved that I could not, on many occasions, understand him at all! Pure science is beyond me, as well as the application of philosophy to politics, and the connection between philosophy and, say, the history of evolution, etc.

I am grateful for this period of rest. I have nothing in the world to do but to read and write, mend socks, with occasional sewing, and a few small errands. A pleasant, humble Irish girl tends to all our wants and serves our dinners in our room. I feel that I can now regain my health, for I have been dangerously thin and weak lately, and the doctor who saw me in Hendaye threatened me severely with serious illness. And so I rest—I lie in bed in the mornings, I go out for a walk before lunch, I read and copy some extracts out of my old journals. I am not ready for creation yet.

April 24. Vain efforts to subdue the disgust I felt last night when Monsieur E., who had taken us out to the theatre, took us to a cabaret where we heard coarse songs and saw such coarse people. Or was it because I was not in the mood for them?

I view with fear the suffering I underwent, through jealousy, for I am horribly, deeply jealous. Hugh admired an odd Russian singer, who sang two songs with guitar accompaniment—admired her in his frank, calm way. To see his eyes, his eyes I love so well, following her gestures caused me intolerable pain. After her came a handsome young Russian violinist, and it was my turn to watch him dreamily, unconsciously (I was thinking of Enric). Once home, I learned that Hugh had suffered over my admiration of the violinist!

He is often jealous, so often that we should be able to laugh at each other, but for me the feeling is followed by such sorrowful imaginings—always my cursed imagination!—I begin to build picture upon picture of a tragedy; how it would be if Hugh grew tired of me, if he loved another woman, how I would act—and suffer.

French books and plays have accentuated this malady. My imagination is sick with Latin impulses, Latin fickleness, Latin fancifulness and unsteadiness. I long for a purer atmosphere, I long for the calm, fearless love of our Richmond Hill home. Whether or not Anglo-Saxon purity is hypocrisy, at least it is a boon to the dreamer's eyes.

April 26. Our most perfect dance—last night, at the Italian soirée to which Guicciardi gave us tickets. Not knowing anybody, we danced together all evening, observed people with a beautiful peace and quiet humor. We also compared this dance with all the others we had been to before we knew each other, and the comparisons ended with a most sentimental and flattering appraisal of the present. Yet once, when they played a tango that I had heard often in Havana, I felt a pang of regret—for what?

April 28. I realize now how deeply I needed this physical rest. I have buried away my puritan detestation of idleness. I am enjoying this most pleasant medicine prescribed to me, enjoying the long, sunny, unfilled hours, the dozing in the early afternoon. And a joyous accent added to my lady's existence: I bought, after long months of privation—no, years—in one day, a black silk coat, a lavender hat, a handbag, a small umbrella and perfume!

And then Hugh completes my demoralization, saying that he loves me more now than when I drudged, *because I am more beautiful.* I threatened him with never again eating a meal cooked by my own hands, a threat which he took with a smile—and no wonder, for he *knows* my cooking.

However, I know that in a month or so he will be sighing after a home again, so I must thoroughly enjoy my present role of "lady" while it lasts.

I am indignant over the undisguised copying done by Nicolas Ségur in his *La Belle Venise*. Each word, every character, every situation, every idea, echo d'Annunzio's *L'Enfant de la Volupté*, and he has the audaciousness, besides, to introduce the vague figure of d'Annunzio himself in André Gallerani. He even makes use of the same form to describe the state of mind of the angelical lady—in *L'Enfant de la Volupté* she wrote a diary; in *La Belle Venise* she writes self-revealing, diarylike letters. Such cold-blooded imitation is infamous. The only right to forgiveness is that Ségur has at least done it well. But how can anyone blacken his soul with the stealing of another's work?

And I had liked the author for his curious and original interpretation of Anatole France in *Les Mélancolies de l'Intelligence*.

May 1. While writing Richard M. and Joaquin, I felt that I was ready for work again, and it made me so hapyy. I began today by working three hours on the copying of my old journals.[1] The bad writing in them saddened me and piqued me. In 1920 particularly, the phrases are affected, even though feelings, I can swear to that, were true enough. But such borrowed phrases, gathered from miscellaneous reading, thousands of them! How difficult it is to find one's true self in style.

May 4. Sadness—inexpressible, unreasonable. Hugh leaves me at 8 o'clock and returns for lunch, but never *entirely*. The bank has taken possession of him—his mind is elsewhere. Nothing I tell him interests him.

And then, I stay alone again until 7:30—but even then he does not return completely. Sometimes we worry over this together, his head on my breast, his hands clinging to my shoulders: "I love you, I love you so," he almost sobs. "You are my best self—save me."

And then he promises everything in those moments—but the next morning he is gone again to give his freshness, his energy, his soul, to his work. Everything disgusts me. I have no desire to write, to walk out in the spring softness, to dress, to arrange my hair. A terrible lassitude, a terrible indifference, take hold of me.

[1] *A.N. began preparing typescripts of her journals.*

And I struggle to cheer him. I talk lightly, I smile, I do not show half of the restlessness and disappointment which devour me. I read feverishly, with a desire to live at last in the imagination. But the realization of my isolation strikes me continuously. It is worse than if I were not married, because I fear to cling to the friendships offered me, such is the desire I have to belong to Hugh entirely, because I love him, and because above every unhappiness I may feel for myself I feel *his* unhappiness first. I don't want to abandon him. I know him too well to think that this absorption is by his own choice. Poor darling! He has to work and he wants to work well, and I admire him for that, but why is the human mind so weak that in order to succeed it has to concentrate wholly on one thing? He cannot relax, he cannot rest, he cannot forget, when he comes home. That does not mean that I want him, after his day's work, to devote himself to me. That would be selfish, but he could at least *come home and be himself*, and that alone would satisfy me.

I want to try and get rid of these thoughts, which are so intolerable, before he arrives. How? Can I think of the things I have to make any woman happy? No housework, peaceful and cheerful surroundings, all the books I want, time which belongs to me, work waiting for me—unfinished stories and essays— modest comfort, security. Oh, today, these seem so little, they shrink to material proportions, while the other assumes the gigantic proportions of a spiritual calamity.

How inconsistent I am. When I apply this single-minded intensity to my writing, I do not blame myself. When Hugh applies it to banking, I fret about his endangered salvation. But it is true that when he comes home, the creative flames drop from me and I become wholly devoted to the filling of his pipe, to giving him his lounging coat, his slippers, to cheering and comforting him, to silly chatter which he asks of me (at least when I am silent he always begs: "Talk to me, little Pussy").

Woman, I suppose, is more flexible for these transformations. She is adapted to the art of pleasing. Ah, now I generalize in the most stupid of ways, confounding Hugh and myself with all the rest of the men and women—when we believed that we were different. But are we not proving that we are not different, with these century-old problems—the selfsame weaknesses and the selfsame blunders?

Why should Hugh be so different from his father? His father started, I know, by being interested in other things. He loved his violin, for example. He ended by resembling all the other American fathers who have amassed comfortable fortunes, and at fifty have attacks of acute indigestion and are already wasted, hardened —a contradiction of their original self.

He came home earlier. I forgot my pain and my pessimism in his tenderness. I even felt remorse at the thought of what I had written in the morning. Still I was fully in power of my reason when I wrote, and it must be the easily softened woman in me who disturbs my sensible description of the situation.

May 6. The fever has begun again. Thoughts about everything are burning me, and on top of this, in the usual sequence, the desire to write. So I am working again to the tune of my Parisian life.

This Parisian life, I am convinced now, is a constant source of irritation to me. Why? I don't know. Deeply, beyond the surface glow, I feel the impurities of it keenly. And yet each morning I greet it with a smile, each morning I approach it with tenderness. Towards nine o'clock, when the rosy-cheeked Irish maid brings me my coffee and rolls on a little tray and I awake to the sounds of the street, a quiet enjoyment fills me. I eat my roll, listening to the thundering of wheels on the cobblestones, to the purring of automobiles, the cries of vendors, the barking of dogs. And then I rise, impatient to meet the day. I walk to the windows to open the shutters, and lean over the iron railing to question the weather. If it is sunny, I am drawn outside, irresistibly. Avenue d'Iéna is wide and clean and aristocratic, and I walk up to the Etoile in the delicate shadow of lacy trees. In the corner I breathe more deeply because the air is heavy with the scent of cut flowers on their stand. In the shadow of this stand sits a painter paying tribute to the Etoile.

Paris is like a giant park, riotous in coloring, festive in its fountains and flowers, glorious in its monuments. When I stand at the top of the Champs-Elysées, with its chestnut trees in flower, its undulations of shining cars, its white spaciousness, I feel as if I were biting into a utopian fruit, something velvety and lustrous and rich and vivid.

But the worms are gnawing it. A repugnant phrase in a book, a coarse breath of the theatre, a look from sacrilegious eyes, the smell of something foul and abysmal, even a talk with Guicciardi, whose clever phrases give every thought the saving, inexplicable

Sculpture of Anaïs Nin by Richard F. Maynard, c. 1924

Hugh Guiler and his brother John, Long Beach, N. Y., July 1924

Rosa Culmell Nin, John Guiler, and Anaïs

Anaïs, Long Beach, July 1924

The bungalow, Richmond Hill

*Portrait of Joaquin by
Paul Swan, 1924*

*Anaïs on her way to
France, December 1924*

Hugh browsing at the bookstalls along the Seine

Hugh in Paris, 1925

The Guilers' apartment, 11 bis Rue Schoelcher

Joaquin, Rue Schoelcher; bust of Anaïs on piano by R. F. Maynard

Anaïs in Paris, c. 1925

Joaquin and Antonio Valencia,
St.-Jean-de-Luz

Hugh and Anaïs, Rue Schoelcher

Hugh and Anaïs, Hendaye, April 1925

Anaïs traveling in France—Mont-St.-Michel and the château country

Anaïs in Luchon, the Pyrénées, 1927

Anaïs aboard ship (probably the De Grasse*), 1927*

Anaïs and Hugh, Luchon

Anaïs and Hugh revisiting their bungalow in Rich-mond Hill, July 1927
Courtesy of Sylvia Maynard

R. F. Maynard

*Anaïs, Lorraine Maynard, and Hugh ready for an outing in the May-
nards' Studebaker, July 1927*
Courtesy of Sylvia Maynard

R. F. Maynard

Lorraine Maynard, Anaïs, and Hugh at Long Beach, July 1927
Courtesy of Sylvia Maynard

R. F. Maynard

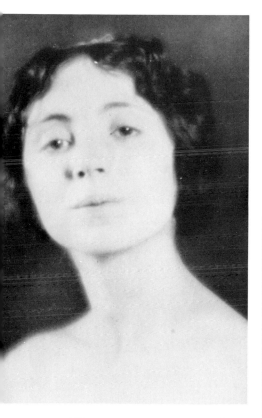

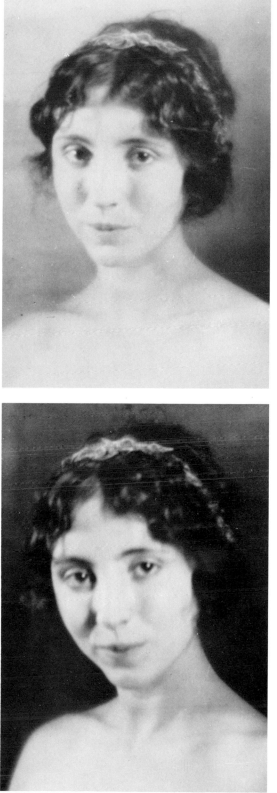

Three studies of Anaïs by
Richard F. Maynard, 1927

Unfinished portrait of Anaïs by Richard F. Maynard, 1927
Courtesy of Joaquin Nin-Culmell

twist, in whose presence idealism suddenly dwindles to a pale sentimentalism, and the fruit turns bitter in my mouth. I stand in the same place, but shivering, nauseated.

My reaction to sensuality causes me infinite pain.

May 7. On the whole, these are happy days. I feel that I am building up a physical root—an enduring one this time. I never want to feel that mortal lassitude, that depressing weakness, I have felt so often. In order to calm my conscience with a determined, reasonable plan, I say to myself: I am going to rest all summer, and grow strong, and then in the autumn I will be ready for my work. This means the making of a home and writing and studying at the Sorbonne.

When I lie on the couch, reading, I drop my book sometimes to contemplate this satisfying plan. The rest and calm and idleness seem a preparation for it.

Idleness! Am I ever truly, truly idle? From these many books I am reading at random, I absorb a quantity of ideas and impressions which are in constant fermentation. Every moment of dreaming adds color to my imaginings. For hours, some days, I sit and ask myself, what do I want to write, what am I fit to write?

The pure novel does not seem free enough. I have a feverish desire to invent a form for myself, to follow my inclinations, my impulses, to give free play to the queerness within me. For I repress my queerness. There is a fund of respectability in me, a sort of puritan literary conscience which looks suspiciously on the dancing flames.

I am not obedient—that came out clearly in the eternal rebellion I felt in the presence of Richard M.'s discipline, his subjection to principles and Columbian dogma. Should I conquer this as a fault?

But I admire restraint and polish. These are the virtues of the white sheep. Do black sheep with restraint and polish exist? Are they all untamable pirates?

A polite, sweet black sheep, that is what I would like to be. Or perhaps not a sheep at all, but an unclassified singing bird with a daring voice.

May 18. Bad health—struggle to keep my good humor in the face of this physical "débacle."

And then underneath it all, a burning restlessness. Ten, fifteen times a day I reach out for my paper and my typewriter, but each time, before I touch them, I realize dejectedly that I am physically unable to work. And I turn to reading, reading which feeds my creative fever and gives my gestures the brooding impatience of caged animals.

May 29. I am alive again, and happy and strong. But lazy. Whenever the active life is presented to me in the form of teas, concerts, dinners, I enter into it with the wholeheartedness of a novice, thinking to myself: Perhaps I have not seen enough of it yet to lie back in my chair and recreate it. So let me live—I will write later.

And that is why, these days, all I have to show is a well-stuffed calendar of events.

Among other things I have met the sweetest American girl imaginable—Mrs. Cushman. Sweetness, sweetness, that is surely a quality which is becoming rare in our century. How beautiful it is.

"Circuitous" is the word I have been seeking to describe part of Horace Guicciardi's manner of thinking.

And then I also have discovered a word that suits my thinking. I believe I am the greatest sophist alive. In fact, Hugh who so seldom condemns, admits it. So it must be true. And I am worried. Or perhaps I think I am worried because I know I should, from a respectable point of view, be worried.

To balance this, I have made pleasant discoveries: [Joseph] Hergesheimer and La Argentina, a Spanish dancer; the fact that by neglect my problem could be effectively disposed of; and that by reading *L'Histoire de France* I could dream more and see the true France.

June 2. Without knowing exactly how it happens, we go out here far more than we ever did in N.Y. I could tell more about this than I have done, but the novelist holds me back, takes the pictures out of my hands to bury them in that inner chamber in which the work of weaving is accomplished, and leaves me nothing but very personal and very uninteresting sensations. It is this novelist who permits me to live, but who urges me at the same time to efface myself and to place another in the settings.

And then there is the physical lethargy that holds me back, and also a sharp sense of disappointment in myself. I don't think I have ever been as painfully conscious of my imperfections—a sense so powerful that it makes a coward of me, and I fear even the writing down of these faults, which could stare at me with such hardness from these pages in which I seek consolation and peace.

Lately I have summarized my belief thus: There is little of the ideal in the world; there is nothing I can do about it except contribute to a general idea by my own individual perfection. And I have struggled to attain this. With what result? That I have become a flamboyant egoist. For the first time I find myself flying from my journal as the most hateful form of this egotism. All my writing gives me a feeling of revulsion. What should I do? Where can I go?

All those who love me do so for what I have *made myself*. Whatever is good in me is a creation of my own ideal, because like all others I am naturally selfish and envious and evil-tempered. How can I turn back and forget myself now? If I forgot this self, would the natural defects live again, uncontrolled?

I throw myself wholeheartedly into my love for Hugh. But here my egotism faces me in a different way. If he hears singing or sees dancing that he admires, immediately I want to do these, to offer them to him myself so that he might possess everything he loves in me.

Oh, I can't write all these things. I see them clearly enough at night when I awake with the weight of them. It is again the torments of the imagination—of an imagination which, for good or for bad, is never, never at rest.

July 1. A month of mental apathy, of normal inanities with a few scratches on a hard surface—such as an argument with Horace Guicciardi on war and an increase in Hugh's salary. Also an absolute end to the Problem in the desired way. Mother's visit was an exchange of devotion in the form of gifts, entertainments, books for Joaquin and medicines for me. We felt again close to each other and very happy. With all this, there are Thorvald's letters, and through this correspondence we have become strongly united. In fact, I have never been so intimately united with my brothers, and I am happy that I can help and understand both of them, and that they both turn to me as to a second mother. As I wrote Mother a few days ago, I am interpreting her—that is, I am mother *plus* writer, and the last is serving the first.

Today two valises lie with open mouths in the room, and I feed them gently and constantly because Friday evening we leave for Brussels, where Hugh will try for a tennis cup. I look forward to Brussels but also to the return home, which will mark the beginning of my real life again. The doctor allows me to write 2 or 3 hours a day. He is more preoccupied with my body than with my mind, and while he administers medicines to the first, I am free in the second, and I intend to use this freedom.

Oh, how I detest days without thought, without reachings and searchings, without dreams and without creation. Even our love, which is supreme, loses in richness without these, and Hugh, while whispering, loverlike, sweeter things than have ever been written, said: "When will you write again?"

"Do you miss it?" I asked incredulously.

"Yes. I feel part of the object of my work is lost. I work so that you may create—for both of us."

This made me happy. I thought my activity tired him, as woman's activity usually does tire. Unconsciously I have tested the power of simplicity on Hugh. I have been merely the agreeable woman, occupied with clothes and outings, with his work and our material life. I find that merely looking neat, daintily dressed, with dainty phrases and a deep love, is not sufficient for him. I rejoice in it.

July 16. In Brussels we visited the Grand' Place, the park, the Hôtel de Ville, the Palais de Justice and Sainte Gudule; we had lunch with the party of tennis players and the members of the Belgian team, who, with the president of the club and a few others, received us; we had tea at the tennis club after the games were played; dinner at the Grand Hôtel, where we were stopping, and danced at the Moulin Rouge; we rode through the Bois de la Cambre to Tervuren and visited the colonial museum. Hugh triumphed at the courts of Vice President Grogan, in his superb garden, where 65 people gathered afterwards to have tea. And then came the final banquet and more dancing.

But all this faded before the loveliness of old Bruges, Bruges and its ancient little houses, its canals, its truly Venetian aspect— that is, Venice without gold and without laciness, for Bruges is Flemish. It is sober and soft-toned and simple. The houses, which rise out of water and crowd, with their little gardens and flower pots, all along the canals, reflect a stolid red-brick face pierced with sleepy windows and surmounted with unexpectedly sharp, pointed roofs of irregular, loosely fitted slabs. The small cobblestone streets are linked with variously shaped bridges over which ivy and moss and rock flowers run and cling and hang. Only a painting could render the haze and depth of Bruges's coloring, the contours which lose themselves in one another, roofs against the sides of the church, turrets into turrets, bridges that meet the water, while the water slaps the black sides of a mossy boat.

We have become restless; we feel tied now to work which keeps us from enchanting wanderings, from seeking and finding beauty throughout the world.

July 17. I cannot rid myself of the dream. It is as if I have gone so far away that I find it difficult to return.

Today, however, I remembered that I wanted to see Uccle. It was in Uccle, about twenty minutes' drive from Brussels, that we lived for three years, from my seventh to my tenth year. Our street, the Avenue Beau Séjour, was lined with neat, suburban homes with small front gardens, and at the end of it, we found the house, No. 74. I saw the bay window of Father and Mother's room. It was there I stood one time watching the street for the coming of Marraine,[1] who had promised me a doll. I believed then that only blond hair was beautiful. Marraine came up the street with a large package. As soon as she saw me behind the window, she opened it and held the doll over her head for me to see. It had a head of luxurious brown curls! I cried bitterly.

Beneath this window was another of the same shape. That was Father's study, which we rarely entered, but there was a nice big table covered with a red rug, and under it Thorvald and I occasionally played "house."

All through that street I had taken Joaquin about in his carriage, and played with Henri, the naughtiest boy in the street, and with Clairette Hostelé, whose father saved my life.[2]

I wished I could have seen the backyard where we spent so many hours and the room where, in desperation, we used to shut Joaquin up with his toys.

The memories rushed through me as I stood before the house. I felt nothing about my own life, but only for Mother. She was unhappy there, she worked for us then as she always did, she

[1] *A.N.'s godmother and aunt, Juana Culmell.*
[2] *By warning A.N.'s father that she would die wihout immediate medical help; she had appendicitis.*

endured, she cried. And Father was selfish, as he is now and always was. I remember his scenes of anger and fussiness—never any kindness.

The house saddened me. It was Mother's life to which I pilgrimed, Mother's sorrow.

How brave she is. She is happy in Hendaye; she has passed through everything and beyond. And it is I who brood over the house in which she lived just before the separation.

July 20. I tried to write a true letter to Eugene, and it was commonplace and spiritless. Why? Is it that thought must be continuous to evolve? It must be that, and I want to find myself again, to move out of this plain, colorless, though eventful life. For one thing, I forced myself to write on Bruges before Bruges's meaning awakened in me. I pursued every shadow which I saw on the still waters, to find color and sound and thought eluding me, and my hands closing around guidebook phrases.

I write while it storms, and this reminds me of the afternoons I spent in Richmond Hill, sitting before my ivory dressing table by the window, watching all the changes in nature, and looking inward at the same time. Those days were clear and simple compared with these, and though I do not complain of today's complications, I wish I knew as well today just how to act and what to seek. Then only words darkened the world for me. Today, thought . . . and thought is far more difficult to pass through.

I should be contented with this free life, with its very small duties, its comparative comfort, and above all with our perfect marriage and Hugh's happiness. And I am. I am happy when I sit in the morning cleaning his big shoes and thinking of the good work he is doing; I am happy when he arrives for lunch and we have two hours together of talk and rest and walking. When we go out with other people, we often glance at each other with the same thought and the same caress in our eyes. Once home, we invariably compare their love, their life, with ours. And we end by falling asleep in each other's arms, with a sigh of satisfaction.

Now and then we discuss the education of our children, the possibility of our being rich someday (Hugh is so sure he is going to make money) and even our plans for our old age.

Occasionally I read to Hugh some of my journal, whatever is connected with our life together. It pleases him, though he does not hesitate to condemn a phrase when I deserve it. He is critical of my writing, as I am of his life.

July 24. Hugh teases me now about my not writing. It is as if it were something I owed to him as much as my care and my love. So today I began thinking of my writing again, dutifully, without results. The play is finished. I dare not read over my first book; though mature as far as it goes, it has stepped out of my hands. I have created people, situations and surroundings I know nothing about, and am treading artificial grounds. Shall I leave this and start another? My sense of orderliness objects to that. Would it not be useful to my writing to go on with it, to force it into its proper mold, to master it?

July 27. There is one thing that *no one* in the world can ever understand, and Hugh least of all—and that is the intolerable pain I get from impurities. *Paris est plein de saletés,*[1] and for that I hate it.

A Parisian yesterday told the kind of stories which *fit* his kind of life about a man I admire intensely, Woodrow Wilson. The Parisians are not only impure themselves, but they enjoy pulling down an Anglo-Saxon into their own filth. They are jealous of purity. The story revolted me, and besides, I did not believe it. Then in some unexpected way it came up in our conversation that evening while Hugh and I were preparing for bed. He had accepted it. The change has begun in him in such a way that he believes an intelligent understanding of the world means granting the possibility of such monstrosities. This disappointed me so deeply that I dropped the subject and slipped quietly into bed, thinking my weariness would explain my silence.

But Hugh felt it and sought explanations, and we talked in vain for an hour. Our talk changed nothing. We fell asleep in each other's arms, seeking, in a nearness of bodies, a union of mind which I at least did not feel.

Of what use is it to talk? I know I am alone, absolutely alone in this as in other things. I must realize this and be quiet about it and love Hugh for all that he gives me, for all that he does understand. And I must remember what I wrote once: that there *must be differences* and that I have no right to lament these differences.

After all, I come back to writing, I come back to self-communion, I come back into the hopeless circle of self, which alone contains the answers of self.

[1] *Paris is full of filth.*

July 30. I have made a curious discovery. That if I had had the courage, it is a man like Eugene I should have married, Eugene with his depths, his limitless seriousness, his severity even. I should have married Eugene and endured hardships with him for the sake of that work which I believe his great mind capable of producing.

But I loved Hugh, who was more pleasing to look upon, Hugh, who was softer, who could appreciate, with Latin sensuousness, the visible beauty which Eugene does not accept. It is Eugene's absolute spirituality which I admire. It is Hugh's more compromising, worldly, tolerant, divided attitude which I chose. Hugh could *dance* with me when I wished to dance. Hugh believed with me in a lovely, soft home, in the beauty of luxury, in the decided advantage of worldly success.

With Eugene, life would have been pure, absolutely pure, stripped of visibility, of weaknesses, of self-coddling. Oh, I love Eugene for that in my best moments. There are times when I long for this severe spirituality, as I long for goodness. There are times when I feel he would *understand* certain things better than Hugh does. Hugh is not strict enough. At least I feel myself more puritan than he is, more *serious*, too painfully serious.

And every now and then I turn with unconquerable devotion to my first *ideal*, to those vague dreams, to those formless, fleshless desires, to those aspirations for invisible beauty. And in these returns to the old, I leave Hugh far away, so far away that I feel the sharp pain of the separation.

At such moments, too, I turn to Eugene. I would like to write Eugene things which Hugh must not see, for they would startle and displease him, and I do not have the courage to contradict his ideas. But what would my life have been if I had realized the somber dreams of my girlhood and loved one like Eugene?

I remember one night in Richmond Hill when Hugh, Eugene and I sat together on the porch—before our marriage. And Hugh was reading Carlyle, and reading it stretched out on the most comfortable chair, the whole length of his big body, with his golf-stockinged legs on a chair. Somehow it shocked me that he should read Carlyle like that; his physical being, his physical relaxation and comfort were so obvious, and the golf stockings . . .

Eugene, meanwhile, sat straight in his chair, thinking with all of himself, with the forward stretch of his head, the intensity of his eyes, of his living, restless body.

This is my secret. These are the things which will cause my journal to be burned when I die.

These days I have been tormented by fears for *my* love for Hugh—not his for me. The fears, this spiritual estrangement, will disappear, fortunately, when I become normal again, when I reenter the fleshly life that is mine as much as these worthless imaginings.

July 31. I felt remorse last night for what I had written. Hugh came in before the words had dried and I delayed the homecoming kiss to pass the blotter over them and to close the book. He came, tender and tired, tired with work he does merely for the sake of such things as I repudiated yesterday. And I felt unworthy of his kiss, unworthy of his devotion, unworthy of everything he gives me. I think too much. There is not a woman in the world who would not be absolutely happy in my place. How complicated I am, how intent on vague, spiritual accords, how *inhuman*!

I will never write Eugene that letter which *he* was not to see. I will never be even spiritually untrue to him. And as for those exaltations, those dreams which are not woman's but the mind's, they will live only here, where they can do no harm.

It will be like the times when, in a fit of temper and fearing what I would do or say under the influence of it, I used to shut myself up alone with my journal and write many silly and unworthy things. My journal is full of those ugly outbursts.

Apparently, I have not gone beyond such "queerness" of character yet.

Now, for the first time, I realize I must get a locked box for my journal. Until now I had trusted, with a share of indifference, knowing little harm would come even if my journal were published.

Is it possible that I misunderstand Hugh because he talks so little? But no: comparing his life in New York with his life here, he said, "This is *softer*."

I feel mysteriously alone, yet in a very little while Hugh will be coming home. I wish I could be *good* again and feel as secure and as calm as I felt in Richmond Hill. Why did no doubts assail me then, no jealousies, no fear of change in him, of cynicism? Why did I find his face always sweetly the same then, while now he has expressions, and phrases particularly, that are older, more *knowing*. Oh, I wish we were out of Paris, and there are moments when the two years which we must spend here seem interminable and terrible to me. If our love can last through this poisoned life of Paris, then I shall believe in it forever.

I try to come out of these dark circles. I worked at my second book for two hours and copied more excerpts out of my old journals with the hope of making a worthwhile piece of work out of them. Often I dread discovering my likeness—Amiel, who wrote nothing but his journal!

While I wrote, the thought of the letter I wanted to write Eugene pursued me, and I was so angry with myself that I finally abandoned everything, and in an expiatory mood I cleaned Hugh's shoes and packed his tennis clothes for tomorrow. Tomorrow is the beginning of our weekend. Will it dissolve my painful self-analysis and my vague unhappiness?

August 1. I have driven away those ugly thoughts, and Hugh helped me by a new proof of his love and with an explanation of his attitude towards E., for example, and his worthless acts. He *tolerates*, he *understands*, he does, in short, what I had preached in *Aline* in relation to evil!

"But you are so quiet about it all," I said. "You never hate or despise or revolt or condemn."

"Of what use is it?" he answered me. "Those things exist, I see them. I realize they exist in others. All I can do is feel that I would not act as the others do."

"Please help me to understand you."

And on this phrase we slept contentedly, although nothing had changed but me, and I had merely shifted my position a little so that I see less of the black monster.

And now I will leave all this and go out on Hugh's arm, in sunny Paris, and be happy with him.

August 2. Every now and then I rediscover the true face of my black monster. It is always my "devilish imagination."

I realized that lately it was ruling me too tyrannically, and with an effort of reason or logic, I shook it off. How fortunate that I *can* control this imagination, for it is the source of all my unhappiness as well as of my pleasures.

August 26. It is not that I have lacked the desire or the time to write, but that I am struggling against one of my worst "crises"—

a deep, unreasonable, intensely painful melancholy. I can neither excuse nor understand myself any more. I have so much to be happy about, and yet the mood will come as irrevocably as age or as the return of the seasons.

First, we have made the discovery of a home. It happened a few days after I last wrote in my journal. I had gone with Countess Guicciardi to look at a gray and banal apartment. A new, white building immediately in front of this old one attracted my eyes. The giant-sized windows made me shiver with desire—studios! Artists! Words that have always and will always have a precious significance in my eyes. I begged Countess G. to let me inquire, to let me see them. There were three apartments available and exactly what I dreamed of having.

Four days later Hugh had signed the lease, and I spent all my nights wide awake planning how I would furnish the place.

And then I worked with all my strength and soul, shopping, overseeing the electrician, the carpenter, the painters, looking into every antique shop, sewing curtains, cleaning, packing and unpacking.

Though we had decided to wait till September 1, we moved in a few days before. I had no regrets on leaving the pension, whose only charm was its light and sun, since we have four times as much of that here. I did secretly regret loosing my freedom from housekeeping, but this selfish attitude did not last. Hugh and I have had more joy from this home than we had from the apartment in Forest Hills or even from the bungalow, for this is, artistically, far more to the likeness of our dream.

We have a studio, then, with two immense windows, no houses in front of us, but the quiet Cimetière de Montparnasse,[1] of which we see only the ivied walls. Next to the studio is an alcove, which we have made into a library. Books cover the walls completely, and there is left just room enough for Hugh's comfortable armchair, a pillow on the floor for me, and a table for his smoking things. And there is a little white kitchen on this level. A small winding staircase leads to a small bedroom and bathroom. I am too restless and impatient to describe the furnishings. That will come later.

Exactly half of my day is spent in housekeeping. The other half will later be devoted to the things I love. For the moment, I

[1] *Montparnasse Cemetery.*

make pillows and sew curtains and prepare for Mother's return and for our vacation on October 3. In between, I read with the same feverishness I had at sixteen.

Everything is perfect, except my moods, which distort the world for me and torment me. What is this feeling which has pursued me through childhood until now and which I can trace all through my journals?

Sometimes I say: I am too alone, I need companionship. And I try that. But I am unhappy when I am with others. Frances disappointed me, and ordinary, everyday people I can't endure.

Then I think it is physical, and I try to rest, as I did in the pension. Still I was unhappy and restless. Writing I dread, though I am doing it now. It accentuates everything. Reasoning about it *dissolves* my troubles, in theory, but not in actuality. And the most maddening thing of all is that tomorrow, for no reason at all, I may be as happy as I am sorrowful today.

I have but one satisfaction, and that is that I have been able to control all outward manifestations of these moods. People think me calm, sweet-tempered and even. Hugh himself never, or very, very seldom, has to suffer from my moods.

That is all I can ask, and I am happy about that. It is as if it were something apart from my character, like a demon never coming out of me before the eyes of others.

October 6. Château de Verneuil, Verneuil-sur-Indre.

At last I have found the words of writers to be true—at last I have seen the beauty they have seen.

The château first appeared to me at the end of a long, straight, white alley. It was already night and I could see only the large and simple white outline of it. But that majestic approach gave me a shiver of aristocracy.

An old man greeted us, and after we gave our valise to a maid, he led us through high doors to the dining room and showed us our table. Faced with a cotton tablecloth and thick white china, I remembered that we were simply boarding in the château, which belonged to the Marquis de Verneuil. The shiver of aristocracy returned, however, when we climbed the broad, white stone staircase to our immense room. I slept calmly and dreamlessly.

The next day, very early, when the mists still covered the world under our windows, the chimes awakened me, loud and near and persistent. My ecstasy began. I discovered infinite beauty in that first day, made additionally awesome by the brilliance of the southern sunshine.

First there was the dungeon.[1] It stands at the left of the château—one square building attached to two round towers with pointed slate roofs. The mellow cream stone walls are half hidden by ivy so ancient that its stem is as thick as the trunk of a young tree.

In front of the dungeon, separated by a quiet, shaded space, stands the old village church. We heard Mass there on Sunday. A thick stone column conceals the aristocrats from the view of the villagers. We kneeled on a straw prie-dieu, since of the former luxury there remained only one red velvet chair. Below the stone we walked on were buried all les marquis de Verneuil.

The burgh lies at the left of the château and its little unpaved streets run from the foot of the wall which surrounds the domain downhill towards the valley. Old women in wide black skirts and tight black waists and shawls, with white lace caps on their scant hair, stand at the doorsteps of their cottages and watch us pass. On Sunday morning when the bells called them to Mass, I saw two of them coming out of their homes together. They stood in the sunlight for a moment and there was something about the fullness of their skirts, the chaste tightness of their blouses, the neatness of the lace caps, that gave me a sharp fear it could not be real.

Hugh and I divide our time between bicycling and the six books we brought. I call him Sir Hugh and he calls me Marquise.

I did not bring my typewriter on purpose. When I have it before me, it is a reproach. And I am tired, and so happy to rest in the calm and beauty of the place.

October 7. When I finished writing yesterday and reread what I had done, I closed my journal with a snap of anger and stared with sadness at the field before me. What bad, rusty writing! I start with an artificial exclamation and continue in falsetto tones all through; it is the truest beauty I tear with my scraping pen.

That confession now lifted from my worried mind, I feel as if I had torn the last pages off. What makes me do that when I approach the subjects I most love? I wrote equally badly about Bruges. I am afraid, then, of my writing. The impression beauti-

[1] *A.N. probably means "prison" or "keep."*

ful things make on my mind intimidates and silences me, outwardly.

Today, for that reason, I chose to turn my back on the castle and the dungeon. I sit under a gigantic fir tree and I can see the rivulet and the park of the château and plain fields—all kinds of simple things, for which I can so easily find words. It would be amusing if I often had to turn my back on beauty in order to recover my power of speech.

With our bicycles we are able to visit many little villages. The first day we went to Saint Hypolite. Only the old people and the children can be seen—the rest are probably at work in the fields. It is in the evenings that these little villages become animated. Then people talk to each other across the streets, men gather in the café, women prepare to go to church for evening prayers. But in the daytime, absolute calm. When we pass on our bicycles, we occasionally see a head appear behind the flower pots, with inquisitive eyes. And that is all. And Hugh and I continue silently, joyfully, pausing always before the old, old church. At 10 o'clock we buy some bread and chocolate, which we eat on the road, sharing it with shepherds' dogs and goats.

At 12 we are back for lunch. The dining room is the size of a Parisian apartment, or two of them, to realize its height. It has a tall brown door, a stone floor, paneled walls painted beige and brown and a ceiling painted sky-blue with clouds in it. The windows are as tall as the room. Our small table is in front of one of them.

On dark days the brown dining room, even with its pale-blue sky, has an antique and sorrowful air, and the wind, when it blew last night, had as hoarse and lamentable a voice as one could expect to hear in any castle.

We are almost the only guests here, besides a painter who monopolizes the best views of the church and the bridges. So in the afternoons, when we start out with our books and the ink bottle, we can choose among a thousand lovely places in the domain one to suit our mood.

I tried to make Hugh write. I told him that I had brought his journal instead of mine and one book. "Would you mind letting me have the book while you write?" I asked suavely. But he offered to go upstairs for my journal instead, so that I was forced to bring it out from underneath my sweater.

We asked the painter if he thought the dungeon interesting

enough to paint. "It is too white," he answered. "It looks new." And there you have an artistic opinion of the awesome tower.

From here my studio appears to my mind more and more worthy of my enthusiasm. I think it is a fitting background to our European life.

As for reading, I hate, abhor and detest Stendhal. D'Annunzio, in his third novel, lets the decay of his character pierce through the magnificent style. I still drink his lyricism, but I feel the acidity of his ideas. Anatole France's *La Vie en Fleur* must be the most beautifully written childhood on earth. No wonder that Hugh prefers it to writing in his journal.

October 9. Yesterday morning we took the train to Châtillon to visit the ruins of a fortress. It was an absolutely round tower of gray stone on which nine hundred years had moved only a few of the top stones and crumbled half of the wall. At the iron gate the thickness of the wall showed to be about 20 ft. Looking through the gate, we saw a hole which took the whole roundness of the tower and was 50 feet deep. The walls showed traces of smoke. There were a few long and narrow apertures. To penetrate into the dungeon, men must have used cord ladders, such as I read about in a book by Walter Scott. Besides the forbidding power of the tower, there was a wall of similar thickness all around it, and to the height of it was added the height of the hill on which the tower stood.

First, because I was tired, and then because it stormed, we stayed in our rooms in the afternoon. The light was bad for writing and for reading, so Hugh and I played checkers. I was secretly glad not to have to write about the tower at Châtillon. But there was no escape from it when we came out into the fields with our ink bottle "to write." I delayed the moment by writing to Mother. Then I boldly attacked my dungeon.

And now I sit in the weak sunshine brooding on the perversity of words. But, as Hugh says, we are living here in the Middle Ages, and at that time women did not know how to write, so I am not an anachronism.

October 13. Tonight we thought of this promise, which I am going to copy down. We laughed over the idea of Hugh ever being forty-five years old and I, forty. And all this because we have been so happy on these many little trips we have taken together, so harmonious, so much affected by the same things, so earnest in our interest; and because we appreciate our youth, which intensifies the joys of this trip, and our love, which colors it.

If twenty years from today we still love each other, we will come through all these places again in which we have been so happy together, in which we have loved and enjoyed each other.

Promised: Anaïs Nin Guiler
Hugh P. Guiler

October 14. The white dungeon of Verneuil means nothing to me now since I have seen the tower of Châtillon and then the beautiful Château de Bridoré and then the awesome Loches. And after Loches I saw Montrésor. Each was more beautiful than the last. The Château de Loches has more history and is more complete, more impressive, but Bridoré had a special charm for me—it was alone, unvisited. And there was less of it, and it appealed to my imagination. Loches is infested with guides, English golfers and post-card vendors. Nevertheless, the cells, the Bishops of Sforza and the "oubliettes"—the dungeon—made a terrible impression on me. The size of Loches is gigantic. And the village is enchanting.

Montrésor is different. The fact that it is inhabited and restored changes the quality of its charm. I lived the past more deeply there because it was so perfectly recreated.

My hands are restless again, aching to create. I make the gestures of "shaping" in my dreams, and even by day. Of course, the ultimate result will be a story, for that is what my writing is, overflowing. When I live, I overflow. When I can't live actually, my imagination burns me until I can live it out in writing. Out of all these sights, three stories have already been born.

Today we are resting and I go over in my mind every pictorial detail of Bridoré and Loches and Montrésor. It is not only their tangible appearances which obsess me; it is their past, it is the intense and persistent effort to recreate from half-effaced fragments. The very sight of crumbled stones gives me a spiritual "malaise," a restlessness. The meaning, the entire life, is there and I cannot see it, and I want to see it. It is the muteness, the mystery of the stone, of the smoked beams, of the barred windows, of the black oubliettes, of the twisted passageways, I want to penetrate. Deep, unknown emotions and ideas agitated those men who feasted in the salon of the château, those who agonized and howled in the torture chambers, those who carved crosses on the stone walls of their cells, those who were left to the terrors of dark and madness in the treacherous oubliette.

It is so strange to see all these fragments, in the sunlight, to see them so coolly. We have the "symbol" of a cruelty, say, 600 years old. The symbol has decayed. We come to look at it as a curiosity. And all the while that cruelty exists; it passed through that century, through many centuries, and it is now among us. It uses other tools, that is all.

I awoke this morning with the desire to write. It may have been due to the reading of the Literary Review, which always has the power to make me restless, or to the clarity and peace of Verneuil. I lay in bed waiting for 8 o'clock breakfast and thought of my stories. Then I concluded pessimistically that to write a novel, one needs maturity and furthermore that I, not having maturity, cannot write a novel.

How I came to feel my immaturity is through the "critics." I can visualize what they would say about my book. In fact, I could write a criticism of *Aline's Choice* far better than they could and kill the book off with more skill and speed. Of course, if I wrote a novel today, it would be older than *Aline*, but not old enough. I know what it is to be old, but I cannot convince others that I do. And I could not hope to convince a critic, and unfortunately they have power for good or for evil, such as was granted to ancient kings.

In short, I am afraid. I have no faith in myself. Which does not mean that I will stop writing, but which means that I can never look at writing as a profession, as a "public" work. I think I am doomed to loving and practicing it in secret, in short, to possessing it as a vice, as a useless and blamable waste of time. By contrast, when a man *works*, with the intention of *giving* his work, of serving the world, his work is respected. Richard M. has already discovered my peculiar religion of self-effacement in relation to publicity. He said it was selfishness to write for oneself. That troubled me at the time. He gave as an example the marvelous effect of my journal on him (I had given him a few pages to read).

Today, however, I have no ambition, no desire to give or to please. For that kind of generosity there are too many virtuous devotees. The list of new books shows that. The critics are overworked and irritable. I don't think it can be very selfish to sit on a log in the sun in an unknown corner of Touraine and to write for one's self.

I have been seriously tormented by Anatole France's belief that one should not try to understand oneself and that one should disregard and ignore oneself as much as possible. There is no way of compromising. It is a flat choice between self and selflessness. And it is in writing that the choice has to be most clearly made. Amiel, Pierre Loti, de Goncourt, de Guérin, d'Annunzio, have explored and utilized their selves. Flaubert, Edith Wharton and others have not—or if they have, it is with disguises. But they give the impression of living outside of themselves. Which, artistically and philosophically, are the greater?

And if I realized today that I have been wrong for the 14 years of my writing life, could I change? Could I come out of this self which I have spent so many years in making habitable for my ideas, this tower whose solitude I have deepened by the digging of moats around it—specializations of tastes, inclinations for abstract thought, for books rather than people—whose windows I have made of amber glass and through which I look at life? And then I am surprised to find it of a different color than my neighbor's life! But am I always in it? Have I not come out of it to work for my mother, to love and serve Hugh, to meet and judge my father? Am I not out of it today while sewing yellow curtains for the white glass windows of our home? When am I really self? Only when I write in my journal. And then I am not kind to this self. I want it to serve, to work, to produce ideas and opinions. I return to it to drive it on. The contemplation of it is no more than the watchfulness of a parent over a child. I began by desiring to make something of this self. I want to finish now. I *have* to remake. I want to improve. It is an instinctive gesture with me. What harm if I experimented with my self first? I still believe one should begin that way rather than the other. "Cultivez votre jardin. . . ."[1]

How mellow is Touraine, how soft its valleys, how calm its rivers. And the château, when the sun strikes it, shines dazzling white out of the darkness of the ancient trees that surround it. I sat all morning at the foot of a tree, and in the afternoon I rested on the easy chair in our room by the big open window. Then Hugh and I

[1] *Cultivate your garden. . . .*

came to the terrace to enjoy the last warming light, and while he writes Eugene, I wonder how I could entertain such worthless thoughts this morning when I might have been writing joyously about Verneuil.

Our last day, and the sun is still caressing us. Our trunk is half packed; there is only one plate left for us to use in my worn camera, and we have already looked back once on the days of our vacation to admit that they were all very full and rich and sweet. That happened the night before last, when it was very cold and when we sat by the log fire in our room. We feel stronger now for the winter that is coming.

I cannot say that it will be happy, for Thorvald is ill in Havana, and Mother and I have been worrying about him. I can understand her desire to be near him and will do all to make that possible. Joaquin, if Mother should leave, would stay with me.

Apart from that, the winter will be full and productive. These are our plans: What I must do first is finish the arranging of our home. We need chairs and a table and another rug, but we can't buy any of these things because we are very short of money. Hugh must work well and wisely to earn another raise in December.

When the house is ready—that is, when I have done all to it that can be done without money—then I will begin giving "business lunches" for Hugh and "social dinners." The social dinners will be for people of the bank whose society we enjoy personally— the lunches, for business talks and for people we owe attention to, but whom I can't stand very long.

Then I will have my studies at the Sorbonne.

Then we want to have "musicales" occasionally, for Mother and Joaquin's sake especially.

In between, I must write at least one book and sculpture something and read. Then there is the serious task of my correspondence with Richard M., with Eugene, with Thorvald, occasionally with Eduardo, with Ruth Morgan and with my relations.

I would like to do all these things well and completely, from the smallest to the largest.

How clear the course of our life appears to me today as I look at it in the peace and transparency of Verneuil. I am glad that I traced the simple outline of it. Later, in the confusion and the weariness, I want to be able to fix my wavering actions, I want to be able to find myself again.

There are also to be remembered my own intimate desires which have been the same these last years. First I want to make

Hugh happy, and to keep his precious love. Then I want Mother, Thorvald and Joaquin's happiness.

And for myself only this: I want to be "good." I want to be unselfish to those I love and I want to give them pleasures.

I get so discouraged with my character, with the eternal struggles I must endure, the constant war against my badness. Sometimes I think the only hope I have is that I can feel *pity* for others, for anyone who suffers, and that in order not to make those I love unhappy, I can find supernatural power to make what I wish out of myself.

[In the above, the young writer, then in her twenty-second year, is found in one of the moods of extreme penitence, in which she blamed herself for every conceivable reason. Always the last to find fault in others, she was the first to accuse herself. As her husband, I can attest that she always remained the purest and noblest spirit, and that she had even at that early age attained a control and management over her character which might be envied in an octogenarian. At this time she was well on the way to the true knowledge of herself and the full expression of her rich mind, to which she aspired.][1]

October 19. Return home, but to even sweeter things. The dream takes shape, the dream I had of an artistic winter. It rains outside. In the studio Joaquin sits before a baby-grand Gaveau playing his compositions by candlelight. Mother is knitting by the lamplight of my wrought-iron stand (reproduction of an antique). I sit in front of the gas stove on a pillow with my journal on my knees and an orange quill pen between my fingers. Hugh, with his spring coat on, sits at the antique Breton bureau, struggling over a letter he has no desire to write, as far as I can make out.

Before I had completed the phrase on Joaquin's playing, he left the piano to read, and now he lies flat on his stomach on my rug with the *History of English People* before him. However, his music has so filled our home that I still feel the vibrations of it.

I read his journal (with his consent) and found it very fine.

October 20. Towards the first part of my plan I have contributed only the arrangement of the books in the library. Hugh wanted them to be classified by kind—novels, poetry, etc.—and I, by

---

[1] *A note added by Hugh Guiler at the time of the journal entry.*

personal liking and harmony of covers, size, and thought. I wanted my favorite books on one shelf with my journals. But finally I did as he wished, as it happens that most of my favorite books are journals, and they have to go near *my* journals. But it saddens me to see the *Meditations of Marcus Aurelius* so far away, among the miscellaneous books, and d'Annunzio's *La Vierge aux Rochers* among ordinary novels.

I had asked Hugh to write his own desires and plans for the winter. Instead, he glanced over my last lines written in Verneuil and wrote the footnote, which, I said to him, seemed as if he had been reading my journal over after my death!

November 30. Poor, abandoned Journal! I have grown accustomed to going about without talking inwardly any more, without consulting my mirror, almost without thinking, and writing even less. Our home has absorbed most of my energy; my husband, what little desire I had to talk; the Sorbonne, my time; and then Frivolity, personified by my Aunt Julia,[1] has occupied my evenings. And now I feel clumsy with my journal, and my thoughts dissolve into nothing as they have been trained to do this month.

At last came a quiet afternoon, during which I wrote Richard M., and I realized how deeply my writing had suffered from this abstinence.

Yesterday, too, when I wrote to Eduardo, the phrases I created to rouse him sounded meaningless to my own spirit. For I thrive on reading, on writing, on intelligent conversation, but when I have to live in mediocrity I freeze inwardly, and my thoughts sink back in sullen indifference.

I liked the atmosphere of the Sorbonne, where I have heard, in all, five conferences on French literature. The conferences themselves disappointed me. The professors gave a meager show of thought and an abundant display of facts—very little new to me, and I divined their phrases as soon as they uttered the first word, sometimes before they opened their mouths. I did not renew my subscription, but decided once more to find my education in my very thorough "chewing" of books.

December 2. Sadness again, uncontrollable irritation against the French, always in connection with my housekeeping, with my life's work. And when I excuse myself to Hugh for my lamenta-

[1] *The wife of A.N.'s uncle, Enrique Culmell.*

tions and tell him that he does not see that weak aspect of France, he admits that he does in his work and that it irritates him too.

I try to conjure the France we saw on our vacation, the France I loved so well—the châteaus, the little villages, the fields and valleys—historical, chivalrous, poetic, legendary France, the France of cathedral builders. I try to remember the unforgettable smile of the French Basque, the taste and delicacy of their writing, the mysticism out of which sprang the beautiful Sainte Chapelle, and I cry, as I cried many years ago about religion: But I *want* to believe!

Out of this struggle and the weariness it brings to me, a new hope is shaping itself. I turn to Italy; in all my thoughts, I long for Italy. I have a premonition that I am going to find Beauty there, that I am going to love it as I had hoped to love France.

And so I read d'Annunzio, and out of the sickness of his soul, out of the putrefaction of his mind, I gather the most musical prose, the most beautiful images, and I seek his secret for writing so clearly of imaginings. If I could learn that from him, then a new and powerful world would be freed from the chains of my weak silences—a world whose clarity, intensity, I have never been able to transmit.

And yet I have turned away from Pierre Loti, who lives also within images, because he is weak. D'Annunzio has an admirable force; that he uses it for evil does not matter—evil in him is only an occasional lapse. But Loti has no such force. He drops into sensations, because one sensation brings another. And he never rises above them with thought. D'Annunzio's physical and mental fever is a search, a desperate, sometimes unscrupulous, search, but it has an Idea, it has its meaning.

They are alike in their egoism and in their exoticism. Reading them side by side brought out the emphasis of the self in their books.

Loti's Journal shows where the journal is the worst betrayer of a character more or less well protected by the cover of impersonal literature and by the kindness of uncritical friends. It was there that I found Loti shallow and weak. And still, he will not be banished from my library. First, because he has a supersensitive "feeling" for things—for the sea, for the Basque country, for color. And because he can write so well about his two cats, about little sick children, about the old mother deprived of her son and about the young bride whose husband drowns—Yann and the jealous sea. Pale, sentimental music, at which one weeps in one's soft moments.

December 3. I should write this so as to never forget it. My tongue is my worst enemy. The thing I must learn above all others is when to be silent. I talk too often—I talk under the pressure of every emotion, irritability, enthusiasm, happiness and despair. And meanwhile, Hugh, who is too often silent, judges me.

Today we had a serious difference, born out of a trifle. He let me talk. I discovered afterwards the meaning of his silence, which I interpreted as an *assent*. He thought me in the wrong and unreasonable and did not believe it worthwhile to "reason" with me. In that one moment I lost the superiority over crowds of women, which I have struggled so earnestly to gain. I have to begin all over again. I am discouraged and miserable. I fled from our bedroom to control the bitterness which overflowed. I came downstairs and sat in the lonely studio, my pulse beating so fast and loud that it makes my writing tremble. It would be sweeter if I could cry on his breast, but I feel far away from him, far away from every human consolation. And I don't want to cry.

December 8. I have changed since that evening. I have been unhappy and lonely. First, because I realized my detestable faults, and second, because Hugh does not help me. I help him. I thought that our love was intelligent enough for us to be frank with each other, and I am frank with him always. But he treats me as all men treat women, like a child, and that has made me shrink into myself and be more silent.

It is stupid, anyhow, to seek a way out of the curse of isolation. From the first moment that circle of fire is traced around you, *no one* can come to you, can come near you—without burning himself. It is not Hugh's fault. It is all the fault of my moods, which are uncontrollable and illimitable, the fault of my temperament, which has marked me as a sick creature, not to be touched, not to be included in the normal life of others.

I feel the intolerable pain of my isolation at all moments, usually when people around me laugh and are happy. One evening a delightful young couple were laughing every minute, it seemed to me. At first I laughed with them, and then I felt a veil falling between them and myself. I had a desire to stretch out my hands, as if to ask someone to hold me. I looked at Hugh. I saw that *everyone* there was united in their cheerfulness.

And with this feeling came a fearful restlessness about other things. My reason *sanctions* these flights from actual life. Other aspirations shaped themselves clearly in my mind: I want to talk with *deeper* people. Is this impossible? Is there only one Amiel in the world, one de la Mare, one Ibsen, one Anatole France? Is it impossible to talk with minds like theirs?

That evening was a result of our "nice" life. Hugh and I chose to compromise. We do not live, like Eugene, exactly as we please. Hugh's banking is a compromise—the "niceness" of our house, our clothes and therefore the "niceness" of our friends. Having chosen this, I have no right to rebel. Today, if I could, I would withdraw entirely from this sweet, nice life. But then the coldness with which the normal world regards rebels would weigh on Hugh's worldly future. And tomorrow I might be sorry for my "sauvagerie." I must find a quiet, unsuspected way to satisfy my peculiar aspirations.

Hugh understands this. He feels exactly what I feel, but more mildly. Sometimes it is this mildness which makes me feel alone. But I must not be unjust, for his understanding is very true and deep.

This book of my journal marks the closing of a spiritual experiment, inspired by Hugh's dislike for my idealism and puritanism —or at least for the response which pushed aside all manifestations of sensuality in either books or people. I spent this year studying these manifestations, I absorbed an unbelievable quantity of French sensuality, calmly—Ségur, France, Prévost, Loti, Stendhal, Flaubert and innumerable dime novels. And I studied d'Annunzio deeply, d'Annunzio who is certainly the most sensual of all men and artists and who, if anyone, should have helped me to understand sensuality, for it was offered to me on golden plates of indescribable beauty.

I understand *everything*. I lived with crime and weakness and brutality and desire, for a thousand reading hours. I *saw* everything, I heard everything.

And then I said to Hugh: "Are you satisfied with my knowledge? Have you tested the intelligence of convictions you thought based on ignorance and innocence? Look at my eyes—they are not vague any more. I know everything now. My intolerance now is not born of surprise and revolt, but of knowledge. Are you satisfied?"

"I am satisfied. But I want you, little Pussy, to stay just as you were when I first met you. You were perfect then. I don't want you to read any more of *those books!*"

And from this manly contradiction I gathered that I had read enough to please his desire for broad-mindedness!

Of course, I am not the same as when he first met me. I am older, naturally, less happy, less dreamful. Europe's old cynicism has not passed over my head without leaving me at least a doubt. But for myself, my ideals are precisely the same, exacting and rigorous. Those books have only convinced me that evil exists and not that it is right. No one can change me enough to prevent me from feeling a sacred adoration for da Vinci's life and revulsion for d'Annunzio's. But I have learned to appreciate d'Annunzio as fully as he is worthy. I have learned tolerance and pity. I think my judgment is at least clear of personal reactions, such as Hugh rightly condemned. And what is most important, I think that Hugh understands my puritanism in the wise, beautiful sense that I have given this ideal. He feels that I have pushed my search far enough, that no blind, instinctive pruderies will guide my intelligence. And he demands again sweetness and clear thoughts and peacefulness in the woman who has been bending over abysms. Could anyone say after this that man is easy to please?

December 9. Lately, Hugh and I have had three differences between us. Oh, they are little enough in themselves, but I don't understand why there should be *any.* I am struggling to discover if it is my fault. I must keep my mind clear, I must realize where it is that our talks turn to wound. How difficult that is! Before I have time to realize anything, I see a breach opening between us, and the distress at the hopelessness of our misunderstanding brings tears to my eyes. There is no anger ever, no temper or violence, just the bitterness of words quietly spoken. All I feel is Hugh's stubbornness and his characteristic spirit of contradiction, which I have often seen turned against others and which, ever since we married, I divined I must at all costs travel around instead of through. I think I have up to now been very careful not to rouse the only demon in his character. And that has been difficult enough since my own character is so positive. If we are to be happy, or at least if he is to be happy, I must never *go against* Hugh, I must not *contradict* him, I must never *argue* with him. As I write this I stare at the words and wish they would carve themselves into my memory. It is not the first time that I have used my journal as a *reminder*, as an emphasizer.

I promise to reread these lines whenever we disagree again. Today, in this calm afternoon, alone, I have looked closely at the problem, I have traced a plan of action. My judgment is cool. It must serve to influence me at other moments when I am moody and illogical.

I am glad to have learned to control myself because I need this control now to be "submissive" in my talk, to be sweet. Let me keep my *real* self here, my opinions, my outbursts, my emotions, my dislikes, my moods, above all—everything that is strong, that takes room, so to speak. Hugh must have a chance to be himself, too, to expand, to assert, and he would be happier if he could do so without obstruction. Silence and self-effacement—that, for the wife. As to these violent overflowings with which I am cursed, this intensity which brings tears and ideas and individualism to such a quick ripening and flowing, these are good enough for the artist and must only show themselves in writing.

December 12. The long-expected holiday has come. I work five days every week in order to deserve this moment. In a little while Hugh will come home to stay, and we will go out with his arm in mine, and all the torments created by my imagination will be dispelled. None of our misunderstandings have ever withstood our desire to understand each other, the profundity of our love. Hugh has always succeeded in making me ashamed of what I write, in making me feel entirely in the wrong, and above all, in convincing me that I am *unfair* to him. In this he is helped by my desire to believe him! And now those pages of lamentations and despair worry me like a stain, and yet I must have them as a punishment. I want to look at this new journal like a new life given me and to feel that everything else is effaced.

December 13. Hugh sits in his favorite armchair in the library, considering whether or not he is to write in his journal, so I decide to influence his decision by setting an example—though I have no desire whatever to write. We were so happy this morning, freezing among the books along the quays in the hopes of finding a rare edition for Eugene. That is the way we spend our Sunday mornings, usually, preceding this literary rite by a more sacred religious one, for I have taken more pleasure in piety since I discovered St. Séverin, where Dante prayed. And I was happy yesterday when we walked about together up and down the Rue du Bac looking for Christmas gifts for Richard M. and Horace. We spent our evening addressing Christmas cards, and every moment, while attending to these things, I remembered New York last year, our last talk with Eugene, my last sitting for Richard M., and the splendor of our expectations concerning Paris. A year, however, is a short time in which to form an opinion. And after all, this first year was spent in readjustment. This coming year alone will count, and I want to be supremely conscious of it.

December 21. Just as Hugh and I were realizing that subtle things were lacking in the new friends we had been making, and just as I cried out for deeper people, John Erskine arrived in Paris and called on Hugh at the bank. It was an answer to all our vague questions; it was the symbolical affirmation of our ideals. We prepared to receive him. The fact that the book he described to us a year ago (when we had lunch with him) had been published this year and that the Times Book Review contains an eulogy of his latest poems served only to increase our admiration and awe.

Sunday afternoon came at last. John Erskine arrived with his wife, his young boy and his little girl. I had worked myself into the highest pitch of nervousness. My hands were frozen, and burning perspiration covered my body. I have never suffered so keenly from this terrible weakness. I served the tea so badly that I thought they would have to laugh at me. Everything conspired to increase my distress. The character of Mrs. Erskine—I can never talk before those who do not understand. One cold, unsympathetic look paralyzes me completely. And there was the arrival of two unexpected visitors. Still, I clung to what I wanted to tell Erskine. I said three things which arrested his attention. I knew I had to win his interest for Hugh's happiness, for our happiness. I triumphed. He said he wanted us to meet a lovely and interesting Frenchwoman, that we did not belong with the "others." He dwelt with pleasure in our little library. He showed a sincere interest in my journals, which Hugh showed him in spite of my objections. And above all, he talked to me sincerely about Italy, about the French provinces, about his method of writing without criticizing each page (as he thought I had) so as not to grow self-conscious—but to continue on and on until the end.

Hugh was happy with the visit. But I knew that on the whole we must have seemed very young. We are too old for the "others" and too young, superficially, for Erskine. All day my hands have trembled, and I am tired. I pray to get calm again. I write slowly, like a child learning a lesson. I am humbled by my defects, by my blunders. Why should my nature intensify experiences until they are like a fever? But I am punished for my ridiculously high aspirations. On Wednesday we are going to a dance!

Evening. How often I have written at this hour while watching the dinner and waiting for the sound of Hugh's homecoming footsteps. But slowly this custom will disappear, perhaps with the comforts which Hugh's work is bringing us. Today, following a second raise, we decided that the heaviest part of housekeeping would be taken out of my hands by a servant, who is coming by the hour. It was Hugh's stubbornness which brought me this joy—for it is a joy! I maintained with equal stubbornness that this luxury should come last. I wanted to work for him, to help him. I was glad to tire my body and to coarsen my hands to make his home beautiful. The argument which finally won my consent was that I was "not writing." This is true, and I suddenly realized I could make him happier and help him more if I wrote successfully. Secretly, that is my greatest desire, and secretly, I have regretted sometimes that all my energy should be spent on housecleaning. But now, due to the thoughtfulness of my Pussy, I am going to be free; and for his sake I must utilize this freedom.

December 27. Happiness, happiness, happiness! First, Dr. Erskine was not bored by us. The very next day after our tea, he invited us out to lunch and to meet the literary Frenchwoman. We are going to see Chartres with her next Saturday. After that Erskine came with his family to see us on Christmas Day. He brought us two of his own books of poetry and dedicated them with "deep affection" and in "memory of a happy Christmas Day spent in their home." He heard Antonio Valencia play, and he played Chopin himself and MacDowell's "Wild Rose." It was a warm and perfect evening.

Hugh and I took a deep pleasure in our holidays, but Horace nearly spoiled them with an experience which has weighed on me like a nightmare. He invited us to dinner to meet a Kate Colby, to whom he proposed marriage a year ago while on board the France with us. Ever since (although she refused him), Kate's name has often returned in his talk.

Hugh and I could not believe our senses when we met her. The disappointment in Horace was deep and disturbing, because she was indescribably common and silly—not in a mild way but in an offensive way. I could see that the evening would have sad results for Horace. In one moment he lost a great deal of our esteem, and with me, as usual, the effects are more serious.

December 29. I have been kept busy shopping with Mrs. Erskine, and evading invitations to places where I might see Horace, for since that evening he has lost my esteem and I feel an unreasonable dislike of him. My affections and my hates are equally strong —in fact, nothing in me is sweet and mild, but hypocritical manners, which deceive everybody.

All my thoughts turn towards Saturday when we are going to visit Chartres with John Erskine and his family and a young American poet. And at the same time I have a great desire to write a description of Horace now that my enthusiasm for him has cooled down so completely. I can see him more clearly, more detachedly. Before, he was the delightful conversationalist whose versatility appealed to my imagination, and he was the mysterious friend who showed his true self only occasionally and unexpectedly, and he was the flattering dancing partner who could find expert and professional compliments for my dancing. Today, he is a weak, unglorious young man who has lost his head over a meaningless face, whose attention is riveted by the cleverness of such remarks as "Oh, my dear!" and "How amusing," uttered in a nasal and blasé voice between two puffs of a cigarette.

And worst of it is that all frankness, all philosophical considerations, such as were so frequent between us, are out of the question today since the subject is a woman, and all criticism of a woman by another is subject to misinterpretation and suspicion. No woman can ever, safely, judge another woman for a man— she may, in a book, and that is where I shall get my revenge someday for all the deceptions I have to practice in life out of kindness for others, or, in this case, out of kindness for myself. Fortunately, Hugh spoke first in this affair. He could not control his clear expression of dislike for Kate. He says he feels now as if Horace had done something immoral—and this, coming from my tolerant husband, adds bulk to my convictions and pepper to my ink. Perhaps it is possible to be truthful with Hugh—at times. But how cautiously I advance in this experiment.

❦ *1 9 2 6* ❧

January 12. La Vita Nuova.[1] Since that day we spent in Chartres, I began to understand John Erskine well, and my admiration for him has grown hour by hour.

We were many in the party, and it was difficult to talk with him alone. There was Mrs. Erskine, their son, Graham, who is fourteen, and their daughter, Anna, who is nine, Mr. Gibney, a very young American poet, and Mlle. Hélène Boussinescq, a middle-aged French teacher of English literature. She was the one who had planned the trip to Chartres, as it seems she has spent several years studying the cathedral during every moment of her vacations. She knew it well indeed and pointed out everything that she thought beautiful, with marked dogmatism which left no room for differences of taste—such as Erskine felt and such as I felt, so that after a short while the party was divided, and we wandered through the cathedral by different ways. Mlle. Boussinescq was telling the stories of each stained-glass window to Hugh. Mrs. Erskine was resting and feeding Anna chocolate and crackers. Graham was taking pictures. Erskine was walking alone and admiring, and as I was doing precisely the same thing, we met, and by common understanding, walked together, talking little but vaguely and poetically about the cathedral, about religious rituals and Catholic theology, about organ music, about Spanish churches, and about Rome. We were all reunited when Mlle. Boussinescq obtained the giant keys to the little door which led to the belfry. We climbed innumerable circular dark stairs to the very top of the immense cathedral bell, in heavy wood frames, which was going to begin ringing the Angelus. The bell ringer was pushing it with his whole weight until it swung freely, and the clamor began, deafening, impressive, fearful, even. We felt the spire sway with the power of its sound and the rhythms of its weight. The young poet had helped the bell ringer, and I wondered what he thought and what Erskine thought of what they both had heard, and whether it would some day be described in two beautiful poems.

For me it was too mechanical, too loud and violent. It made

[1] *The New Life.*

me think again of people who dissect writing or music with chilling exactness, and who cannot conceive the beauty of the whole. Knowing that I could stand inside of Chartres's chimes did not mean as much to me as it would if I had heard the Angelus while walking up the aisle of the somber cathedral alone, with fathomless imaginings.

Mlle. Boussinescq had exactly the opposite attitude. She even took us inside of the roof of the cathedral so that we might see the framework of the silhouette we admired from below. She had a remarkable knowledge of every detail of the cathedral and a sincere love of it, which roused my sympathy, but she remained, for me, absolutely unapproachable. It was in vain that Erskine tried to make friends of us.

In spite of this, Hugh and I were drawn closer and closer to him, and coming back in the train we had an intimate talk together about his book and about journal writing. He told us that he had tried keeping a journal during his trip, but that he abandoned the idea because he found he was always missing the truly important things. It was out of a discussion on this subject that he formed his request to read some of my Journal—a wish Hugh ardently expected and I feared.

A week later Erskine came to our home for dinner with his family. Antonio Valencia came, too, and after dinner we sat in Mother's studio[1] and Antonio played while Mother sang. Erskine grew enthusiastic and played a great deal himself and sang Scottish songs with Hugh and teased Joaquin on the absoluteness of his musical opinion. I did nothing but listen to Erskine's every word and watch his face. I was trembling with the joy of having received praise from him about my writing, which he had seen during the week.

It is having received encouragement from Erskine which I consider the "vita nuova," an encouragement which embraced the kind of life we have chosen and the ideas and aspirations which guide it. He said that my writing was "exquisite," that the most interesting thing I had done was that essay on journal writing, that he would have wished more of that and that if I finish the essay, I must send it to him and he will get it published. He chose what I loved best, what I wrote most freely and most joyfully. He chose my most daring and most undisciplined work.

[1] *The Guilers and Mrs. Nin had facing apartments in the same building, at 11bis Rue Schoelcher.*

He criticized me for my early writing—my girlhood vagueness and for my "reticence." He thinks I do not tell enough, in particular about my posing, which I merely "sketched." He also thought I was extremely sensitive, and he did not want me to lose that. This he told Hugh the other night after the dinner offered him by Columbia graduates. He repeated that my writing was beautiful and penetrating.

All this made me deeply eager to work, eager to grow up to Erskine's intelligence so that I can appreciate more deeply one of the most talented men alive today. By writing well, I may be admitted into the circle of his life and allowed to listen to him and allowed to talk with him about his work. This was the feeling his praise gave me. Only a month ago I dreaded that Erskine should find us too young and uninteresting and that he might turn away from us, when to know him was to have our whole life made beautiful and deep.

January 13. I have just returned from Gare St.-Lazare, where Hugh and I went to see Erskine off. He looked tired. Though he has never said anything, we have seen signs that make it clear his marriage and his home life conflict with his ideals and his philosophy. Hugh and I have divined the things which hurt him. We feel that all the weaknesses of his situation must have come out more blatantly during this trip through Italy and France.

If I alone had felt this, I might mistrust my perceptions and attribute the ideas to my "Foolish Imagination," but Hugh, the wiser one, felt it too, and not only while being with him but while reading his book.

These days our other friends have become pale and meaningless shadows. We went to a large reception, where I saw Horace again, and it was with an effort that I fixed my attention on the description of his doings. He had, among other things, met an American woman who was "always drunk," and always "saying very funny things," and she amused him as a "type." The very night we were receiving Erskine, he was out dancing with E. and R. in a "delightful Chinese cabaret." They had discussed whether they would call on us and invite us to their party.

My whole life is clear now. I work every day towards that development which is to bring me nearer to Erskine and all that he represents. I will never be weak again—as I have been for a whole year. Since March 1925, I have done nothing. It was then I wrote what pleased Erskine. An empty year, which has brought no beauty into our life. I have been too much the woman—our house can show that, and the list of our social affairs. And the worst of such a weakness is that I am responsible for Hugh's soul as well as my own. But we are starting anew, and Erskine has blessed our struggles.

January 14. I must be careful not to let my housekeeping swallow me up entirely, as it has been doing lately. There is as much danger in it as there is in Hugh's banking, and although I have been wise enough in warning him of his absorption, I have neglected my own salvation. The machinery of our home does demand a great deal of attention, but it has no right to submerge me. I hate to see that it has brought my mind down to the level of the most ordinary woman. Today I resolved to push it all out of my mind, to restore it to its humble place and to keep it there. I write to remember. . . . To write every day—that will be the first rule of my life from now on. Erskine said that he did not believe in the legend of the "tired businessman who has no time for anything outside of his work," that the truth was that these men had the time but wasted it. He proved that by writing only three-quarters of an hour a day, one could write a book a year.

Hugh was impressed by Erskine's ideas and by the example of his activity, for Erskine has written the whole of another book during his trip, which started in September. Yesterday, Hugh stood before me with the traces of much thought on his face and announced that he was going to write poetry. I believe he would if other people did not write so much all around him and keep him busy reading, beginning with his own wife. He has added to my happiness these days by a statement I had never hoped to hear from him. It was after the evening with Erskine, when the Master had sung: "Drink to Me Only with Thine Eyes." Hugh said that he had realized during that evening that there was a purity in English ideals which the Latin could never hope to reach or understand—a purity he loved. It was all we needed to restore our understanding, for it was my one bitter feeling against Europe, that it had deprived Hugh of the poetic ideal, and though I never mentioned it in so many words, the pain never left me. Europe has done me enough harm; it has robbed me of peace about love, and I no longer believe in an eternal love.

January 15. My imperfections torment me to an unendurable degree, and it is all the more difficult for me to make war against them because they are really just the other face of my good qualities. For example, Erskine spoke of my sensitiveness, which on some occasions takes on the most infernal character because it is extreme and uncontrolled. It has made something monstrous of my puritanism, something inhuman and unbelievable. At the least shock, at the mere sight of coarseness, my imagination is struck as by something fiery and immense and destructive. The acute pain I feel, so acute that sometimes I think I have been physically struck, works inside of me like an illness. Conscious of the abnormal feeling and of its ugliness, I never express it, and it hurts me all the more. This defect, this distorted view of something natural and universal, would be enough to isolate me, but there are a million others, so that I am doomed to great suffering, and I ask myself wonderingly: How long will I have the courage to endure it? A great fear of marring the perfect beauty of our marriage haunts me perpetually, for I know now that everything weak or sorrowful comes from me, from this intensity of feeling which unhinges my reasoning. And every moment I make an effort to distinguish the mind from the impressionable and diabolical spirit, so that I may at least know when I must not trust myself. With my journal, I may grow accustomed to recognizing the expressions of the contradictory faces of my character.

January 19. I sit in Mother's studio, and while she sits in her armchair, sewing peacefully, and while Joaquin writes with equal serenity here at my right, I wonder how I can live so normally among sane people and yet be haunted by eternal sorrows. My latest mania has been brooding upon my imperfections, night and day. Today I promised myself to face my problems as clearly as possible, to trace a plan of conduct with which to solve these problems and to live by this plan or else punish myself by never writing in my journal again. These are the faults which have most clearly shown themselves to me these last months. First of all: I am self-conscious. I have watched my own character too long, in the hopes of making it better, and as a result I can never forget myself. To control this I am going to cultivate an objective philosophy; I am going to look out, to take an interest in others, and punish myself for vain or egotistical thoughts by confessing them to you. Second: I am irritable, quick to sorrow and never quick enough to see the humorous side. I must watch how often I feel angry and unhappy in a day and see how often it is all due to my own ways. Third: I am capricious and weak about my writing. I leave too much to impulse, to desire. I cover up an ordinary laziness with the word "temperament." I elude an effort of will, discipline, regularity. This temperament has made a whole year empty. When I should be writing, I do insignificant things which fill the hours, and I deceive myself into believing that I have been busy. Then I have to watch my egoism, my temper and my temperament, ridiculous moods of emotionalism, of many whims.

Where to begin? I have to call Hugh because he called me at ten minutes past one when my lunch was all ready to tell me a client detained him and he would have to eat downtown. I answered him calmly, in a neutral voice, knowing perfectly well that by omitting "dear" and making the conversation short, I could make him feel bad. But I had made a special lunch, and he could have called me a half-hour earlier. However, I was strong. It humiliates me to call him, but I will do it. As to the egoism and the temperament, opportunities to practice my new resolve will come up within five minutes—they always do come up, all day long. And every day, to begin with, I will write for an hour at least.

Now that all this is settled, I want to begin to live reasonably again. I have been reading Amiel's *Journal* and making sketches for my essay. Mother has been in bed with a cold for a week, and the semblance of activity which I felt while preparing her special meals, keeping her company and sewing with her deceived me. Eduardo writes, and wants me to help him with his indecisions, his lack of central purpose. Of the group of young people who at one time planned and aspired together, I seemed the most successful in the art of living. Is it possible that this is an illusion and that I have really failed? No, no. I have been weak in little things but not altogether wrong. Erskine did approve my life and my writing.

January 20. Today I have been good. I hummed while I did my marketing, and I thought of others. It may have been because the sun was out, and I will never be able to describe accurately the immense influence of the sun on my life. Or it may have been because Hugh loves me again—he would object to "again," but what I mean is that he talks to me openly, and we even ventured on the subject of our sad misunderstandings: French life, as compared with American life. He thinks now that I believe and feel exactly as he does and that I keep my secret well for fear of antagonizing him and making a more stubborn European out of him. My secret is that I hate Parisian life, I hate it, hate it, hate it. I have been happy only when away from Paris—in Verneuil, in Bruges, and I will be happy in Italy—but Paris is a nightmare to me. Of course, not every day. There are times when I am reconciled to it, but the fact that I am alone in my detestation adds bitterness to my feeling. I will have to plot so carefully for the future.

I wish I could learn to resign myself to any life. I wish I could dislike things more mildly. And what worries me most is that it is not New York I desire to live in more than Paris, but just a place that would be *clean*—any place where people don't kiss and embrace in the streets, where men would not follow me and whisper ugly invitations, and where women, so many of them, don't prowl everywhere with crimson lips and expressions that awake a lasting disgust in me. Above all, I would like to see real men, men who are not thinking of women every single minute of their lives—women in relation to physical love only. J'en suis dégoûtée.[1]

Mother's studio grows dark early. At four o'clock it seems the end of the day, and I no longer feel the joy of living in light and warmth. Mother sews. Her hair is half gray now and her shoulders droop a little. Joaquin is practicing. His nimble fingers race over the keys, monotonously. They are peaceful and industrious, both of them. I look at them, and then at the thoughts which torment me, and I remember all my promises.

January 25. On Saturday afternoon we visited Mlle. Boussinescq. She received us simply in her little apartment on Boulevard du Montparnasse. We talked about Erskine and his family, about his book and his poem of the Sleeping Beauty. Next fall his book on Sir Galahad will come out, to be followed by one which will tell how the marriage of Cinderella to the Prince turned out.

We discussed the marriages of great literary men. It was only natural that Mlle. B. should dominate the conversation. She was well informed, clever, assertive. She spoke of her acquaintance with Sherwood Anderson and intimated a million other connections with the literary and theatrical worlds, which filled us with awe and pleasure. She advised us to read *L'Europe* for monthly contact with general "doings." A moment later this advice was accentuated by the arrival of Monsieur Léon Bazalgette, one of the directors of the review, the translator of Whitman's *Leaves of*

[1] *I am disgusted by it.*

Grass and of Thoreau—a keen, smooth-spoken man. From the moment of his coming, Hugh and I felt ourselves on unknown grounds, but I listened intently and understood everything though I could contribute nothing. Over our heads, figuratively speaking, passed mentions of Waldo Frank, René Lalou, Thomas Mann and Heinrich Mann; vague allusions to the doings of certain critics, scarcely named, as if everyone should have their names so clear and near that to articulate them would be banal—all this with sharpness, quickness, almost irritation. Hugh and I, though elated by the nearness of our long-sought dream, were wounded by the metallic surface of it, by a quality of impatience and "toughness," which made it unapproachable.

It may have been due to the character of Mlle. Boussinescq herself—sharp, unpoetic, a bit hard and matter-of-fact. Facts! They were the key to her power, her assurance, and the key to the atmosphere we love. We decided to master these facts, to conquer our sensitiveness, to disregard her lack of faith, her mockery, to push on through obstacles to our ends. From her apartment we walked to the library where I borrow books; we bought magazines she had mentioned.

Before we see her again I will have read those very well-known books. The widest separation between us lay in her interest in modern works, which we have ignored. I do not question her arguments for and against modern work—we have a natural, illogical bent for the old. But I recognize the gaps in our impulsive education. In fact, humility is what I condemn Mlle. B. for not perceiving and accepting.

It seems now that the ideal is to commute between New York and Paris! Both the Significant and Insignificant people around us are doing it. All of them, in passing through Paris, continue to "drop in" on us. Slowly, we have discouraged the Insignificant ones. We have found our true life. Tonight we are going to a concert. Next week we are inviting Mlle. Boussinescq to the theatre. I work persistently on my essay, although I am annoyed by ideas that multiply themselves and grow while I try to fix them. We have preparations to make for Italy, too, books to read, a language to learn, notebooks to arrange. As for myself, I would not show myself in all completeness if I did not confess that I am planning for clothes! A new entry—a phonograph, by which we compromise with our nice friends. Poor Horace has felt that we were forgetting him, and insists on coming to see us Wednesday evening. This abandonment may have helped him to realize how completely our friendship could dissolve. I see more clearly now how much of a dilettante he is, how few are the things he has gone into deeply. Hugh and I tend to specialize, to embrace thoroughly. He slides over the surface—he is fluid, evanescent, changeable, complex. Some great passion could hold him together, fix him, but he is incapable of such a passion because he mocks his impulses, entertains others at the expense of his seriousness, and every desire, every dream, every effort, dissolves itself in delightful conversation.

We have famous neighbors. Janet Scudder has her studio on Rue Notre-Dame des Champs. Jo Davidson has his on Avenue du Maine. Christopher Morley is one of the "commuters." Edith Wharton has a home on the Riviera. When will I earn the right to live among the Significant?

January 27. Today I cannot work merely because Joaquin has blackened my horizon with an ugly mood of obstinacy and conceit. Thoughts about his character, fears of his uncertain future, all fill my mind to the exclusion of everything else. In an effort to control myself I took a walk up the Boulevard du Montparnasse to look for pottery and for Waldo Frank's *City Block*. I confronted myself with this very disturbing question: Suppose I wrote *everything I thought*? Considering the fact that I am perpetually in effervescence, my production would be rich, if not profound. For a moment I saw again, very clearly (as I do occasionally), what I *might* do, and the vision is always accompanied by a *certainty of greatness*, which never stays with me to help me in my daily writing. It is like a kind of intoxication, a moment of utter madness. Without this moment, I am small, reticent, humble, secretive—and the ideas, the flights of imagination, which shoot through me every moment, illuminating the secrets of all things, remain hidden. And Erskine divined them; he suspected how false I was to my desires of becoming an artist, because I shirked the first virtue of the artist, to give all he knows—to express all that he is capable of expressing.

February [?]. While we walked through the Jardins du Louvre, Hugh asked me whether I was aware of ugly things. *Aware?* I flared, *more* than aware, I see it all, feel it all, far more than anybody else—far more than those who write of ugly things so vividly, far more than the modern superrealist . . . I would have expanded, but Hugh cut me short: "You don't give that impression."

Reticence again. I see now that although I see the world in a clear way, see all of it, I will never write clearly unless I can give my writing the lucidity, the painful clairvoyance, of my thoughts, and their frankness. I have revolved around this discovery for many days now. I have asked myself all possible questions and have answered them truthfully, inwardly. Have I a right to select what I am going to say—to accentuate the beautiful, for example, when no such accentuation of beauty exists in reality?

Didn't my first book suffer mainly from this unbalanced view of the world? I evaded squalidness, grimness, naturalness, cynicism, physical or mental ugliness. I falsified in order to beautify. If the beautiful stood alone, it would not be beautiful.

The principal point is this. I *see* the ugly. Why do I elude it, cover it up, disguise it, omit it? I lack the common sense with which some people make ugliness harmless and natural. My imagination, my intuitions, exaggerate, deform, augment, accentuate the size and color of ugliness so that I am more aware of it than the people who think me floating over it.

February 18. The Humorous Banker, who does not take banking humorously enough, worked so strenuously that he caught a light grippe. The Management, who knows nothing about our budget, and to whom the Humorous Banker's salary appears very bulky since they pay it out (without having to live on it)—the Management, then, ordered him to go to the Riviera for a rest. The Wife, who dutifully keeps track of the Household Finances and who every day tries in vain to subtract 6 from 3 (3 stands for income and 6 for expenses)—the Wife then calculated that the Riviera was unreasonable unless the Management paid for it. But the Humorous Banker knew without asking that the Management never pays. So we went to Tours with two bicycles, two valises, Young's *History of the Medicis*, a gastronomic guide and the money that was originally intended for the Rent.

February 24. The force of a person cannot be of any use unless the possessor is conscious of it. I discovered mine last Friday, and the discovery gave me great joy. I discovered the power of my prettiness. I had gone down to the bank to have lunch with the Humorous Banker. He and then the Management and then Horace all commented admiringly on my good looks—supposedly results of the vacation in Tours. But I knew that it had come like a wave, with the softness of the air, with a few days of sunshine, with the exhilarating state of my mind. It is really the manifestation of a spiritual revolution, of a spiritual overflowing or a sudden conquering, a dropping of chains. I had gained, miraculously, a magnificent poise. That evening we went to a party at the house of Mrs. F. I made a triumphant entry in a ruby-colored velvet dress. I had a great desire to tell everyone: "This is a great evening for me. I have broken the hard shell of a stifling reticence. For many days I have gone through a spiritual struggle—I am free, poised, older. Do I not express with my eyes, my voice, my movements, this superb freedom that has come to me?" Such blossomings are frequent in the process of constant thought. But I had never felt the moment of transition so sharply—I had never been so conscious of the step higher. That night was extraordinarily lucid. Ordinary people might have summarized my experience thus: "Here is a shy person who has conquered her shyness." But to me, it meant an immense change, it meant that I had understood Erskine's penetrating criticism, and that I had broken through a reticence that extended all through my life and my writing. That evening I acted out my freedom. My tongue seemed magically loosened. I talked in an extraordinary way to Horace, startling and amusing him. I was more myself because I talked as I thought. It was my turn to wonder why other girls looked so self-conscious and afraid of moving or speaking naturally.

I spent half the evening talking and dancing with Horace, the most interesting man there. The rest of it was divided between a stupid American and an Italian, who tried to charm me with his dark eyes and who succeeded merely in awakening H.'s jealousy, so that when we came home my Love said we would never go to another party. Mrs. F. said that before she had seen me she did not believe miniatures looked like people. In short, I shone, as I need to shine to believe in myself. The results of such an evening: I take up my writing with new vigor. My head is full of new thoughts, new characters, new understanding, simply because I have renewed an artificial illusion of power, renewed my supply of self-reliance.

Soon the struggle will begin again. I will not trust my thoughts, my own eyes. I will waver. Still, I believe now I am steadier, more mature. Perhaps the days of spiritless self-criticism will come less often, the black moods, the weak health, all the things which interrupt my work. I took joy Friday evening in watching Hugh also undergoing a change somewhat similar to mine. His manners, his talk, his voice, were steadier and more graceful. After all, this is natural. We are growing older. Hugh celebrated his 28th birthday on February 15, and I my 23rd on February 21. Some people might say that this mere dropping of youthful shyness should have taken place sooner, much sooner. But for us there was so much involved, so much that was small and subtle and delicate.

March 2. We had Horace to dinner for the first time since we met Kate. He was at his best, sincere, brilliant, rich with ideas, but always lacking in unity—always "éparpillé."[1] We discussed, among many things, our three characters. Hugh thought Horace slightly changed after a harrowing experience he went through at the bank, which made him less careless in his flowing talks, less self-reliant, but more mature. Horace thought Hugh very little changed since he met him in New York, but he went off into an exaggerated tirade about the change in me. He said when he first met me he thought me sweet and pretty and nothing else. He did not like my voice, which was high-pitched and interrupted by nervous giggling; he did not like my manners, which were cute and young, and he did not like a certain way I had of pressing my lips into a sort of pout; furthermore, my talk was nothing out of the ordinary. Oh, he was frank enough! But *now* in the last year I had become *very interesting*. I had ideas, I talked well, he enjoyed hearing me, he was interested in what I thought. And my manners, oh! And my well-modulated voice without giggle, my mature and sharp expression, the way I stood, sat or talked or looked—*everything! Wonderful!* I was amused. Hugh was insulted. Later, when we were alone, he admitted that I was not as mature as he felt himself to be, but that this was the only thing he could reproach me for. He thought Horace did not have enough intuition or perception to discover how interesting I always was—though in a shyer, more elusive and less mature way. He continued with as much warmth as Horace had displayed to emphasize my present charm.

Why did Horace not get interested in me at first? I was forced,

[1] *Scattered.*

by Hugh, to think that the change may have taken place in him rather than in me. Hugh believes I taught Horace to appreciate what I represent.

What Horace does not see is the change in Hugh. As usual, it is slower in showing itself, slower in crystallizing, but I see it growing. In fact, every change in the two of us will always bear the same characteristic qualities—speed in me, lucidity, intuitiveness (I realize something almost *before* it happens); in Hugh, slowness, thoroughness. He will realize it all much later, perhaps more entirely. It is so with all the opinions we form, with each step we take.

March 4. I am passing through a crisis in my writing, though my imagination is in effervescence. I seem incapable of application. So many things have the power to divert me—a visit to make or to receive; an evening out, which requires preparations; a lunch for someone from the bank, which demands a morning of work; alterations in the studio for the time when Hugh's mother will see it; and preoccupation with new clothes. I have moments when I would like to have nothing else to worry about except looking pretty. So many women take that as a justification of their existence. I have other moments when I wonder if the people who merely enjoy life are not the wisest. Why am I so intent on working, on understanding, on growing more intelligent, on putting spirit into other people? To maintain this power of spirit-giving which I have been granted, I must believe in it first. And I do. But secretly, I fail even myself occasionally. Meanwhile, I see Hugh grow brighter and more active under my influence, I see Horace disturbed in his ancient belief in mere existence, I see Eduardo make a new and unexpected effort to obtain his degree—all through my words, my influence. Eugene, even, tries to write long and frequent letters. Can't I work the same charm upon my useless, wasted days?

March 5. Sometimes I doubt whether writing is my true vocation. But my marriage prevents me from experimenting with other things, and with the stage, particularly. I read the memoirs of Sarah Bernhardt and the life of Eleonora Duse with an emotion which no literature has ever given me. I know I could be a tragedienne. But there are two other things I could have done and for which I long secretly on days when my writing shows its ugly face—dancing, Spanish dancing, and sculpturing, in the style of

Mrs. Vonnoh.[1] I realize the childishness of these desires. In them there is the same monotonous labor, the same petty difficulties, the same homeliness of the mechanics and technique. Besides, I have chosen a career. I am Hugh's wife, first of all. I write because this is the only outside occupation which does not conflict with his happiness and his comfort. But today I hate writing, I hate the capriciousness of it, the elusiveness of it. I feel deprived of the smallest share of talent. I am rebellious, untrained and unreliable. Can it be that, like my father, I am incapable of creating—that I can criticize, understand, appreciate and talk, but that I cannot invent? This fear terrorizes me on days which bring nothing beautiful to my writing.

March 6. In talking to the Cat[2] about my troubles, I found the true reason for them. I was told I was acting like Joaquin when he is asked to play. He rubs his hands, he hesitates; he does not take his playing naturally and simply. He wishes to surprise, to be different. We often condemn him for it: "Don't make such a fuss about it! Play like Antonio, without affected preparations and pretentions. Just go to it!" Well, here I have been, for days, in front of my new and comfortable desk, sifting paper, dusting my typewriter, rearranging my old writing, thinking no subject big enough, reaching out to fantastic plans, writing nothing. As soon as I realized this, I changed. I went to work this morning and polished my play, for which I have a great affection, as the ideas are a direct offspring of my whole life's experiences and philosophy. I was humbling myself by rewriting, which I detest, so that Monday I may start spiritedly on something new, naturally, without fuss and pretentions and hesitations. Of course, Saturday afternoon does not count for work. The Cat is home. It is his holiday. He is here to be petted, fed and taken out for walks. When I write, he frowns. I can only do so when he reads the *History of the Medicis.*

Tonight we invite Mlle. Boussinescq to the theatre. I have no desire to go. There are certain days when I should be left alone to brood, owllike, on whatever I please. Above all, I detest having to face her ironic smile, her acid remarks, her dryness, her intolerance, her extreme opinions. She is an assertive, disagreeable woman of charming accomplishments. But she carries in herself

[1] *Bessie Vonnoh, American sculptor.*
[2] *Hugh.*

the essence of French grouchiness. I admire her and at the same time I bristle at the very sound of her voice. How few people I love! And how often I try to increase their number!

March 7. Nauseating reaction from the ridiculous play last night, *Irma*, and from B.'s enjoyment of it. Consoled somewhat by H.'s feeling towards it, which resembled mine with the exception of the intensity. All evening I remembered Pirandello's *Henri IV* and was deeply struck by the difference between what I admire and French comedy, which I execrate. Is there anything closer to the animal than the French, despite all their varnish of civilization? It there any humor quite as low, quite as humiliating? Their comedies are elaborations of dogs pursuing each other in the streets. Last night I distinctly saw the two young "lovers" turned into dogs. I wish someone had staged them without the fashionable suits, the smart ties, the polished hair and manners. Denuded of these embellishments, the animal shows itself so clearly that you see it crawl with its nose on the ground, smelling; you see it satisfy its appetites out of a garbage can or by pursuing the first female on the road, however ugly, mud-covered, crook-legged or mange-eaten.

March 13. Saturday is always sweet. The morning is short and full with preparations for the weekend. The Cat comes home for good, which makes a remarkable difference in his attitude. He truly drops the bank and turns his mind to me, to his books, to diversions, to rest. We are happy, although we are both passing through a period of very bad health. We are lying down in the little perched bedroom with three Rubáiyát scenes around us, the two Oriental windows, the black furniture and dark-red hangings. I have finished the first volume of the *History of the Medicis* and am waiting for H. to finish the second, which I am constantly reading over his shoulder. It distracts me from my journal writing and keeps my thoughts revolving on a magnificent subject.

March 20. Hugh passed through a very bad crisis of his old stomach troubles. We saw a big specialist, and ever since, I have been taking infinite care of him according to the doctor's instructions. He has become thinner and pale. But I hope all this will disappear in Italy, and I make the preparations for the trip with greater impatience. We go first to the Italian Riviera, where H. can rest and grow well. And from there to Florence for a calm and thorough visit of the long-imagined city. Last night Horace came for a farewell visit. We discussed the subjects which interest us— life and how it should be lived; people, whom we are trying to elucidate; books we have read; ideas we have acquired lately. We always sit in the little library. The smoke of the two pipes makes the appearance of both people and books slightly more soft and unreal, so that at moments I am not certain that our voices do not come from the books, or that Horace is not just a fiction. Of Hugh's reality I am more convinced. After the door is closed on Horace and I have taken away the coffee cups and emptied the ashtrays and turned off the little lamp, he slips his arm around my waist, and says: "You looked lovely tonight, my darling." We climb the narrow, curving stairs to our bedroom, sighing happily, and talk about Horace and his ideas. We compare his life with ours, and always close the subject with: "Poor Horace!"

April [?]. Nervi, Italy. We arrived at Turin at 1 o'clock at night and had to wait until 4 o'clock for the train to Genoa. We went to the cold waiting room and sat on red-plush chairs. Hugh dozed, with his cap over his eyes and his head on my shoulder, but I could not relax and my eyes wandered restlessly over the large room. I observed the antics of an English caravan who would not break decorum to sleep as others did. They laughed at the Italians, the French, the Germans, and us, who were making the best of the situation. Afterwards, seeing that no one was observing them (except me, with my eyes hidden in the shadows of my broad-brimmed hat), they closed their eyes and let their heads droop. After a moment of this, they slipped down in their chairs and opened their mouths; a moment more, after looking around again to see if anyone could see and condemn them (everybody else was sleeping), they imitated us and stretched their legs immodestly on their valises. An hour or so later, they were entirely demoralized. Some had unfolded their blankets on the floor and were lying stretched on these with their heads on their valises; others had blown air into their rubber pillows and were snoring over them; still others slept with their heads on friends' knees, while the friends rested on other friends' shoulders, in a long chain of human frailty. One Englishman slept soundly lying on a marble mantelpiece. By the time they were all at rest, the train arrived whistling into the station.

Hugh and I found an empty compartment and slept until we arrived at Genoa. There we had breakfast on a park bench, and took a carriage ride through the city and along the seashore. We liked the port, with its many ships. It was there that I discovered the first pastel-colored houses, with almond-green shutters, and blankets and rugs and shawls hanging out of the windows, and balconies full of plants. We took our train to Camogli, as we had been advised. On the way we passed through Nervi, and a mere passing glance made me say, "I wish we were stopping here!" Once in Camogli, which we found noisy and full of unexpectedly tall houses and inhospitable-looking hotels, we remembered this exclamation and after lunch returned straight to Nervi. And here we are, in an ordinary hotel that stands next to the sea, waiting to get a room.

These are the facts. I had no burning sensations when I stepped on Italian soil. I was so tired, but I knew already that if I should want to buy oil, I should ask for Olio di Sasso, having seen this advertised at every Italian station in letters larger than the name of the place. Also I knew that there was a mineral water named after La Gioconda,[1] which gave me a little chill of fear at the commercialism in Italy.

April 7. The softness I love so much—the brilliancy and warmth which dissolves my restlessness and my anguish. Everything sings: the very gentle winds, the wandering musicians, the fishermen on the sea, the workmen in the streets. We sit on our balcony with the glowing Mediterranean below us—sleepily content, like two well-fed cats. Hugh's nose has become very red, and I have freckles on mine, from so much basking. But he has written beautifully in his journal, whereas I have only dreamed.

I was apathetic in the train all the way here, from the reaction to the very excited last days. (I had rented the apartment to an artist, and was obliged to move all my belongings to Mother's apartment; I had to attend to a thousand details.) It was only when we had found a hotel in Nervi, were stretched on our beds, resting, and some street musicians came to play a serenade under our window that I came awake and stirred. Hugh was bewildered by my joy. I sat up in bed and uttered various exclamations, while making operatic gestures.

On Easter Sunday, I became deeply responsive to everything after a concert of Italian chimes, ringing light and clear in the

[1] *The Mona Lisa.*

delicate atmosphere. Dreamless nights and long-sought-after peace. Paris looms far in the future, dark and sour and mocking.

"Don't you find yourself using 'we' most of the time, now?" asked Hugh, raising his head over his own journal.

"I was just going to write about this," I answered. "I have been feeling very confused in the use of the person—it is so seldom that your life is bound to mine, that we do everything together. I am not used to writing 'we.'" Fortunately, there is no need of moving our chairs closer; the balcony is small. We just have to lean over our journals a little for a kiss.

April 8. During the night, the Mediterranean had a serious fit of temper, and the sun was afraid to come out. Suddenly plunged into darkness and cold again. I shivered, body and soul, and cursed the whims of an effeminate sea who dares appear in blue one day, turquoise the next, and green on the third. The heavings and rolling awakened us in the middle of the night. Hugh is sleeping now to replace those lost hours, but I sat disconsolately before the closed window and wrote letters.

I have finished counting our money (a task of short duration because here they believe in cheating with a smile). But who can condemn such handsome and cheerful rascals?

April 11. Was struck yesterday by an important discovery. Paris kills my writing. I have been oppressed and belittled and silenced in Paris. As soon as I leave it, I feel free again, vivid, enthusiastic, fervent, creative. Why? Because Paris has a passion for vicious criticism, because Paris is old, envious of youth, an enemy of individualism, an enemy of mysticism, an enemy of energy. I am stifled by the tone of its theatre, by the deadness of its old traditions, by the leering expressions of its crowds, by the decay of its modern literature. I have been spiritually crucified in Paris, and this torment has broken out into all kinds of small irritations, in rebellions against the eternally gray weather. Outside of Paris, I live. I lived in Verneuil, in Tours, in Hendaye, here in Italy. My impulses return, my tongue loosens, I feel my shoulders lighter from the weight of critical, dull, mocking eyes, from the weight of an envious curiosity. Hugh suggests I should take pleasure in this combat, this clash of temperaments. He loves a fight; I don't, at least not now. I had just begun to raise my head when I arrived in Paris, and its superiority passed over me like a violent and unexpected storm, leaving me bewildered and crushed. I must conquer this vulnerability, I must have courage. I act under the glaring eyes of Paris as I do before the cold—I shrink and shiver. While Hugh says always, "Breathe deeply, throw out your chest, fight the cold, and you won't feel it."

Calm days, these. We read, we write letters, we sit in the sun, we dress for dinner and talk softly across the little table on safe philosophical subjects. We fly from the crowd, from the entertainments, even from the walk along the sea which is, as usual, a parade.

I listen with pleasure to the serenade of the wandering musicians, who stand on the long terrace below our balcony. The rain of silver pieces distracts them from their melody, particularly when this rain threatens to roll away into the sea. We write Horace, teasing him about his arguments in favor of sociability, telling him how we live on our balcony and cultivate sauvagerie more than ever. I tease him, too, about his refusal to write me a letter in which he would tell me what he felt on his visit to Florence years ago, an experience which I divined to have been the most important in his spiritual life, and which his adaptation to Parisian life is slowly effacing. He suspected me of wanting to resuscitate a state of mind which was more in harmony with my own temperament, and as he is always combatting the "spirituality" of this temperament, he chose to remain towards me more the Frenchman than the exalted Italian.

The Legend of Paris. There is a monster in Paris called the Literary Tradition. You come from young America stamped with a respect of it which you have gathered from reading. Professors and those who have traveled and wish to awe you with the importance of what they have seen agree that there are impressive arts in Europe which you must fear and admire. You come to Paris penetrated with Reverence. You read the literary magazines and newspapers. They are celebrating the centenary of some French writer. They are weeping over the loss of a never-known-before genius, essentially French in his virtues, an example of French elegance in style, of French philosophy, of French wit. You are impressed with the opinion of the world (as represented by a French critic) towards another great French writer—they are all great, and they are all French—one thing follows another. You go to the Sorbonne. The voices there are deep and solemn, scholarly and elegant. The sound of it alone and the impeccable intelligence, the impeccable style, are guarantees of intelligence and wisdom. You are again impressed with the awful gravity and awful divinity of French literature.

You wander through French streets, where one café is followed by a library, and a library by a café, and so on. You wander along the quays, and you are again impressed by the perpetual presence of Letters. The Monster swells at every step. It has become immense and fearful. You have become a little mortal of diminutive importance, a speechless worshiper. The whole Nation has agreed to deceive you. The legend arrests the meager flowings of your own pen. It swallows your individuality. At last you can write home to young America and say that you are studying Art in the most artistic city, where the atmosphere is so ideal for growth. Growth of what? Not yourself. Perhaps the growth of Paris and its Legend.

Hugh and I together discover many things. We were talking about my lost battles in Paris. We compared my feelings with those he had in N.Y. towards his work. In N.Y. the Businessman is strong in his success— he is rough, intolerant of weakness, critical of others. It is his field, and he arrogantly crushes the weaker players. Hugh felt weak there. But coming to Paris, where the French are weak in business, he became superior. He felt freer and he worked better. This breathing spell gave him a chance to develop his talents and to gain self-confidence. He was free of criticism and sharpness and was able to grow.

Exactly the reverse happened to me. The French had the authority and the intolerance and the sharpness of the successful man. I had the eyes of the Monster on me, and I had no breathing spell except when I ran away and listened to my own voice. All I need now is a chance to develop in a place where I am allowed to breathe. I have learned enormously, even though I have not worked. I have studied the Monster carefully. I have absorbed everything with great docility. Such rough experiences are salutary if one survives them.

April 12. I am spending the day in bed with a cold, due to the rain and cold of the famed Italian Riviera. H. read me my essay on the journal, and I made a very detached judgment of it, without, however, attempting to reform it. The pulse of my life is beating very slowly now, and the fever had died down. I take to wondering all day, in a feeble way, about ridiculous things. This morning I mocked my own serious ideals about journal writing, which never seems to influence my own journal, or to bear any relation to my writing. While working I am unconscious of laws. That is the fault of primitive man. Civilization tends to make a man conscious with the hope that laws are wiser than impulses.

A marvelous philosopher, Ferrero,[1] divides art into puissance and perfection.

April 13. Another day to be spent in bed. But it is a consolation to see H. feeling well, and looking healthily sunburned. We spent yesterday in thought and philosophical discussions. Before we married, we did little else but theorize about life. Afterwards, we tried the adaptation of our ideas. I remember writing then of how ideas should flow into little actions, and large conceptions should be condensed into the perfection of everyday life. I find that now and then it is necessary to return to those theoretical examinations. In a mild way I do this constantly through my journal, with which I criticize and examine, and control, insofar as thought can control. I cannot do it every day, and particularly when it concerns the philosophy of our own immediate life. Besides, now I have H. to help me. We have been discussing such a problem as: What do we want, and what limit shall we put on our desires? Ferrero has impressed us with the wisdom of limitation, with the necessity of knowing what you want and of eliminating many desires in order to fulfill a few completely. This teaching has affected H. more than it has me. I have always been more decided, more condensed, more unswerving, more certain of my desires. Hugh has hesitated between things and seldom found the courage to select, for fear of missing something. Ferrero dealt Hugh's weakness a deep blow, and he has been making resolutions in his journal, and brooding, with his eyes on the sea.

It is contentment Ferrero preaches, appreciation of what one has, enjoyment of things contained within the boundary lines of H.'s salary, of our health, of our characters. He reaches, through intelligence, the ancient and spiritual teachings of the Church: restraint, contentment, resignation. H. and I have been influenced by the spirit of our time, which is a regular ascension of ambition, a continuous race ahead of one's material means. We have traveled through parts of France, and now through Italy, and yet we sigh because the exchange makes it impossible for us to visit Spain and Scotland. Before, I would have thought it a deep blessing in itself

[1] *Guglielmo Ferrero, the Italian historian.*

to possess 400 books, but today, I forget to enjoy them while planning how to beautify their bindings. Our apartment is light, comfortable, but we sigh before the antique-shop windows for the rich hangings, rugs, ancient coffers and candelabra. I never had lovelier clothes—a black velvet coat trimmed with squirrel, a gold lace evening dress, an almond-green duveteen dress, a red silk dress, a lavender chiffon dress, a purple ensemble, a ruby-colored velvet evening dress, a sea-green velvet dress, dainty lingerie, etc. H. takes pleasure in my smartness, but I keep my eyes fixed on smarter women of great wealth and waste time inventing ways of achieving the same luxurious effect. I have taken an inventory of my sins.

Hugh laughs at the womanly twist I give to great intellectual truths. Yet he agrees that it would be useful if we wrote down what it is we want and set aside what we cannot have. And then he adds, with characteristic cautiousness: "But you must also have moderation in limitation." With all this, we submit to one general ambition, for the sake of home and children. And we have agreed that in a year we must return to N.Y. and end our "vacation in Europe." In this I know we are wise. We are going to win money as Americans win, but we shall be deeply different in the way we spend it.

April 15. We arrived in Florence when it was too dark to see anything but the outline of the Duomo and the Palazzo Vecchio. I had conceived a calm, sunny city, with the Arno flowing gently under deserted bridges. The Duomo, in my mind, stood impressively alone in the center of a vast piazza, and small, crooked, colorful streets, full of old shops and Italians, connected the Duomo with Santa Croce, Santa Maria Novella and other churches; the palaces, the museums, were abandoned to our dreamy pilgrimage.

Whereas Florence is different. The streets are crowded with all nationalities and lined with English and Parisian shops displaying the newest fashions. The Duomo stands stifling in a small piazza overrun with restaurants, tourist shops and a network of trolleys. The bridges over the Arno are heavy with traffic and foreigners. The palaces and museums and churches are dense with noisy visitors. An army of persistent guides, dishonest cab-drivers, obtrusive postcard sellers, obstinate beggars, officious waiters, hunts down the traveler, interrupts his walks, his sight-seeing, and sours his temper.

This morning we came out of the darkness of our hotel room,

where we had tried to sleep away the first discordant notes, and came into the dazzling sunlit whiteness of the Piazza della Signoria. From there we wandered all morning, looking for a more cheerful and quieter room, wishing we could afford a room overlooking the Arno, and finally consoling ourselves with the first room, from which we can see the Bargello.

April 16. This morning, after wandering for an hour, looking at the architecture and at the people, we turned our steps naturally to the Uffizi Gallery. We sought Botticelli first, because he always pleased us, and his frescoes in the Louvre are always in our minds.

We did not stay as long as we intended. The room was full of glossy-haired, smart young men from college, young women in sport suits with Baedekers, and old English couples. The young men were always interested in the same paintings which the young ladies studied, and the eyes of these ladies were always wandering off towards the glossy-haired and living works of art.

April 17. Took a carriage to the Museum Stibbert because I had read that there was furniture and clothing there. We came unexpectedly upon a beautiful burnt-sienna house, with a terrace surrounded by a lacy colonnade. Within, we found an astonishing cavalcade of men in iron armor—Spaniards, French, Germans and Italians riding in a silent, still procession across the long hall. In other rooms there were elaborate costumes belonging to lords, ladies and the Church, all richly embroidered, most tastefully designed, and so beautiful that our modern clothes seemed monstrous beside them. There were rooms full of delicate, elaborate, varied-colored Venetian furniture and jewelry, with brilliant-toned Spanish leather on the walls, as in the French châteaux. After seeing a thousand things, of which I noted a few, we sat in the park for a long while, in complete silence. But Hugh wrote of it in his journal, and his description is so pleasing that I prefer to read it when I wish to recall the last hours of that day.

April 18. In the Bargello, saw Donatello's work without interest. We liked della Robbia's terra-cotta reliefs immensely; and were impressed by Dante's death mask. In the Palazzo Vecchio, I was interested in the apartments of the Duchessa Eleonora. The walls are of sea-green-colored stucco, the architecture of a style particularly pleasing to me, expressed chiefly in arches that have an

Oriental delicacy, in arched ceilings, doors, and windows with thin spiral colonnades. The windows are in deep recesses with two stone steps leading up to them. The scene there must have been one of royal charm, when the ladies in long dresses with trailing folds climbed them to look out into the piazza.

From the palazzo we went to the Church of the Annunziata, and there, for the first time in Florence, I found Mockery, and this is the way it was treated: In a fresco by Andrea del Sarto, a saint is seen clothing a poor man. Meanwhile, three gamblers stand in a corner and mock him, *and they are struck by lightning*. Applicable to the French. After this the rain drove us into the movies, where we saw a beautiful story—the Legend of Santa Simplicia, the delicate white-robed sister (played by Eva May with fine soberness) in a tale of the power of good over evil, which made both Hugh and me cry. It was all in harmony with our life here, our surroundings, our emotions.

April 19. In the Academia I was distressed by the enormous proportions of Michelangelo's work, although his face and his life had moved me deeply. It is strange that I cannot appreciate giant reproductions of the human body when all manifestations of intellectual greatness and power awe me.

April 21. We sit dolefully in our ugly hotel room, watching the rain fall on the Piazza Firenze. Florence looks as gray as Paris, even though the streets are enlivened by the green-and-red flag in honor of the birth of Rome.

To console myself, I spread before me the postcards we bought of the places and paintings we loved. And also the jeweled cross and bracelet Hugh gave me, delicate products of Florentine art. I am warm, inwardly, with the deep glow of a thousand paintings. We saw more yesterday in the immense Pitti Gallery, room after room of fixed and ever different faces, of immutable smiles, of coloring that will never alter, of gestures that will never melt into another—a kind of calm eternity.

The Palazzo Pitti, apart from its works of art, seemed to me in supreme bad taste. Gilt is used in it with a heavy, showy hand; the coloring is harsh and the designs are heavy and luxurious. Nor do I like the cathedral. Its heaviness of line, the complicated mingling of colored marbles, express neither the spirit of Florentine art nor any religious ideal. It does not have the character of a rising hymn, of a swelling organ note, the grace of a long white taper. It is a pretentious, expensive building planned by men to glorify their strength, not God's. And God's punishment is that it has remained "matter," tied to the earth, crouching lifelessly.

The Italians are more like children than anything else. Witness their love of holidays. Everything is closed—you cannot buy even a newspaper. They loaf in the streets; the cafés are full. They run before the military bands and watch the parades with childlike pleasure. Work is their school, which they prefer to be away from, in order to see the soldiers pass with the music.

We wrote letters, made notes, read over our Baedeker, made a careful list of the things we had missed, which we will see tomorrow, and then decided to act as if we owned umbrellas, raincoats and rubbers, although we had none of these things, thanks to my faith in Italian sunshine. Hugh found occasion to deliver his usual neat Scottish sermon on cautiousness and preparation against bad weather. This time I listened with drooping head.

The Palazzo Vecchio was illumined that night to celebrate the birth of Rome. In every space between the protruding stones of the roof and the top of the campanile there was a burning torch.

April 22. Hugh said that he had learned in college that the individual had little inherent taste, but needed training and developing; in short, he learned to distrust his own opinion.

My own untutored, undisciplined education brought out the opposite habit in me. I always had the daring of ignorant people who judge by their instinct. I have taken delight in forming and developing these opinions. I have tried to discover things alone. In Florence Hugh carries the guidebook, and I only my natural habits. Out of fun, he sometimes compared my judgments with those of authority and found them very often correct. After seeing this, he began to find equal delight in the exercise of his own senses and intelligence. He agreed to free himself more, although I, in return, promised to be careful and more considerate, as there is more danger in my daring than in his cautiousness.

April 27. We took a trolley to Fiesole for a dutiful visit we had promised to make. It rained so hard that we decided not to leave the trolley but to go to the end and return. But at the end was delectable Fiesole, and we found ourselves before the very door of a hotel, whose balconies, we noticed, commanded a surprising view of all Florence.

We left our trolley and engaged a room immediately. Hugh

and I had understood with magical shrewdness that it was here we should spend our last week instead of Nervi. We came back the next day with a renewed supply of ink (this little detail was afterwards to play a large role in our destiny) and chocolate, newspapers and a new book for me to read.

The continuous rain has kept us in our room, but we have written letters, written in our journals and had long talks, which have brought a deep and joyous understanding between us. My year's bitter loneliness in Paris, all because I hated it and Hugh admired it, is past. So much is the fault of our different occupations. H., in the bank, sees nothing, is conscious only of a few pleasant facts about his successful work. I, at home, have to adjust myself to a life for which I am temperamentally unfit. The people, the literature, the theatre, the faces in the street, my dealings with all those on whom depend the beauty of our home, Hugh's health and Hugh's comfort, all these have tried me. I have understood the language better, have divined, with an inexorable sharpness of vision, characters, attitudes, atmospheres, which Hugh could not see. But at last he realizes everything, his eyes have opened suddenly, with the help of his new spiritual awakening. Modern Paris is the cabaret and the divorce court of the world. Why should one have to live near ugly things when there are cities like Florence, and even New York, where at least there is secrecy about evil, and men and women hide their vicious faces, instead of boasting of, praising, flaunting their sensuality. Florence's true artistic character preserves it yet from the claws of fools. Not that Florence proved entirely a stainless dream. The modern Italian seems to us a political fanatic, an idle café-haunter with an immense and unquenchable greed. I have never seen such exploitation of museums, of palaces, of sacred houses, cloisters and churches, such a deliberate attack on the tourist. We have not spent our money; it has been taken from us with the same treachery of old-fashioned bandits.

We are weary, now, of traveling. Beauty, which we came so far to see, demands much from its pale-faced adorers. One has to fight for it with lance and armor and a strong body. An ardent spirit does not suffice.

I should not spend this sunny day (our first in Fiesole) brooding on sorrowful things.

May [2]. Last day of vacation. Terrible depression, felt first in a physical way when we came down from Fiesole to Florence on a heavy, damp day; felt spiritually on the train when I realized I was returning irrevocably to Paris, my hell on earth.

May 5. I have startled my whole family by my irrepressible joy-ousness, and Mother has been looking at me with a faintly suspicious and worried expression, wondering whether she should not call the doctor.

Nothing explains it. However, in the bus, on our way downtown, I leaned over to tell Hugh, "Florence has changed me. I feel stronger and calmer. Don't you?" He answered that he had been wondering what was the matter with me and that he thought it might be my new black hat, but that I did look more mature. Whereas I thought he had changed. "Before," I explained, "your face seemed to be perpetually questioning and unsettled. It seemed to be always saying, 'Yes?' in a mild tone." "I'm glad," said Hugh.

We looked at Paris with the same eyes. We admitted that nothing but the lead-and-pearl coloring suited it. We were on our way, for the first time, to the American Library. After spending a whole year reading nothing but French novels, I think I deserved this. And we stumbled upon the most vivid contrast imaginable—on the delicate, whimsical, subtle and delicious Stella Benson. It was not entirely an accident, because we had been reading Christopher Morley's *Thunder on the Left,* and he is an admitted admirer (also an imitator) of Stella Benson. Morley has attempted a deeper book than Erskine's (I believe they are frankly enemies), but it got drowned in American crudeness. It is a case of someone trying to catch the crowd with a bait and falling overboard. Of Stella Benson I have read only half a book, but with a shock of pleasure and a conviction that it was an important discovery.

Hugh is unrecognizable. Instead of Commercial Reports, he has been reading Morley in the bus on his way to and from the bank. Tonight he forgets to relight his pipe while reading Stella Benson, and I hear him chuckle occasionally. Joaquin makes discoveries too: first, that I look older, and second, that I laugh like a "noiseless piano," a "noiseless keyboard." (He explains that I looked older, but that he could not find the "wrinkles.") Mother still looks at me questioningly over her book. It is May, and we are shivering with cold, but I am happy.

May 9. I am afraid of the people who do not believe in me—I am afraid because I know they are right. Before them I remember all my weaknesses. When will I convince myself that I am not bad?

Only then will they believe. And yet their lack of faith is an obstacle in my way. It disturbs and discourages me. It makes me hate myself, it makes me feel bad for many days. Their eyes seem to say: "I know you are *pretending* to be good. You are not naturally so."

All this proves to me that the most interesting thing about me is my husband. Nobody can suspect him. He is more solid, more dependable. He has no diabolical inheritances, and very few struggles. He has fewer moods, fewer fancies, and he never *guesses* things. However, all his troubles, as well as his fortune, come from me.

Modernism, Waldo Frank, sound like Stravinsky's music—all are at first only discordant, harsh and mad. Later, one begins to see their meaning: desire to return to absolute truth in expression, discarding words and tones to which we are accustomed, in order to seek again the primitive, the exact, the vigorous word. The complexities and discords of our lives and ideas are well suggested, but why should they always deal with the poisoned and fetid wounds? Newness in itself is not art. It is right only insofar as it surpasses the old, by expressing more than the old in a more truthful way. I recognize the power of modern efforts, but I feel it is still a crude and undeveloped art.

May 10. Hugh says to "stop speculation and begin work." So I cleaned all his shoes, mended his socks and bought some necessities which he has been asking for for a week and continue to pretend I don't know which kind of work he means.

May 13. I can't forget Horace or his troubled, moody, restless face. And Hugh tells me he has been acting queerly even with him. I cannot understand exactly why he is so unhappy, except when I realize that he is losing himself more every day, growing more and more confused in his desires and taking refuge from his unrealized troubles in social activity. We are going to see him Saturday, but not alone, and I await impatiently the moment when I may talk with him and perhaps soothe him.

We went again to the American Library and took out another book by Stella Benson—her latest one. She has disappointed us deeply. At first, we were intoxicated by the sharpness and lightness of her prose, by all that she promised with that fantastic approach of hers to unreal and wonderful worlds, and by her madness. *This Is the End*, particularly, contained much of that intangible promise, but in the end it was all a deception. She enters her worlds but cannot breathe in them more than a moment without laughing so loudly that everything around her runs away. And they stay away because she continues to laugh so loudly. Some of her phrases were marvelously crisp and wise, but she destroyed the delicate balance of her fine work by caricature, by too ready a love of the ridiculous and by vagueness. In her latest book, *The Poor Man*, she is just morbid. But someone should collect her occasional paragraphs on dogs—I have never read more delightful descriptions.

Another book helped to draw my attention away from Stella Benson. It was Geoffrey Scott's *Portrait of Zélide*. I have a predilection for biography, and particularly for biographies of intelligent women. The life of Zélide held me in a trance for two days. I seem to have been living inside her intensely lively and vigorous mind. The quality of her mentality did not appeal to me so much as the vividness and swiftness of it. She had character, which I worship, she had this fever of thought, this habit of analysis which I can understand so well since I possess the seeds of it myself. And then, she was alone, and this won my tenderness. I would give many years of my life (and this at present is the greatest sacrifice I could offer) to talk one evening with a woman like Zélide.

Talking with Eugene, Horace or Hugh is different. Men are slower and too irritatingly cautious. And then Ideas do not "excite" them. Ideas come to them as a natural result of a working logic, as normal conclusions. They come to women by supernatural channels, and they bring with them a supernatural fever, such as mystics feel, such as discoverers and witches and others must feel. I think men fear the lucidity of ideas whose parentage is so unearthly and unsound. Their ideas are begotten of domesticated and legitimized Reason. That is why they look with suspicion on the woman who thinks; in fact, it is the same kind of fear which burned people suspected of witchcraft.

Men deal with powerful weapons. They say: "We shall banish you from love." And this is enough to subjugate most women. Few are brave enough, and when they are, they suffer. All the intelligent and thoughtful women I have read of have suffered. They have been deprived of love. The terror which Zélide inspires is ludicrous and tragic. But she, at least, found Benjamin Constant for a short while. Zélide is scientific and masculine in her manner of thought. She is also downright invulnerable (except in the matter of her lost Benjamin), outspoken, strong—but none of these words define her entirely. Scott portrays her will so well that when Benjamin Constant is attracted by Mme. de Staël, I hated her and her sentimentalism and her faith and her ardor. It must be true that to possess the sympathy of a person is to possess everything. Even Zélide's husband won a little of my sympathy—the quiet, slow, pathetically gentle man who could not follow his restless and too-brilliant wife.

This problem of isolation is troubling me. There must be in the world today minds whose knowledge would alter my whole life in the same way some of these old minds have done. Why do I never feel or hear or meet them? I don't understand that this should be a law among minds: "You shall never meet your likeness in this world."

May 16. Yesterday I lived through a day of madness, not my madness but that of other people, which is very different and more impossible to understand.

I went in the morning to hear Rosamond Frost play the piano at the American Women's club. R. is about twenty, comfortably healthy, with short blond hair and absolutely meaningless, wide blue eyes. She described herself one evening in this way: "No one ever wanted to paint me, but occasionally I have been told I could pose well for a huge Statue of Liberty or Peace or anything of that kind." She is perfectly cool, perfectly harmless and more like a healthy, handsome boy. She also says often, with untroubled eyes (her eyes never change, whether she is talking about a person, a painting or a chair or a cold), that she thinks Europeans make so much fuss about love, and she does not see what there is to it to hold one's attention.

I have seen R. stride across a room like a strong swimmer, and I have also seen Horace's little eyes speculating on the value of such a person. Today I know what his speculations have been. R., he has said, would make fine children and a comfortable marriage. Eventually, he will marry one of the three Frost sisters, and for the moment they are the three Fates of Horace's life. If he marries R., I give him up. If he marries M., he will give me up. If he marries E., we shall keep him, but I may hate him profoundly. There is in Horace too much of his father—of the greedy rover obsessed by Woman. Yesterday afternoon, after lunching with Horace, his father and mother and Mrs. Payton (the Greek lady

Hugh and I liked), we sat in the salon. Mrs. G. sat looking at me and repeating: "Elle s'est trompée de siècle, cette petite. C'est un portrait du 18ième siècle, de ces belles françaises des salons."[1]

Mrs. Payton, over her demitasse, thought I looked Florentine, whereas Hugh brought out proofs against that, which he had lovingly collected in Florence. Horace sat before our phonograph listening to Debussy and pretending not to hear. He always hates people who give me compliments because, he says, "she likes them." (I told him once I did not know how he had had a chance to find this out.) After heated, quarrelsome conversation in the salon (Monsieur and Madame disagreed, Horace scolded everybody, Mrs. Payton dropped a noisy spoon, Hugh said nothing but wound the phonograph and I tried to agree with everybody and pacify them all), Horace took H. and me to his room. But there was no peace to be had there either. Horace's mood was decidedly combative. He attacked our ideas (our behavior the night of his party had irritated him). There had been a Mr. Brown that night whose name we used as a figure of speech. "We don't want to meet any more Mr. Browns," we said.

"That's silly," said Horace. "If you stay home, you will never learn about life."

"We learn more about life going to Florence, reading or talking to people like Erskine," I said. "The trouble with you is that you have nothing to interest you about your own life—you have no work, no hobby, nothing to occupy you."

"I like to come out of myself," said Horace. "You are too interested in *your* life, your ideas."

"Our life is interesting, we are absorbed by it. We don't want to come out of it and out of ourselves just to talk with more Mr. Browns!"

"You should not be so absolute, so exclusive," said Horace.

"You should not waste your time in futile, empty experiments," we said.

"You don't understand me," said Horace. "I like to be brilliant in company. I like to say clever things. Inwardly, I am like you. I am genuine, and I like simplicity."

"We know that. Besides, for you to go out is different. You are looking for a wife. But we have everything we want."

---

[1] *"She is in the wrong century, this little one. She's a portrait from the 18th century, one of those beautiful French women of fashion."*

"We must talk about this again," said Horace. "Your attitude is all wrong."

"Some other day," I said. "You have a cold today, and you are not feeling well."

A thousand questions and answers exploded between us in a few minutes, illogical, extreme, but serious and anxious. Much more was said than I reported. We are each pulling our own way violently. Just at this moment the Frosts, the mother and two of her daughters, arrived, and the maid came to Horace's room with the news.

I had grown terribly excited in the talk and was in no mood to return to social restraint, which I hate more every day. With the excuse of a tea at home, we hurried away with Mrs. Payton. Mother was waiting for us, with Antonio and Joaquin and a young American composer. We spent the rest of the afternoon peacefully listening to music. But my whole mind was still beating wildly after that encounter with Horace and the vehemence with which we had to defend our life. My last picture was of a feverish, restless, irritable, mad Horace standing before two of his cool Fates, lighting his pipe to give himself time to "adapt."

May 17. I forgot to record an important day in the life of my writing. After reading *Zélide*, I felt a close sympathy for biography, for which I have always had a particular worship, and I felt again a great desire to write the life of Someone. The "form" itself appeals to me, the informed, free style, the telling of character without story. But whose life could I write? Whose, as well as an imaginary character's? And I found her. It is Chantal.

Chantal, a dream, to be fitted in the framework of my life, for I am impatient of facts and do not like to seek new ones. Chantal's name is from Savoie. It is expressive and living. Chantal is a ghost; Chantal will be all the dreams which torment, fascinate and exalt me, all of them unspoken yet, even in my journal. But Chantal is not me, because I am vain, egotistical, self-conscious, and I have no soul. The only things worthwhile about me are my dreams, and she will possess them. I shall give away the only treasures I have to someone worthy of them. If I accomplish this, I may repay the world for the life given me, which I have at least lived with all my strength.

Afternoon. Chantal was shy and frightened when I faced her today and would not cross the threshold between thought and action. I became irritated and abandoned her for my essay, to which I gave, at last, a semblance of reason. It runs evenly now, not, as before, in explosions of animated thought. When writing of Amiel I had to subtract one exalted adjective to every half-phrase. I also found a modern, direct, lively beginning, mistrusting my pedantic instincts. In every other part I give way to them, however. I would like to know once and for all whether I can be myself without being immediately murdered or ostracized. But would it not be better to write much first and find out afterwards?

May 18. I don't need to ask myself any longer what I make of life to find "qu'elle s'écoule en encre."[1] I am satisfied that it is full. Yet I am glad that after a year of idleness I have begun to write again. Today I worked four hours. Aside from writing, I have been busy discovering Joaquin's character and its ridiculous resemblance to my own. His compositions are like my writing—generally somber and deep, as if they were for an organ. His moments of good humor and of witticism are fitful and intense. He has the same moods of detachment from everything, accompanied by sadness. He has the same audacity in criticism—of people, places or art. He has the same fever, the same restlessness; a vanity which is fundamentally a tragic and intense lack of self-confidence; a strong admiration for goodness and purity. He is, furthermore, impatient of details and technique, impatient of other's teachings, unless from someone he admires. His mind is critical, his heart is sensitive; he will do anything if appealed to by pity.

He eats quickly, as if eating were an interruption to more interesting things. He reads quickly, voraciously, but shrewdly, and marks his reading with original, individual ideas. Above everything else, he thinks for himself. He is occasionally apathetic but more often feverishly active and wide awake. His sense of humor is there sometimes; at other times he has a sense for tragedy, for the dramatic. When younger, he turned often, in moments of anger or despair, to the idea of suicide. He is not always sincere. His imagination is sometimes stronger than his integrity. This imagination makes him talk exaggeratedly sometimes, or write with a view to effect an artistic roundness. But this imagination brings him inspiration in his music. He is precocious, intuitive, original and interesting.

We understand each other, and as I am older, he willingly

---

[1] *That it flows away in ink.*

imitates me in little things. He is keeping his journal on the pattern of mine, he reads the books I love, he likes to borrow my candles to fix his studio like mine, he believes much of what I tell him. These things will serve him until he finds himself entirely. I believe he will be more than I am, because he has a clear and positive genius in music. And then he is a man. He is free.

He understands my writing better than anyone I know, and when he is older, he will understand me. We are and shall be close friends. I feel his music, his compositions, his way of playing, his choices, and I think I understand him. My imagination can follow his movements and I can guess his moods.

Meanwhile, he has been writing about me! This is what he says: "Anaïs is outwardly surprising in her changings. From pensive mood to elation over dresses, it seems she transforms herself, yet she remains the same—serious, thoughtful, quick in her decisions. She writes well, observes deeply, feels intensely, understands her character more than she understands life, battles with few, almost unnoticeable faults, which her imagination enlarges and her conscience loves to torment. She smiles at me, she understands me. Does she understand the music in me? Must one understand to feel? She feels and thinks that is enough."

May 24. The Cat and I have made a discovery—our whole life is going to be affected by it.

It came after we had gone to the Luxembourg this morning, to read and write. There is no peace to be had there. The park is crowded and noisy. We left it early, discouraged and, as usual, making wishes for an empty world. In a desperate moment, we asked the concierge if we might sit on the roof. She answered that we might, that it sloped downward a little but that it was otherwise very pleasant. Of course, there is no railing. At this, the Cat and I, who have fear of heights, winced. The concierge then offered to lend us a servant's room, now unoccupied, which has a balcony. We came up to see it. I am writing now on the balcony. We have no desire to return to New York. On this little terrace, seeing Paris from such a high plane, nothing can affect us. I shall write many books here, the Cat will read many more, and we are near the sky, we breathe pure air, we have peace. This is the most delightful discovery. I am as happy here as I was in Nervi. We want to rent the room and terrace, to own it, to turn it into a Secret Refuge, a workroom. We shall have plants here, books, and sit here on summer evenings, in the dark, to talk. The Cat has christened it, more accurately, the High Place. And the High Place it will be. Only Significant people shall reach it (by the elevator).

I have been reading a most uninteresting Journal, that of Josephine Peabody, an American poetess who died in 1922. The writing was exclamatory and very young throughout the book. She was charming, delicate, impressionable, endowed perhaps with a gift for pretty poetry and nice plays, but everything she has to tell in her diary is on such a youthful and minor key. It is true she had no opportunity for development, but even then I do not see how she could have ever been mature or intellectual. She is poetical, sensitive, always in a small way, and her style is more often banal than anything else. One cannot help liking her—she was so genuine, so aspiring, so eager, but this is a case where the French attitude, so intolerant of unintelligence, so mocking of naïveté and immaturity, seems well deserved, even if it is cruel. Before such an American, I, too, feel impatient and critical, in spite of my habitual pity for those who strive with childish confidence, in the face of a tragic lack of genius, to speak when they have nothing to tell.

May 25. The three of us are in the High Place. Joaquin is studying *Faust*, Hugh is reading Stevenson, and I have just given up Edith Wharton's *The Writing of Fiction*. I am tired to death of reading about writing, talking about writing and thinking about writing. Such consciousness is petrifying, and particularly for me when I am already so critical by instinct and inheritance. Joaquin is the same about music. Antonio has already warned him of the dangers of an overcritical mind.

Today the self that is elated by Dress predominated. Mother and I went shopping. Joaquin watched me with amusement, but I knew what he was thinking and told him why. He pretends to be displeased if I read his journal, but he truly likes it. And he also likes to see what I am writing. I showed him my letter to Richard and he said, "It sounds so natural—just as if you were talking." Later he made me listen to his last composition, which was wise and smooth. Tonight I think about all these things and conclude that my life is interesting. I seem to possess more than Enric, who is directing a jazz orchestra in Havana; more than Eduardo, who has rebelled against his family and is struggling to become an actor in New York; more than Miguel, who is tied to a lawyer's office in Havana, like Charles. We all started at the same age with immense expectations. Which one has lived more, deeper, and given more? It is too soon to tell. We all promised so much.

The Cat deserves long descriptions, but I like to keep him to myself and think of his character while I am sewing or while I am waiting for him to come home. I love him almost too much to write about him. It is bad for my eyes, too, because they always get dim, like warm apartment windows on frosty nights, as soon as I begin to think of his ways, his eyes, the roughness of his cheeks and the furriness of his wrists.

May 28. Hugh is often more violent or vehement than people think. The other night I asked him playfully if he loved me, and he said he did not. "Then I must find a lover," I said. He pinched me impulsively and cruelly—hurting me physically for the first time. "You Spanish tyrant!" I called him, but I showed my enjoyment of his masterful ways, and this new discovery amused him. He attributes my primitive actions to my Spanish descent. Jealousy is primitive. In him it is explained by the origin of his name, changed gradually from Aguilera to Guiler.

May 29. Yesterday evening I passed through a black crisis of the fever—in spite of a cheerful survey of my life in the morning. I had a fear of not living enough, a desire to run away from my home, to run away from the beloved but strict cords which bind me to a peaceful, virtuous solitude. I don't want the companionship of ordinary people, but I cannot endure this whole day's waiting for Hugh, to see him for an hour only, to sleep with him afterwards. I do not wait idly. I have my housekeeping, my sewing, my writing, a few dutiful visits, and my thoughts.

But this activity, of thinking and writing, is exactly what brings me such a desperate thirst for living. How different it would be if I were not married! I would work without interruptions by the house. I could dance and act on the stage. I could find companions during the day when I felt utterly alone. And still, I could make Hugh happy, since he needs me only in the evening, at night and on weekends. But why should all my whole long, exciting days be made to wait for those few hours—to stand still. I cannot have a few, rare friends without making him unhappy. I make great, continuous efforts to link our lives, but they are too different. I must have my life apart from his during the day, but dedicate it to him by filling it with occupations centering around him. That is the way I keep near him. I want to stay near him, but I can't. A million things draw me away. I want to be a rover; I want nobody to expect happiness from me. My very real self is not wifely, not good. It is wayward, moody, desperately active and hungry. I control myself only because I love—because of love I am sweet, I dress and act to please. I control my writing, my imagination, my bursts of cruel frankness.

How monstrously selfish I am with this big, noisy, voracious, passionate Self, turning wildly within its harmless-looking shell. Hugh, so good, so unselfish, works hard for our love. He is not to blame for not being a genius in art, for not having work to do at home so that our lives may flow together. When he is here, I am tamed. I am content to be his wife. His goodness makes me good. I crave no other companionship. My spirit rests. But he is seldom here. Oh, what a curse it is to be so much alive, so impatient, I, who have so much, so perfect a love and home. What a curse it is to aspire forever to more and more when happiness is in my hands. I shall be punished.

Marriage is in itself a Destiny which decides the character of the wife's life by that of her husband. Even in an enlightened age, she must follow him wherever he pleases. I have made my choice.

Against these fantastic moods I have only one weapon: my absolute, passionate loyalty to my Darling—to him, to his every wish, to his most timid expectations. My imagination alone is willful, and disloyal, but then my imagination is the Demon in me.

Our neighbor, the owner of our apartment, advised a sculpturing school for me, where he himself goes. I saw Hugh's brow darken, and though he said nothing, I offered, again, to remain at home, and I saw his happiness.

So here I am, making dresses to please his family when they come in July, shelling peas with Mother for his dinner, thinking of him. While I write now, he plays his guitar, which inevitably reminds me of the evenings in Richmond Hill before our marriage. Marrying him seemed then just as fantastic a dream as flying from him does today, if I dared.

Sunday we went to hear the organ at St. Séverin and returned directly home to the new books drawn from the library yesterday. Conrad for Hugh, and Bazalgetti's *Thoreau* for me. But I am unable to read it, being still under the powerful impression of Beethoven's life by Romain Rolland. Beethoven was one of the

Pure Gods—like da Vinci. After breathing in that rarefied air, I suffocate when I return to my world.

Horrible, horrible loneliness!

May 31. The last words of yesterday were written in the blindness of hot tears while Antonio played his own sonata, which d'Indy marked flatteringly in pencil. Hugh realized about half of my torment and restlessness, enough to drop his Conrad for a while. I feel sorry for him for having such a wife. He is soft, sensitive, capable of pain, but his imagination is normal. It serves him to understand poetry, not to invent tortures. He reasons and dissolves the things which worried me so that even I am convinced there is nothing really wrong with my life. I told him half. But he dissolved the whole, and all I kept was a bruise. The fact of my loneliness still exists. But just that alone cannot wreck his work and our home. Things will stay as they are because they are sound and sane as they are. My dissatisfaction, my doubts, my desires, my restlessness, are a kind of madness. Hugh, in a gentle way, practically said they were. He thought when I spoke of the difference between our lives and how impossible it would be to keep them together that I could not be feeling well. Madness and rebellion pass away. I shall continue the Wife. I have my journal and the art school, to which I am going next week. I shall dance for him alone.

I love like most women, and I shall live like most women, as a punishment.

June 13. Living like an ordinary woman—it is sometimes possible. I have done so for the last thirteen days. My madness returned only when I heard the marvelous Segovia playing his guitar, and also last night when Horace came to dinner and was most delightfully himself. It struck me last night that Horace is the most "insaisissable"[1] person I know. What I feel every time he comes into a room is that I have to begin all over again to recapture his attention, to win his interest, to reconquer his affection. At first he eludes my eyes; his talk is shifting, vague, restless. After a moment I feel his attention fixing itself. I feel that he is pulling himself together, becoming whole. Then his eyes cease wandering and his mind, too, and I know I have won the struggle. His real self arrives late everywhere. The first part, which is always on time, is

[1] *Inapprehensible.*

a habitual and empty flow of talk, eyes that roam over the surface, seeing everything and feeling nothing. We introduced him to the High Place. He admired the peace and beauty of it.

We spent the rest of the evening in the little library and talked of Florence. Several times our eyes met in perfect understanding. They are very Latin, his eyes, extremely brilliant, expressive and caressing. While he talks, they seem to say very contradictory things, just as Enric's eyes did, a kind of prayer to be believed in, to be liked, an appeal to cover the irrelevance of their phrases, the *irresponsibility* of them, and of their actions. Eyes like that I find in persons without will, and they make me disregard the reality of the spoken word and of the gesture, to accept the desire and the aspiration.

Rain, rain, maddening rain and cold. This to me means misery, bodily and mentally. I never want to go out, and I can never go to the High Place. I have spent my time making our home beautiful. When I feel less cross I shall make a description of it. Meanwhile, I find satisfaction in the pleasure I give Hugh and all those who see the place. Yes, in those little, insignificant things, I have talent. With little money and much work, I can make a room beautiful, like a stage setting. I have a feeling for clothes, for coloring, for beautiful ceremony. My dinners are smooth, special. I am essentially a Producer, and an Actor occasionally, not yet an Author!

Inwardly, wordlessly, secretly, I am Everything. Hugh said some time ago, "The stage will get you yet." It is the only way I shall live out the multitude of lives, characters, emotions, vibrations, that live in me. The stage! The stage! The life of the imagination, the unreality, the fantasy, the outlet for this overflow of life, an end to my pointless, useless exaltations.

Would I find Eduardo satisfying now, as I did in those days in Richmond Hill when his responsiveness almost frightened me? And Eugene, who just wrote us such a stilted young letter? Oh, why was I made so queer that my only companion should be myself? Freaks in the circuses sometimes have twins—the whole world is usually divided off into twos—but I turn around in my calmly beautiful studio and find no one listening to me, encouraging me, talking back to me, smiling at me, but Myself.

June 14. We are reading and writing in bed. Today in spite of the rain I conquered my egoist's mood, which is so hateful. I have been thinking of other things. Antonio, for one, has been occupying my mind. He is with us often now because he feels lonely and homesick. Il est la sagesse même,[1] beautifully balanced, extremely intelligent and pure. He has very fine, soft eyes. His devotion to Joaquin is remarkably unselfish and active and beneficial to my thoughtless brother. He has gentleness, very modestly hidden learning, and no desire to shine at all. And he is talented. His quiet manner makes most people overlook him—people like Horace, at least. But at concerts, he has won admiration and sympathy before beginning to play, just by the way he comes on and by a charming simplicity. Last Christmas I gave him a journal book like mine, which he is filling slowly. It is strange to see, with Horace, how necessary talk is to keep pleasure alive. With Antonio it is not. He is one of the very few persons with whom you can be absolutely silent.

July 19. Days so full that I have not even remembered my journal. I have been preparing the house for the arrival of my New Family.[2] I made pillows, lampshades, dark-red velvet covers for the table; I bought candles, extra dishes and glasses; I looked over Hugh's clothes and shoes and my dresses. When I felt too tired from perpetual and intense bustling, I came up to the High Place and lay on the couch for a little while, looking at the sky through the open window and at the terrace through the open door. This terrace was also prepared, with wicker armchairs, orange cretonne pillows, green chairs, and a little green table. Meanwhile, Mother and Joaquin were preparing to leave for Hendaye. And on the 30th we were all three standing on the two trunks in a struggle to close them. That night I could not sleep. I missed Mother and Joaquin deeply. Our new neighbors were laughing and playing "Sweetheart" on the piano. Lying there in bed, I used to listen to Joaquin's playing, and I could also hear their voices when Mother spoke to him from upstairs, where he lay reading in bed.

This sadness, however, was drowned in another busy day. At six o'clock the next evening we were waiting for my New Family. I found two girls of my age,[3] in neat, fashionable little suits, for whom I felt an instant sympathy. We had dinner with the Guilers at their hotel. They were all sweet to me, and the past was certainly effaced. Still, I did not win them altogether until after

[1] *He is wisdom itself.*
[2] *Hugh's family.*
[3] *Edith and Ethel Guiler.*

dinner, when mother and daughters came to see the house—a living expression of my ideals, my tastes, my work.

The house won their hearts. They are all artistic and unspoiled and appreciative, and they walked through it with exclamations which thrilled my Darling and compensated me.

The next evening we gave a dance for the "girls," as my New Family calls them. That was to be my second test: as a hostess. I triumphed again. It was a success, thanks to the liveliness of Edith and Ethel, to the pâté sandwiches, the delicacies, and the perseverance with which I filled the punch glasses and talked to Mother and Father Guiler. That night I was kissed really as a daughter, and when everybody had gone—even Hugh, to accompany his family to a taxi stand—I sat in one of the big armchairs and contemplated our marvelous life. This reconciliation is really exceptional.

To Eugene:

We waited impatiently for Erskine's book—and no gift was more wisely chosen—because he was here, and we saw him often. . . . At first I thought him too jolly, and although this may seem an unreasonable accusation, to me it is a very serious keystone of character, and it is something which usually hurts and estranges me, like something foreign and unsympathetic. However, I had to retract this judgment. When we knew him better, I found him mellower than I had expected, mellow and deep, and even sad. He has the very deceiving coat of mockery, so peculiarly European, the inclination to follow the curves of a neat phrase at the expense of sincerity, for the sake of a charming flash, sometimes as a protection from sensitiveness, sometimes from habit, sometimes from the sheer love of brilliant conversation.

You can easily trace the European influence in his talk and in his writing—Rabelais, Montaigne, Voltaire, Anatole France. He admits it. . . .

He is not happy, as you could see in his *Helen of Troy*. He raises many problems which he does not pretend to solve, as he said. He seems to be certain only that one must have love of life. But what wonderful things he has told us in that book! I found Helen slightly domineering and decidedly hard. It seems to be impossible to be intelligent without being cruel. I think Erskine is not as detached from the philosophical problem he handles as he should be. . . . Another thought I had was that often the disappointments of his life, his own experiences, finished his phrases for him in a way he did not at first intend.

July 29. On Tuesday at five thirty Hugh kissed me as usual before taking off his coat, but instead of "Hello, Pussy," he said: "We are going to London tomorrow."

The Omnipotent Bank was sending him with expenses paid. Immediately Hugh planned to take me with him; the two of us would live there as cheaply as one. That problem being settled, I attended to the rest. There was trouble in the air. The franc was dying down to nothing. A few business houses were closing down. Foreigners were hissed and hooted at in the tourist buses. Banks were beginning to feel the panic.

That evening, at Hugh's suggestion, I placed in a valise all my journals, his own and Joaquin's, Hugh's letters to me, Eugene's, Joaquin's, a copy of *Aline* and my essay and my play, my photograph album and a few more odds and ends, and the next morning Hugh took these things to the bank to be kept safely.

Towards nine o'clock, while I was packing, Clementine, the dayworker, came in out of breath and with a red face.

"Ah, madame, what will become of us! They are demonstrating against the foreigners in the streets. The shops are closing because the franc is worse than ever. And monsieur, who *looks so* American—he is tall, and he wears glasses. Oh, dear, oh, dear. And to think that on this very spot in 1871 millions were massacred during one of those revolutions." (She was referring to the time of the Commune. Our house was built on a spot where thousands of skeletons were found during the digging!)

I was pinning a flower to the lapel of my traveling suit while Clementine talked. My hands were trembling. Visions passed before my eyes of an angry mob bursting into our home, harming Hugh, pillaging.

"Quick, Clementine," I said, "get me a taxi. It is time for me to go. Take the keys to the apartment. I leave everything in your care. You will put the silver in the cellar, and take this away with you and keep it for me (my Florentine coffer). As soon as I get to London I will send you my address and you will write me, and tell me about everything. If things go worse, I won't let my husband come back from London."

I was eager, desperately eager, to be back at the station, to see Hugh again, to be sure that he was safe. With what relief I saw him coming to meet me at the appointed hour, and how happy I was that we were going to London.

We arrived in London in a very characteristic moment: it was raining. We walked from hotel to hotel in search of a room. Then we had dinner at a chop suey which I had spied on the way. It was there I saw for the first time the handsome men of India, carefully dressed in European clothes and speaking a soft, cultured English.

My impression of London during the three days we had of it was a mingling of New York and Paris, solidity with occasional beauty, as in the House of Parliament; of tall, handsome men, and women resembling men too much to be liked as women; numerous and attractive tobacco shops and sport shops; smooth-running, comfortable red buses from whose top seats much can be observed; charming, wild, untrimmed parks with sheep grazing; and the lovely statue of Peter Pan; an entrancing river of dark moods; one busy and vulgar street, the Strand; a remarkable, quiet and charming section behind Parliament of neatly kept houses, ivy-covered, with doorways in blue or green or white. This section, I discovered, was a continuation of the Chelsea district, chosen by artists to dwell in—by Carlyle, Rossetti, William Morris, and others.

We went to Chelsea one afternoon to look for Carlyle's house. A man we asked information from insisted on not only taking us there but showing us Old Church, so often sketched, he said, and the houses of modern artists. He told us all about the neighborhood and nothing about himself, in true English fashion, but I suspected he was an artist himself; first, because time seemed altogether his own; second, because of his face; third, because of his way of looking at the neighborhood. Ordinary people's eyes are only half opened compared with an artist's eyes.

Carlyle's house was simple and extremely touching. It is kept by an old Scottish lady, whose sympathetic way of showing you through it was in perfect harmony with the meaning of all things in it. We saw his cane, his pipe, his dressing gown, letters and little verses by him, a cast of his face after death and of his hands. We preserve all these little things that prove his life. And all of them to show the same thing: the importance of the soul and the frailty of the body, the immortality which preserves the invisible life, the gifts of the spirit, the products of intellect.

The Scottish lady said that the unhappiness of Carlyle's marriage was grossly exaggerated. She believed that they were both very high-strung persons and may have had their troubles, but that they were happy together in spite of it.

"You would be surprised at the things people say," she added. "There was an American couple here the other day. When I showed them the only two plates remaining of the Carlyles' breakfast set, she said: 'Of course, Mrs. Carlyle threw the rest of it at him.' "

Among the visitors, the Scottish lady had received Paul Bourget, before the war. This fact completed my admiration of him. He won me entirely with his *Voyageuses* and *Reconnaissancements*. In the first there is an exquisite story of a place near Florence which reproduces with peculiar exactness my own impressions of Fiesole and the surroundings of Florence, its people, paintings, churches—everything I would have written if I had his talent, without perhaps quite as sentimental an ending. In the second book there is a perfect story of an artist's disappointment in life redeemed by his fulfillment in art—an idea I love.

It was strange that Bourget should be one of the very few French visitors—that Bourget should admire Carlyle, when the French mind is eminently created to misunderstand him in exactly the way Taine misunderstands him in his worthless *English Literature*.

To finish with my fugitive impressions of London: I was glad to have come in the summer, if only to see in the crowd an occasional veteran in his scarlet coat. I liked also the guard before the building where the court horses are kept.[1] He is all in white and red, and wears a shining steel helmet and beautiful white gauntlets. What handsome men! Straight, tall, healthy, as magnificent as their virile breakfasts.

Such breakfasts! They did not suit the character of my appetite, but I liked the quiet-mannered waiters and the very small pieces of sugar.

I liked other things, too: the absence of nervousness in people, the absence of the Parisian falsetto, screechy horns; the smooth control and solidity of things, the comfortable seats in the buses, the veiled lights in the subway, the eternal afternoon tea. Everything is modest in London, except the wind, which respects nothing, and the dirt. But then baths are free and not a luxury, as in Paris.

I spent three mornings in the National Gallery. I saw paint-

[1] *The Horse Guards.*

ings by Murillo, Goya, and Velásquez, which convinced me that it is for Spain and Spain's art that I have the greatest *affection*, a thing to be separated from admiration. I also concluded that Rubens and his people ate and drank too much for my taste. His paintings are orgies of flesh. I prefer van Dyck's aristocracy.

In the Wallace Collection I was nauseated by the rosy insipidity of Boucher, touched as always by the daintiness of Watteau, by the supreme expression of innocence of Greuze. Hugh and I said we wished our little girl would have a face like that [in his painting].

How I regretted having only three days. Between the visits to Carlyle's house, to Keats's house in Hampstead, to the Peter Pan statue in Kensington Gardens, we lived on top of buses, from which I could see people, houses, monuments, and shops. It was from these trips that I obtained a quick general impression; and from slow walks that we gained a more intimate knowledge of London.

I was followed everywhere by the street organ, the street singer, the street violinists, and immediately the sharp outline of buildings disappeared, and I was given a sense of the *feelings* of the city, feelings like those of a person who suddenly confides in you one evening when there is no light by which you can look at his face.

Both times the Channel showed its teeth; it coughed and sneezed and spat angrily on the decks and heaved as if it hoped to get rid of this small ship running across its chest. Hugh had to leave me alone on deck both times.

Though he is such a bad sailor, he has become in every other respect a very expert traveler. We have both acquired this talent. We have poise, tolerance, endurance and efficiency. Hugh loses neither his tickets nor his head nor his temper. I take care of the lunch, his medicines, the camera and my jewels. The value of these jewels is personal and imaginary, seeing that they are all glass and tin, but how could I replace my Florentine cross, my Breton rings?

It was very sweet on Sunday, when we came home after the rough crossing of the Channel, the dirty, shaking train, to find warm-toned peace. Everything at home seemed smooth, soft, harmonious. The sun was shining through the sun-colored curtains. The rooms were warm and clean and quiet. We both bathed and changed into fresh clothes and then had dinner in the cheerful little kitchen. After every trip, we enjoy this feeling. After every trip we say: "Now we'll stay home forever."

One word, one glimpse of a place on a railroad station poster, the smallest opportunity, and off we are again, eager, curious, restless, with our camera, Hugh's medicines and our notebooks.

Just at this moment, our life at home is very pleasing to study. Clementine deserves a formal introduction. She is Breton, a widow for seven years, with two girls to care for. She is honest, good, devoted, religious, slow in her work, fond of long monologues from which my "work" is a refuge. Clementine arrives at nine o'clock. I give my orders for the morning, make the list for marketing and come upstairs to "work" until twelve thirty. At this time I go downstairs, powder for lunch, and then Hugh arrives. We have a quiet lunch during which I have great difficulty in keeping myself from jumping up to wait on Hugh. However, I am slowly growing used to all these extraordinary comforts.

Hugh leaves immediately after lunch (they have the American short-lunch system at the bank now) and I come to the High Place to rest until time to go out with Frances Hyde[1] or to receive some Flying Friend for tea or to call on some other friend. At 6 o'clock I am free again. I fix a little dinner in the kitchen, and the long evenings are ours. Hugh sings sometimes or smokes, when he is thinking of the bank, or reads and talks to me. I write our day's expenses in a fat book or read or dress up for Hugh in my Russian red shawl to look Spanish, and then we play tangos or violin pieces on the phonograph. Or we talk about the people we have seen, and we end by wishing ourselves in some less popular city where the Letter of Introduction would not keep us in constant fear and disappointment of meeting new people.

Tonight we have Horace to dinner. We have not seen him since the dance for Hugh's sisters. As usual, I feel sorry for him, have forgiven and forgotten and secretly hope for a beautiful talk.

July 21. In the studio, by the lamplight. I have been entertaining Hugh with mimic dances—the Follies girl, Spanish dancer, Japanese, and others. I made him laugh with the silliest characterizations. A shawl, a fan, a rose, little hesitating steps, clicking of heels in swift, short rhythms or plain, distinctly Revue kicking and sprawling—these things amused him. He laughed his loud, frank, sonorous laugh.

[1] *An American, a friend of her cousin Eduardo.*

In dancing, I shake off sorrow. A different self is freed. Movement, color, simple, direct, primitive expressions, absorb me. I need this to find balance, to poise myself. Everything else—life, love, writing, people, traveling, music—all hurt me. Dancing heals me. In dancing, my imagination at last is given free play—this restless and burning imagination which otherwise serves only to get me into trouble.

My life will be more beautiful with dancing because I will have more to give Hugh.

From now on then, you are the Journal of a Spanish Dancer!

How well it would read in headlines: the confessions of an artist's model, a society girl, the wife of an American Banker living in Paris, a Spanish dancer . . .

The very unapproachable, unlovely, unlovable, gloomy side of me never appears on the surface, it seems. Clementine thinks I resemble the Little Flower, my most beloved saint. From Clementine down to the concierge, the iceman, the baker, the grocer, the shoemaker, the cleaner, they all seem to think me kind and sweet, and when there is waiting to be done, or favors to be asked, I am chosen.

It appears that I spend my days in a hypocritical state of gentle cheerfulness. Now that I think of it, it is true—I seem that way. I am glad that I have kept my ugly despair for paper, just as I used to keep my childish fits of temper. For a while it did seem as if Paris would break my cheerfulness. No city has ever tried my nerves so, with its climate, its manners, its customs and its noises. But I think now I have this under control, too.

And dancing will help me in this eternal war against my character.

The Three Fates have abandoned Horace to another Fate. (Our dinner was postponed—this is indirect news.) Horace's peculiar habit of praising one girl to another has made me appear as the dangerous married woman who prevents him from noticing "jeune fille"[1] charm. Or at least, so the Three Fates have imagined, and numerous were the signs of hostility I received from them. They are all gone away from Paris now. And Horace is praising me to Frances Hyde and asking her in a worried way whether she really thinks I like him or not. Our little warfare of ideas and of temperament has gone too far. At bottom, though we quarrel, we have a true affection for each other. He should not doubt it. But

[1] *Young girl.*

just the same, I wish he were married so that marriageable girls might not misinterpret our interest in each other.

Through these high-toned and frivolous patterns there runs, as always, a deep undercurrent of wonderful books. Now it is Dickinson's[1] *Appearances,* in which I find the description of a religion I have discovered too late and in which I might have worshiped.

Listen: "It was the religion of the East, not of the West. It refused all significance to the temporal world; it took no account of society and its needs; it sought to destroy, not to develop, the sense and the power of Individuality. It did not say, but it implied that creation was a mistake; and if it did not profess pessimism, pessimism was its logical outcome. I do not know whether it is the religion of a wise race; but I am sure it could never be that of a strong one . . ."

Too late, because the Ego is now too old and tough, too completely developed; because of the fever of desire and action; and the vice of power, once caught, is never cured. And I would not want peace and painlessness at the cost of selflessness.

August 5. In the High Place. Busy, happy days. I love my new family and was saddened when they went away this morning. Monday and Friday afternoons I spent shopping with "Mother" and my "two sisters." We like the same things, and I enjoyed what is usually more a burden than a pleasure. With them I laugh a great deal over little things.

At 6 o'clock we returned to the hotel to find "Father," and Hugh was waiting for us. Both evenings we had dinner together "Chez Francis," and one night we took a carriage ride through the Bois. They all like me. Hugh is proud and happy.

I find it hard today to regain my calm, to relax. I am obsessed by the beautiful things I have seen and touched: luxurious dresses, ancient jewelry, perfume and evening slippers, Spanish shawls. My hands and my eyes are still restless with desire. This frailty, which strikes Joaquin as a great inconsistency in my character, is fortunately weaker than other characteristics, and soon I shall be obsessed by ideas again, by some new book. A very intellectual mood calms my fever, and my fingers close naturally around the pen and forget the touch of silk and velvet.

---

[1] *Goldsworthy Lowes Dickinson.*

August 6. Coming out of the moving pictures, where we had just seen *Salammbô*, Hugh said to me: "Do you know what the difference is between you and the modern woman? The modern woman was born yesterday, and you were born ages ago—your soul is very old. You have been all these women: Salammbô and Mona Lisa and others. You are so deep. And no one knows you, no one understands you, no one guesses all that you are. But I do. You cannot deceive me. Others may see in you just a sweet girl; they treat you as if you were an ordinary woman. But I know. Tonight you are Salammbô. I love your deep, deep soul. Like her, you would be capable of such devotion to an ideal that you would sacrifice your love. Would you sacrifice me to an ideal?"

"No, because you are that ideal," I answered.

That night Hugh loved me because he believed he had seen all the beauties in my soul; he loved all beauty in me, through me.

He is surprised because I laugh oftener and no longer silently. "Until now," he said, "you had a fear of life. You were a fatalist. Have I made you confident?"

"You have made me believe."

"The joy of our life together is healing you."

"You have made me happy."

I know why families were created, with all their imperfections. They humanize you. They are made to make you forget yourself occasionally, so that the beautiful balance of life is not destroyed. When the labor of art obsesses you, when creation and thought isolate you and congeal your heart, they come with petty requests and little tyrannies totally unrelated to your mind's life—and you take care of their colds, shop with them, help them with their hobbies, tolerate their intrusions, and you live their life with them for a little while.

Still, Hugh and I remain willfully isolated most of the time. We are individuals. The world stands there, and we here. We are alone by choice, by temperament, and because that is the only way we can live. One man has convinced us of the reality of such a life: Unamuno.[1] We are now forever given to it.

August 7. Thinking about my essay: I am a little fearful of starting with such "high-brow" stuff—I may never be given another chance! I would like to follow this first one by studies of Loti,

[1] *Miguel de Unamuno y Jugo, Spanish philosopher and writer.*

Stendhal, Lamartine and the *Philosophe sous les Toits*. All of them would be united by one idea: that of having a definite philosophy of life.

I have a passion for direct and swift writing and a great impatience for detail. This way I often find truth and vividness, but what I say does not seem very clear to others.

Have I talent for criticism? I have read somewhere that it is "un don, un tact, un flair, une intuition, un instinct."[1]

August 10. Instead of working on my essay, I write Horace a letter. Silly thing to do—to try and force him to understand us better by the persuasion of the pen. I am softer with him than he deserves, but that is my way, and it always fails. It changes nothing, except that it makes people ashamed of themselves, more determined to earn the pleasure of coming to me with their confidences and winning forgiveness. Hugh alone is growing taller than my expectations. Straight, clear-headed in business, soft and kind at home and understanding all. We are reading together an author who will deeply influence us. Unamuno. Of all men, he most clearly represents our desires and the philosophy for which we have hungered. For me it is an answer to all uncertainties and the end of all seeking.

August 12. There was trouble last night when the Humorous Banker criticized my newly rewritten essay. He discovered three things: that I cannot do objective writing; that when I leave personal writing and adopt a form, it becomes deadened; and that I have gained a new power in my writing which first showed itself in my letter to Horace (which, by the way, proved quite a success). This power Hugh describes as "incisive and vivid, and direct." Unfortunately, there is no trace of it in my essay. But how can I be personal forever? And why should I be interesting only when I am personal?

The High Place has a peculiar effect on me. Nothing up here has the power to worry me, even the death of my essay. If I can't write, I'll dance!

I was just remembering a visit I received from a Swedish lady with a letter of introduction. She is the head of therapy in a hospital in New York, a mature woman with cold, unflinching blue eyes and extreme theories about birth control. She left her

[1] *A gift, a feeling, etc.*

husband in New York and came to enjoy a vacation in Europe, paid with her own money. When she left me I realized I had been impressed by her character, that her fearlessness of life pleased me, that I admired her control and her steadiness, and just for a moment life appeared to me exactly like her eyes—something clear, hard, simple, practical, steady, absolutely devoid of soul and of tragedy. Only for a moment, and then I sank again into black, ageless depths. But now I have no fear. I am fighting cold and criticism and many other monsters. For days I have felt no tyrannical moods. Unamuno alone could understand, for he has described my feeling: "I am serious and happy."

August 13. This morning there is no wind in the High Place, and there is no fever in me. I read for two hours about Meredith, read broodingly and took many notes, and as soon as I had finished I began to fret because I was wasting time and doing nothing myself. This rigorous conscience I condemned in Richard, and I just discovered it in myself. Why *must* I write? I love work. I detest idleness. I detest an empty, purposeless life. I have a passionate desire to create. But none of these things are within one's control, and my war against nothingness is childish. The truth is that I am unhappy when I merely live without giving. Yet I should face the fact that I have nothing in particular to give and realize that I am made to *appreciate* keenly, to listen intelligently, to feel things thoroughly, and that is all. I cannot admit this. I dream now of a play, now of an essay—dead things both.

Before falling asleep last night I made a curious mental inventory of the little things which deceived me into believing myself an artist. When we first arrived in New York, we went to a nearby parochial school. I had had barely six months of English when there was a competitive essay on Columbus, which I won. I had written it on a bench in Central Park while watching Joaquin at play. I remember distinctly the image I had of Columbus in his ship, approaching America, and the joy with which I strove to reproduce this image and the feelings it gave me with words that were new to me and which I weighed carefully. I won a very small statue of the Virgin, to be carried in a pocket. Then in public school, a year or so later, there was a contest for a composition on "Why We Should Buy Liberty Bonds." Mine was the best. I won $5 and had to read it to younger classes. But before this I had attracted the attention of my English teacher by smaller, daily tasks. Then later, at Columbia, I carried off the highest marks. The teacher called me to his office, questioned me on my reading and gave me extra help. In between, I sold two poems to magazines. Such little, little signs! But there was the faith of Hugh, Eugene and Richard. Faith! I have it, too, some days, but I have fears more often that, like Amiel, I should write nothing but my Journal.

August 15. Delicious day. I rewrote my entire essay without looking at the old copy, and it was alive and strong. I cannot force my writing. It is as willful and as independent as I am myself. I have to let it come. It came.

I walked down eight floors very lightly when lunchtime came, but I did not forget to dress and powder for the Humorous Banker. No essay will ever make up for unattractiveness. And this was Saturday, the lovely, merry, free Saturday for which we wait 5 days.

On Saturday, Hugh's ringing of the bell has a special character. It announces the beginning of a holiday. He is coming not for a visit but for good. We sit down by the long table to a quieter, longer lunch, served as usual by a flushed and respectful Clementine—respectful because the lord is home, the true master of the house. I am nothing, contrary to American standards. I am even supposed to fear His wrath if the soup is burned or if the butter is forgotten. The dinner is cooked to please Him. He is asked to pronounce upon the taste of it. And Clementine honestly believes that it depends on Him whether I keep her or not.

Hugh enjoys this prestige and fully lives up to it. In the end I am impressed myself by his importance. Besides, I am too Latin not to admire a European husband, and I secretly admire dignity, authority. I like to see a man of character at the head of a table and at the head of a house, provided that in intimacy he shows the greatest weakness for me and the greatest softness.

But this is Saturday, and it is forbidden to be serious. While we eat, we wonder what we shall do with our afternoon.

"Should we continue to visit Paris? Shall we see Le Marais or Cluny?"

"Wouldn't you prefer the quays and picking up old books?"

"Do you want to go to the library and then take a walk in the Bois?"

"Well . . . let us first rest a little while in the High Place."

"Good idea."

The afternoon is *climatically* perfect. We rest, we read, we lie in the sun in the wicker armchairs. We talk. We examine the view. And we remain there all afternoon. And then we have a quiet dinner downstairs and we come up again and sit talking and watching the sun set behind the hill of St. Symphorien until bedtime.

Every morning now we awake to a sight of sky alone. The air is pure and sweet. Hugh takes his exercises on the terrace and I look at his profile against the clouds from my warm, comfortable bed. He cannot make me rise in the mornings to do them, but we do them together at night. I stand before him in my pyjamas, and my "cuteness" distracts him from his grave purpose. My short curls used to flutter, but my hair is completely different now. It had to follow the change in my character. It is half cut, and I part it in the middle and wear it absolutely straight, down to below the ears. There it curves over towards my cheek. The back half, which has retained its old length, is tied in a feminine way pre- cisely to hold a Spanish comb and to escape the ugly modern shaved neck. The effect is more classical, more serious. My brow is free, and there is nothing fluffy and curly and young any more. It is the kind of coiffure which harmonizes with maturity and with ancient jewelry. It pleases Hugh, and is not that the aim of my existence?

But I was speaking of Sunday morning. We visited Old Paris —the Hôtel de Sens near the Quai des Célestins, the Place des Vosges, Rue des Francs-Bourgeois.

After lunch, we came up to the High Place. Always the High Place. It means peace and books and sunshine. It is so clear today that I can almost count the houses on Montmartre, Sacre Coeur shines white, and below us the cemetery is full of visitors and as colorful as a garden.

The face of Paris is beautiful, but it loses in beauty when you know its true character. I try always to admire it plastically, re- gardless of its significance, but it is seldom that I can see the features without the spirit that lies behind them. Its coloring, its regularity, are perfect, but the expression is ugly.

I leaned over to examine the cemetery. The corner near us belongs to the Jews. There are no crosses on the graves, but many little stones are laid there by visitors. I would like to know why. From our studio we see only the ivied wall. I know too little about death to feel sadness.

We are absolutely alone these days. Our families are away.

Mother in Hendaye, the Guilers in England and my Aunt Julia in Switzerland; half of the Parisians are on vacation, and Frances Hyde is in Brittany. The letters of introduction have not upset our life now for two long weeks. This solitude is necessary occasionally, necessary and restful. I feel that we are gathering strength for the winter. I am so happy, so relaxed, so poised. I love solitude —this kind of solitude, with Hugh at my side reading. I love calm. I like this Eastern escape from desire and the southern softness in the air. I like to sit here looking at the very little, very insignificant details of our life instead of thinking what lies behind its simple appearances. Softness, warmth, disarm my energy, dissolve my will and soothe my body. Our white house with its square roof looks like the palace of Salammbô in Carthage. But I am not Salammbô, I am an indolent Spanish wife.

August 18. I sit in the studio waiting for Frances in my chiffon lavender dress. I have been good. I have attended to the house. I have arranged flowers in the vases. I keep cheerful and practical and tame. But as usual, secretly, I would rather run away. I would rather be up in the High Place writing. I want Hugh as a companion, or else to be alone. When I am alone, then I am lonely. But why cannot I find more people like Hugh?

Yesterday he said: "I could not be true to an ordinary marriage. I am true to you, to you." And I answered: "I never want you to be true to marriage, to be true as a duty—never. What is more, if you ever find someone more fitted to make you happy, I want you to feel free to love her. I shall never hold you."

This makes Hugh angry. "Don't talk like that," he always says sharply. He likes it better when I threaten to kill him the day he ceases loving me! He likes an exchange of tyrannies and jealousies. Our love is certainly not modern. We find no satisfying descriptions of it except in poetry. Hugh begs me to write my own descriptions, but I cannot, I truly cannot.

August 20. Spent 3 hours awake last night because I did not feel well, and during those three hours I thought of *everything*. Frances is staying through the winter. That means social life. I wish Horace might fall in love with her and marry her—I like her enough for that. Then she would not be lonely anymore or need me. And neither would Horace need us. We are happiest alone. Nobody else can understand what makes us happy, what amuses us, what pleases us. Eugene has been the only exception. He would understand everything. He would enjoy sitting with us in the High Place to read Unamuno. Unamuno is affecting Hugh deeply. He says Unamuno has the philosophy he has always sought. Horace would laugh if we gave him the book. The title alone, *The Tragic Sense of Life*, would seem characteristic of us and of our life, which he does not understand.

I'm glad Hugh thinks exactly as I do about it. How alike we are. We love the same books, the same people, the same ideas, the same pleasures, the same plays and walks and places. Both of us are jealous, dependent on the other, lonely with other people, serious but happy, free only with each other. We travel well together, we dance well together, we talk so pleasurably together, we enjoy our home, music and people like Erskine.

If anything happened to our love, it would be unnatural and could not last. It would be a moment of utter madness, because it includes everything whose lack has driven others into unfaithfulness. We have passion, we have harmony, we have enough contrast in our temperaments to amuse each other, we have patience for each other's faults, faith in each other, the desire to care for each other.

Enric, who used to think me cold, and Eduardo, who did not believe me human—if they could see me when I come down to dance for Hugh in the evenings, dressed in the ways which please him, to dance and rouse his desires, to tease and tempt and give.

August 27. Modern life does not affect us very much. In some ways, Hugh and I are feeling more and more detached from it, and we laughingly comment upon the fact that we are growing old. Four years ago, I could dance at a college dance quite successfully. Today, what would become of me? I don't drink cocktails, I don't smoke. I don't dance the Charleston. A flat failure! And we don't play bridge, we don't own a radio, we don't use slang profusely—in fact, we really attempt to talk intelligibly. We don't take a broad-minded and indifferent view of marriage. We have a phonograph, yes, on which we play violin pieces and tangos and a few of the jazz pieces in which there remains a trace of melody. I alter fashion to suit my own character. Hugh does not wear golf suits and checkered socks and checkered sweaters and checkered ties. We don't sacrifice everything to own an automobile.

As for politics, modern history, I know an impressive amount of things about Coolidge, about the French government, about exchange, about the debt question, about fascism and anarchy and communism, and more and more about banking.

If only Hugh would finish Unamuno's book. I am growing impatient. Today I asked him if it was not time to have Horace again.

"I couldn't stand him just now, not while I'm reading this book. You won't either, so we will have to invite him when I have finished it and before you begin it."

Next week I shall know and understand everything. Meanwhile, I work at different things. I am making a copy of Hugh's notes on Italy to encourage him in his writing, copying things out of my own journal and lengthening them, and struggling over the first paragraph of my essay, which, like the first phrase of a conversation, seems rather awkward and fatally important. In between, I read two books. Hugh Walpole, in his *Dark Forest*, gives a very impressive and vivid image of the war and some interesting descriptions of Russians. But I suspect a melodramatic quality, which, as a Latin, I am not so very sharp at discovering—at least, not as sharp as my Hugh. If I have changed him, he has influenced me too.

I have taught him independence of thought, the habit of self-reliance, and strengthened him in will and decision. But he has taught me more important things: the value of *facts* as a foundation, the importance of knowledge, and how to recognize good English writing. I was and remain an *outsider* in English. That is exactly where Hugh helps me. He is so quick to detect cheapness, mediocrity, banality, sentimentalism, falseness, affectation.

In *The Tale of Genji*, by Lady Muraski, I find a thinly disguised imitation of a French novel.[1] A man falls into various women's arms with remarkable facility and nonchalance, and women seem to abound who are always quite ready for this amusing occupation.

The face I stare at every night while I brush my hair is changing. Sweetness, so overpowering before, is holding a less steady reign. Extreme innocence has completely disappeared. The eyes no longer question with owllike fixity and swim in weak distress before everything; they open steadily and more knowingly. My mouth does not regret, but it is often amused, ironic, tolerant, or set and

[1] *A.N. seems to be unaware that* The Tale of Genji *was written in the 11th century.*

firm. There is nothing left of the idiotic angel; there is now more humanity, more will. This winter I would like to see if I can receive all experience without stumbling.

August 30. Saturday morning I had begun to work when Hugh called me up to tell me that Countess G. was very ill. I was there beside her in a short time, but she was asleep, having been given an injection to calm her pain. There was nothing for me to do but wait in case she should wake and need me. So I went to Horace's room and took a book out of his bookcase and sat on an armchair by the window. There was, of course, a new photograph of a new lady on his night table. He had been reading *The History of Florence* and the fat book lay in a corner with a paper cutter in the middle of it. The wallpaper was ugly and so were the curtains and the pillows on the divan, but there were fine paintings on the walls. I could not imagine Frances adapting herself to this background—modern, brittle, simple Frances, who had thought the whole apartment "horrible." No. It is not all horrible—not after you have seen certain things against their true background, and not when you know the beauty of certain pieces of furniture and of the paintings.

And would Frances share Horace's love of Dante, and of Florence? And would pictures of new ladies keep appearing on his night table while she was there? And could she give Horace's mother all the attention she loves? Frances, symbolically, would not fit in Horace's life. She would not understand his complexities, his wanderings, his fickleness, his fluidity, his "evaporations."

That morning Horace's character interested me more than my lemon-colored book. Towards twelve o'clock my watching was justified. Mrs. G. began to awake slowly, and I was there to hold her fevered hand and to smooth her pillow. While I sat there soothing her, Mr. G. and Horace arrived.

I was not needed anymore. Horace wanted to take me to the trolley stop, so we walked down the sunny avenue, talking about his mother, about my suit, which he thought very becoming, about my letter, which he wanted to answer. He seemed elated about something or other. I discovered it was because of my kind forgiveness of him.

"Your letter was very good, but of course, I don't agree with you. You should not take anything I say seriously." That is his eternal phrase. But his eyes said more: "No matter what I say, what I do, you must not mind. I really cannot help it. I can't live up to what you think. I'm sorry."

The same old prayer. Eduardo, Enric—all the weaker ones— the artists, the poets, with flickering wills. "You cannot judge me as other men. I am special, special."

Their eyes beg for softness. I always give it. That morning I gave it to Horace, too. But something happened to me at the same moment. I saw *through* them all. Love them, pity them, help them, yes, but my truest love should go to the nobler man—to Hugh, who never fails, who never needs forgiveness, who works faithfully and disciplines himself, who controls his whims and his weaknesses, who strives to attain, who advances unflinchingly.

I told all this to the Modern Knight. He said quietly: "You would never have said this a year ago." And then he caressed my hand.

All my sins date from a year or so ago. What are all these changes? The most startling is my awakening to the sensousness of love. My senses were dead before and my flesh cold, but today, hour by hour, I become more woman, and I feel very deep desires running through my blood. My body is very warm now, very sensitive, and all these currents of a deeper, burning life pass from my flesh into my thoughts, to vivify them, to humanize them, as my Love has melted my coldly sleeping senses.

There were other sins. My distress at ugliness and my diffidence among people. Yesterday I passed through another trial and triumphed. A year ago we had been invited to ride with Monsieur E. from the Bank, a Frenchman I sat by his side in the car, surrounded by intimidating monsters—his cynicism, first of all, his sensuality, his crudity and his utter indifference to the things Hugh and I love. Conversation came with difficulty, and I was tense, strained, miserable. For a year I evaded a renewal of this experience. Finally it could no longer be evaded—the weather was beautiful, relatives were gone, Hugh's health was good now—no more excuses.

It *was* a beautiful day—cool and sunny, with autumn's coloring everywhere. I wore my lavender chiffon dress, a flimsy, soft, quivering dress of the very Parisian air, with a lavender hat. Monsieur E. arrived. I met him with great ease and naturalness and took my place in front by his side while Hugh stretched his long legs comfortably on the back seat.

It was a long, enjoyable ride, interrupted by lunch in Sens.

We chatted very easily. We talked about the past war, about the possibilities of a future one, about President Wilson. Last year, Wilson was mentioned in connection with debauchery—which afterwards brought on a scene in a discussion with Hugh. This year, there was another story on the same subject. We also talked about women in general, about people from the bank: "Mr. So-and-So had a little friend whom he was getting tired of. . . ." As we passed through a village, two women sunning on their door-steps brought out this description: "Deux poules en retraite!"[1]

I understood all. I brought my share of teasing and joking. Nothing *distressed* me. All that is gone. Prostitution, etc. is merely a cold fact which I accept like rain. Crude things *exist*—I know now. Enough that they are not in my life, that is all.

Tolerance, indifference—kindness, even—for Monsieur E. I even found a quality to admire: his unswerving patriotism. The national spirit is the only instinct in him not killed by cynicism; it is his only fervor and the only thing for which he would give up his life. That is something in a man. I hope he invites us out again.

We had supper by candlelight in the blue-and-white kitchen. Hugh was enthusiastic about everything: "You have never looked so beautiful before—so poised, so clever. You were so different a year ago."

Monsieur E. saw a difference too. He *noticed* me. While we were having tea in a chalet in the heart of the Fontainebleau forest, he gave me a long, cold-blooded, up-and-down examination, in which he took in everything. When he had finished, I almost asked: "Well, you usually like them a little fatter, no?"

In Mont-St.-Michel one evening we settled the matter of our future. Life is softer here, easier, and more enjoyable because of the traveling we can do, but it leads us nowhere in the desire to build our life on a solid foundation. Hugh, is, above all, ambitious. He wants financial independence; we want travel but with full freedom, and I want Hugh ultimately to leave the bank while yet strong and young. To have that, we must return to New York. And we will return as soon as we can. We have traveled, and we have aged. But you can't go on traveling forever and getting old without risking the poorhouse. And then there is the future war that looks so inevitable. Monsieur E. is right: "With all your laws, you cannot keep a family from quarreling—from killing each

[1] *Two retired broads.*

other occasionally. How can you prevent nations? You can't change human nature."

I never knew I would talk as much and hear as much politics, for I always hated it. I cannot look at it yet with composure. Ignorance exasperates me, injustice makes me boil, intrigue gives me a fever, and dishonesty enrages me. And as I am really trying to get stronger, none of these things are good for me.

It is like the Parisian. I cannot write about him and his city with equanimity. He is in the most complete sense "un gamin de la rue,"[1] with whom I don't know how to deal. If you smile at him, he robs you. If you beat him, he smiles.

The Modern Knight said that he would be home early because it was such a beautiful day. He will abandon his war against Bad Loans and will put away his Credit Folders and dismiss his stenographer earlier than usual. Sometimes the business of making money for your home and wife seems like a gigantic mistake in which you waste the best moments of your life. When we go to New York, I want to help him, as it will all finish sooner and we can take a holiday together.

I used to laugh at Capital letters, but sometimes they are really useful to distinguish things from ordinary words.

September 10. The other evening Horace, Hugh and I sat in the High Place and made our peace. Horace said: "I have passed through a crisis this winter. I was fighting against the self which resembles you, and as you represented that self, my struggle was directed against you. You were too absolute in wanting me to be that self to the exclusion of the other. I was too absolute in wishing to unite the two things I cared for by mixing you up, against your will, with my 'party life.' But now I understand everything. I must have both lives. I belong equally to both. I want you and I want my parties!"

"But not together," we insisted.

"No, not together."

A few nights before, he had had a party at his house—with a vulgar English girl, a faded chorus girl, an American couple "out for a good time," Frances, and miscellaneous men. They were all drunk, and danced, flirted and quarreled until 5 in the morning.

With us Horace was enjoying the peace and freshness of the night. Hugh was silent and still intolerant, but Horace shrewdly

[1] *A street urchin.*

guessed that I was not and said, "Anaïs understands me better—she is softening. It seems to me that she is becoming more like me." I did not protest. Hugh's face was grim and unhappy.

When we were alone, he said, "Now that at last I have become as you wished me to be, are *you* going to change?"

"My darling, never. But I do believe in intolerance for one's self and tolerance for others. I no longer will fight against the impossible, as you once laughed at me for doing. But remember, I understand Horace and am soft on his weaknesses, but I don't *admire* him. I admire you, you who are strong and noble and absolute. And it is only you I love." The grimness left his face, and he was deeply happy.

Frances, too, I am patient with, though she falters constantly. She is afraid of sadness, she has no philosophy, no depth whatever, but a certain wisdom born out of much rough contact with life, shrewdness; her eyes laugh constantly, she is sweet, determined, a little thoughtless and superficial, a devotee of the humorous outlook, and she tires me like a child who wants to play all the time. But for the moment, seeing her is as inevitable as seeing a relative, because she needs me, because Eduardo entrusted her to me, because her knowledge of life charms me, because I feel helpless before her invasions. In short, I like her. I seldom wriggle out of our appointments together. Hugh calls our visits my "bridge parties," with a frown, but in a few days he is going to play *golf* with a business partner. The man is uninteresting, but Hugh likes him because he is a good banker and a just and friendly businessman. So there! How I detest these compromises!

September 19. Yesterday was a sacred day. Hugh and I sat talking together in the evening, I on a pillow on the floor with my head on his knees, and for the first time I understood my Love's great wisdom. He was the first to wake me from my imaginative life and to take me into the real world. He made me human—but why? So that I might be a stronger and truer mystic. And now, with his guidance, I am to unite the two, to reach one through the other instead of separating them. My trial is over. I understand. We are at last completely united spiritually because of this knowledge.

My wise, deep-running Hugh, with all his mysterious longings, explained and justified his hardness and what I termed his cruelty. I know now it was only an effort to reveal things to me. We have a secret. When we look at each other now, our eyes do not question, do not seek, do not plead. They assert a conscious knowledge, a knowledge that makes our life extraordinarily beautiful.

September 21. Belated summer days, efforts to build up physical strength, no writing, much dreaming, intolerable moods which drive me out into the street, loneliness. Fear of the High Place, where I am alone with my ideas, alone with my hate of Paris.

Both of us taken by the moving-picture fever, begun by seeing *The Black Pirate*, which drove us to seeking other wonders and ended in disgust after seeing *Bossu*,[1] *L'Abbé Constantin*,[2] and *La Neuvaine*,[3] a distortion of the book [by Colette].

Yesterday we went to the tailor's to order a suit for the Cat. I felt happy after the evening of our talk, happy but restless. What is wrong with me? Why the aching desire when I saw the costumes in the Printemps—jeweled headdresses and Oriental veils and Spanish dresses and Russian gowns. I believe it is a struggle between my imaginings and my physical limitations. I wondered about this, and then forgot to wonder in order to think about the Cat, who was standing before me being measured for his green suit and wanting to know my opinion. Well, my life is useless, but it is not mine—it is his. And because it is his, I find it easier to work on it, to try and make something of it.

September 22. I find in Pirandello for the first time the convictions so dear to me of the reality of acting. He alone could understand that when I think of life as a play, it is more real to me than life itself because the play is a concentration and an intensification of life as movement, uninterrupted by details which do not matter. Thus a perfectly lived life *is* a play. That is why I believe in the fashioning of events, in the power of the author, in the importance of the idea behind the movement, in consciousness of what is going on and its meaning.

And to come down to the details of a play, that is why I believe in the setting, in the furniture, jewelry and costumes. That is why I believe in the exclusion of puerile actors, in shutting off all foreign and hampering material, in eliminating the action which diverges and wanders from the central theme; and that is

[1] *Hunchback.*
[2] *The Abbot Constantin.*
[3] *The Novena.*

why I believe in excluding the people who spoil the play, who giggle at the wrong moments, who think of other things while it is going on, who *interrupt*, who pervert the theme and destroy its significance.

And why, someone might ask, should I give so much importance to My Play? If Pirandello had effaced himself before Shaw, we would have lost Pirandello. But Pirandello lives and Shaw lives, too, and we possess both and they are both important. Each one of us carries the germ of a new personality, and it can only be a personality if we attend to it instead of idly watching our neighbor's play.

Evening. Waiting for the Cat in the early gloom of shorter days. How I love the summer and how little I have had of it— exactly two months of loveliness in a year, and of that, two weeks of warmth. And it is already winter.

Mother, Joaquin and Antonio will arrive at the beginning of October. The Spanish dancing teacher is still on her vacation. Meanwhile, I gather energy for all of them, I force myself to keep calm and not too busy, which is the most difficult thing in the world for me to do. Impossible to sit still for hours—I must write, read, sew, walk, see and hear things, and all the while things buzz and ferment in my head; lying in bed for a rest means such a desperate attack of thinking that I am forced to rise and begin to do something again.

I listen for his long footsteps. He is everything to me now. I love him much more than in the first or second year. I look up to him. I need him. It has taken time for me to know him because he talks so little. But as soon as I know more, he grows more, and I have to tiptoe again and draw him out patiently, draw out those quiet thoughts he thinks so secretly and silently, a much deeper, slower, more thorough revelation of the ideas which I reach earlier, quicker and less deeply.

I think in the beginning I looked down a little on his slowness and his occasional literalness and rationalism, his obstinate thoroughness and carefulness, but of the two ways, his and mine, I have come to admire his the most.

October 2. Even He disappoints me. In the end his love of the body will estrange us. I have followed his as far as I can. I have become deeply sensuous and physically sensitive. I have danced for him, invented ways of mingling stories, imaginings, the loves of others, with our own love, intensifying, multiplying it. And I thought he was now different from other men. Of course he isn't. He has been exalted for days by Hindu tales in which sensuous love is made incredibly beautiful, and then he goes to his tailor, and while waiting contentedly examines the photographs of Revue women, a display of obvious, unpoetic, coarsely beckoning nakedness. And a few hours after he wants to play with my own body, a desire created probably by the sight of the others, so that I am confused with them in his mind, probably compared.

No, I cannot understand, I cannot accept. I believed in him above all men. If he fails, I can no longer love him—his body will disgust me. I need and believe in love as the "poetry of sex"— sex without love I hate.

Evening. He is reading not far from me. I have forgiven, consoled, made little of it all, caressed him, but *something* is changed in *me*.

Antonio is here. Mother arrives tomorrow with Joaquin and Tio Enrique and Tia Julia. What an end to our spiritually and physically perfect summer. What a way to begin a winter of blind- ing activities—no more dreaming, no more long talks and unin- terrupted companionship. Perhaps it is better so. Thinking is a curse. It serves only to discover ugliness.

October 11. Lying on the couch in the studio with tonsillitis. My sadness is over. Hugh understood, regretted, is pure again and has all my love.

Mother arrived with Joaquin—many days of talk, readjust- ment, surprises and noise. I was spoiled with a small Basque coffer and table linen. The best present of all was a short part in Joaquin's journal, in which I found that I meant something to him and had the power to influence and help him. He is taller, with eyes that shine more than ever, large, intense, feverish. We have had intimate talks; he came to sit at the foot of the couch to talk about his work. He is studying now. Mother is shopping. Tia Julia pursues her interest in cabarets, but without us.

Antonio's health is bad, and he is unhappy, lonely, more childish and weak than I believed him, pitiable.

No writing done since the days spent in the High Place. But I read—Fannie Hurst's *Appassionata*, a revelation in style and ideas which I am obliged to admire. It is new blood flowing through an anemic literature, destroying the last vestiges of pale conven- tionality, tradition, familiar words. Her idea of pity, of course, entrances me. It will be my salvation, my only link with a life I am too anxious to despise, the only feeling which can conquer my rebellion, my cruel criticism, my disgust, my obsessions. *Dark Laughter*, by Sherwood Anderson, is pleasing, too, though *too* incoherent and harsh, inferior to *Appassionata*, which contains a beautiful character.

I am again preoccupied with my reticence. The largest part of my life is secret, even from Hugh. Here and there a writer uncovers my thoughts with more courage than I have.

October 14. Sick in bed with the grippe which followed the tonsillitis. Time to think about everything, though I seem to have always more time to think than to live stupidly, as a doctor advised the Tzarina of Russia to do for her health: "Vivre bêtement"—a healthy thing, a joyous thing, a blessing.

Tia Julia, and a million others—"vivent bêtement." Action, impulse, *indifference*, selfishness, thoughtlessness; it is very simple. Cursed are the thinkers, the men with scruples, pity, vulnerability . . . and the idealists.

I did not need the grippe to think, then, but it served me well against the invasion of social duties. With Mother as the most dangerous leader, I was almost caught. In a week, a theatre party, a lunch, an evening reception, an afternoon tea, a visit—and in these seemingly harmless things, the danger of *multiplication*, which is the joy of the society worshiper.

"At the house of So-and-So, I met Mrs. So-and-So, who invited me to tea. And *she* wants me to meet the famous Mrs. X.!"

All this terrifies me, kills me. In spite of my newly acquired poise, I do not talk very much, and I am tortured by the passionate longing to run away. Besides, now I have a right to run away. Before, Mother had need of these people, and I owed them *gratitude*. Today, I owe them nothing. I am free. I exult in this freedom. I even turn away from my relatives.

They helped Mother in exchange for slavery. They paid with money for the right to criticize our clothes, occupations, ideas and marriages.

I owe this freedom to Hugh and love him for it.

My grippe does not interfere with their plans, and so Mother and Joaquin are out to lunch with relatives, and my room is quiet. I recall a vivid evening as if a play were enacted again before me: Horace invited us to dinner at his house to meet a friend of his.

I did not want to go—have I ever willingly gone forward to meet a new person? I almost missed knowing Hugh that way, Eugene, Horace.

But I also evaded the acquaintance of faded chorus girls, an American woman who is always drunk, another in pursuit of a "good time," and other objects in Horace's collection.

What is right? Because I have Hugh now, I suppose I have no more doubts or fears of missing anything. It is a question of arithmetic. Horace takes *all* the chances; I, none. I live more with abstract things and divide devotion among few people—a *concentrated* devotion.

But I was speaking of Horace's evening. R. was a man of Hugh's age, long and thin with curly hair and sharply chiseled face and long sickly hands hanging limply from the wrist. He had temperament, culture, effeminate mannerisms, which suggested Freud, whom I have not read, and Proust, whom I hope not to read again. Both of these influences he admitted to during the course of the evening.

We sat in Horace's room by the log fire, Mr. R. and I nearest the heat, Horace balancing himself on his desk chair, and Hugh quietly smoking. We talked about the senses. Each of us mentioned the one most keenly developed. R. loved to *touch* things, and as he said this his shivery, restless hands became significant. "The touch of velvet, of old silks . . ."

Horace chose the sense of smell—rooms, women, perfumes, dead leaves, incense, wine, coffee. Hugh and I, vision—I spoke of the color of things, their shape, but Hugh did not continue. He felt other things which he could not describe, and I guessed—love, akin to touch; hair to caress; mouth and tongue and their secret, immense joys.

R. sat shrunk in his armchair with feverish eyes. Horace was casual but charmingly and surprisingly *decided* about his ideas, siding with me against R.

We discussed da Vinci. R. spoke of his bisexualism—of the masculine and feminine mixed in his painting, particularly in the equivocal St. John the Baptist. He found the face of Mona Lisa sophisticated, displeasing to him, ugly, insinuating, suggestive.

"Do you mean that she expresses knowledge of evil?"

"Oh, let us not get involved in morals," said R.

"But sophistication must include knowledge of evil," I insisted. "She cannot be *knowing* without it."

He cast shadows over da Vinci's life and purpose.

"You could not feel that way if you had read his life by Merezhkovski," said Horace and I simultaneously, and a look of sympathy passed between us while R. sent out Freudian fumes to confuse us, but in vain.

Inconsistently, R. preferred Michelangelo's simplicity. "He is elemental," I said. They caught the word and used it to continue.

In conversation, that is my only gift. I always give the exact word, I prevent others from stumbling, from hesitation, and I dispel vagueness. I have much less knowledge, but I help them to bring out theirs and to vivify it.

Hugh is slower to expose ideas, more content to listen sympathetically, occasionally forcible and honest in his statements, slightly annoying to men like R. He is vague in his language, though his understanding is deep. Men like R. think him less intelligent, but I know he is *more* intelligent, and it is a question of rhythm—ideas not born simultaneously with utterance.

We talked much of painting. R. was interested in the baroque style, where painting is not suggestive, but final in its expressions and exaggerated. To close this subject, he classified me as belonging to the first half of the 19th century, being a perfect reproduction of Madame de Récamier by Ingres, his favorite at the Louvre.

Then one evening we saw the Chauve-Souris,[1] invited by Count Guicciardi, and sat in a box with Horace and an American lady. Thrilling production—passing from tragedy to the comic in the only way that ever pleases me. Faces beautifully expressive, voices delightful, movements graceful, spirit witty and colorful.

Horace had given me an impression of harmony, and suddenly it was all destroyed again. He chose a noisy, sociable, empty, stupid vacation instead of Florence and solitude. I feel like using Sherwood Anderson's suggestive *dots* and no more.

October 18. Joaquin moving in the society I knew so well as a girl—the rich and idle Cubans. He played for them with much success and gifts of money (6,000 frs.), very much appreciated and very much deserved by my bewildered and happy brother.

I refused to go to the reception. It would seem different today with my opened eyes. Long ago, it was a fairylike thing, in which I read my own meaning—the pleasure of being loved and courted,

---

[1] *Strauss's* Die Fledermaus.

the joy of dancing. The people remained shadows. My imagination transformed them. I shall see one of the shadows Thursday. He was then a Personage, a Marquis,[1] who danced exquisitely, with whom it was a pleasure to have tea and to sit out under the palms on lovely evenings. A woman guesses at such things—he loved me, I am sure. I would have been a Marquise!

October 19. Enric Madriguera is here! He came to see us last night with his mother. He has changed. He is strong, determined, and much handsomer. The roguishness of his character is more emphatic. He showed me a drawing of my head which he had made from memory some time ago. His hands, which I had forgotten, impressed me with their sensitiveness. One cold winter night in Richmond Hill we were crossing a field on our way home and Enric had asked permission to put his right hand in the pocket of my thick warm white sweater. "I am cold," he said. I let him, but I withdrew my own hand. For that withdrawn hand he has never quite forgiven me. Last night he looked at me now indifferently, not sentimentally, and I could see that the indifference was not real. He remembers everything. I do, too, but I regret nothing.

And the Cat, watching everything, said brusquely: "How the devil did you get to look so well suddenly?"

This morning he woke me with numerous long, stifling kisses.

The winter will be full. I shall have all I desire—life, love, peace, writing, music, dancing, and intelligent friends—Horace, Enric, Antonio. I will continue my war against "la vie et les gens bêtes,"[2] against bad health, against false, ugly and weak things.

October 22. Walking down the Boulevard Saint Michel; I did not want to come out. I am afraid of the cold. So early, and it is dark. The people's faces are hidden in their coat collars. The street lights are blinking. I walk very lightly, very swiftly, but the wind is swifter and lighter and I feel it pushing me. There is a leaden mist over things, and the automobile horns are slightly muffled. It all reminds me of two years ago when we first arrived, of the terrible chill I felt . . . Parisian winter . . . there is nothing sadder. In New York winter is white, blue and gold. In Paris it is gray and black and wet.

[1] *The Marquis de Avilés.*
[2] *A stupid life and stupid people.*

Mother mocked my desire to stay at home. "Tu veux devenir une fleur exotique—une fleur des pays chauds."[1]

I don't want to, but I *am*. But Hugh said I should conquer cold. Breathe deeply, straighten yourself, you weak thing. Conquer the cold, conquer the chill, fear not the grayness, be strong.

Home! I sink among the brilliant pillows on the divan near the "poêle"[2] . . . softness, warmth, peace . . .

October 26. Joaquin and I had a happy talk through the Rue des Saint Pères and Rue Bonaparte, arm in arm, stopping to flatten our noses on the windowpanes of antique shops, thrilled by the same things, mingling talk about life, books, music and interior decoration with discussions about Antonio. The trouble with poor Antonio is that he is in disgrace with Mother, justly or unjustly, I cannot say—a little of both. But I am fated to be a lawyer, and I had to take Antonio's case in hand when he came to me with tears in his eyes. I had to explain him to Joaquin, Joaquin to Antonio, Mother to Joaquin, Antonio to Mother and Mother to Antonio! I succeeded in making Antonio happier and Joaquin more just. I can't change Mother, but I can slip in between her little warfares and temper her blows. With this way of soft words I have also made Mother love Hugh and Hugh understand Mother. A few months ago I was busy explaining Thorvald to Joaquin and Joaquin to Thorvald. Who am I that I can understand both my brothers, who cannot understand each other, and my family's friends better than they do themselves? And Horace better than he understands me? It is my desire for justice, my desire to understand and my detachment.

I have sometimes helped Hugh in the bank with my sudden discoveries of men's characters, those he works with, made after a moment's meeting. When I make a mistake, it is that of *always* expecting more than there is. In that, I show no discernment. I should not have spoken of detachment—that is untrue. I care a great deal for the fate of all these people. I listen and defend. So far, my affections and intuitions have never betrayed my judgment.

I have begun to write. I have set order in my papers. I have nine black book binders on my desk: "Quotations," made by Eugene, Hugh and me; "Letters," vols. 1 and 2—Richard's letters and

---

[1] *"You want to become an exotic flower—a tropical flower."*
[2] *Stove.*

mine, Joaquin's and Eugene's; "Journal Notes" made by Hugh in Italy and on other trips; "Essay" on the journal, finally condensed to five pages; "Journal" I and II—I, being the selection made for Erskine, and II, everything I ever copied out of my books; *Aline* (no description necessary); and Novel II, about the pianist Joseph and his wife, unfinished and useless. In slimmer holders I have my *Blind Men*, which I reread occasionally and cannot abandon, and several beginnings for novels, my *Chantal* being among them, only three pages, old, pathetically insistent.

My journal sometimes thrills me, when I find in it the truest writing I can give, and next to it all my other writing sounds curiously stilted. At other times I read it coldly and critically and find it sadly naïve or highly comical. When this happens, I give up the idea of writing and dream of my dancing. . . . I see myself expressing rhythms and moods and ideas so simply and yet so brilliantly, stirring desires for beauty and for life such as no words could stir, except d'Annunzio's. I love color. Words have no color. I love sound, and words have no sound in themselves. They may create both, but not as vividly as a tangible figure, moving, swaying, with a tinkling of feet and earrings, a flashing of arms and eyes . . . and the crackling castanets.

I am influenced by gaudy arts! The gentle ones, the quiet, aristocratic art of writing, the first practiced by women, if we exclude Saint Cecilia's singing, will be supplanted—unless my journal should thrill and satisfy me again.

What is to be done with such a wavering faith? The best thing, I found, was to buy a new notebook, a fresh, clean one, which tempts me. I have not changed since the time I wore braids, when a notebook given by Emilia Quintero,[1] and a later one from Eduardo, drove me to write hurriedly in the old to finish it. Fickleness, vanity, unconquered.

October 28. Certain things Joaquin plays next door disturb me deeply. I write in rhythm with the notes, but afterwards, I am dissatisfied and unhappy with the results. I am not frank yet. I have more inhibitions than my most puritan friends. Afraid to hurt people's feelings, afraid to mock, afraid to uncover ugliness—three shameful fears which silence me. And then I have vanity—for the sake of my own faith, I deceive myself about myself, and that makes some of my descriptions of character childish. Or am I still

[1] *A pianist and family friend.*

childish, really? I would give years of my life, which I love so much, to be an impersonal writer. I suffer from being too conscious of myself. Every description is turned against me, naturally, since self-knowledge is my only knowledge, and though I am convinced that I use this self-knowledge for noble ends, it hurts me like something tyrannical and obsessing.

October 29. Such little things torment me. Hugh may have to go away for two days on a visit of industrial cities. Immediately I become *bad*. I try to prove that I don't care by planning mad ways to fill the day. I have often done that. When he has gone to play golf, I have gone to three movies; I have walked all through the city, through the shops, until late, so that I might arrive home after him. The pain and restlessness of waiting alone with my cursed imagination is intolerable. If he goes, I must become hard and indifferent in order to bear it. I will go out with Horace to dance, to the theatre, to all the things I hate on ordinary days but which satisfy me in this struggle against feeling.

My sweet weekend is ruined. We have a three-day holiday, and we are going to see an artists' village near here. But all the sweetness of this little trip has gone. That is the way I am, and I have done all I can to change myself. I can reason, but I cannot control my feelings. Hugh does not know that when he leaves me physically, I leave him spiritually, in self-protection against the pain he inflicts on me. I write here because I want to be quiet and not torment him. Again, I want to be bad inwardly and in my journal, but I will show it to no one and hurt no one.

I am so convinced that *apart* from my feelings such sacrifices are wrong. The Bank is a wolf. We give it all we can to eat, in exchange for gold, but we should not give *all* our freedom because then our gold is worthless. Hugh obeys blindly. I struggle against useless sacrifices. His way of loving me is to go away bravely and forget about the sentimental part. My way of loving is to see first whether going away is absolutely necessary for our ultimate good. But I can't often explain my *reasoning* to Hugh. I can't explain it simply because I reason and cry at the same time. Hugh mistrusts me on account of the crying, because he doesn't cry. And I mistrust his reasoning *because* he never cries, never feels soon enough, but too late.

He trusted me. He understood. He was astounded at his own way of blindly accepting duty, without reasoning, because of his *racial* habit of self-control and control of feelings. He would have realized the feelings only later, perhaps when alone in the hotel room.

With tears and caresses he begged me to forgive him for not understanding me and thanked me for watching over our true happiness. Now he will go if it is absolutely *necessary*, and I shall send him away sweetly, but he must not go blindly and serve the Bank so well for the sake of our happiness that this happiness will be destroyed.

November 5. Hateful gray days—short and dark and oppressing, wrapped in mists, with a pale, powerless sun appearing occasionally through them like a mockery. You see the copper circle, but its rays cannot reach you—the fog swallows them and cuts up the warmth halfway. And to me it is even sadder to see the sun and not to feel it, to be reminded that on other worlds it shines so deliciously.

Sometimes I have no desire to rise in the morning, and often when I am resting after lunch I have no desire to rouse myself— I try hard to keep on sleeping, drowsily, because it is so dark, so lifeless, all around me.

Enric cannot stand it. He wants to go to Nice. I want to go *anywhere*, but away from loathesome Paris.

November 12. Powerless to bring an idea or an image out of this world that is full of suggestions and full of images. The city is full of sounds that tell stories, full of faces that scream tragedies, full of whispers that reveal secrets.

A man shouts every morning: "Marchand d'habits, chiffons."[1] Where does he come from, where does he sleep at night when his bag is full of rags?

The studio is quiet while life trickles into it. The bells of the cemetery, the horns, the snoring wheels, the hoarse voice of street singers. Over the roofs smoke curls out of a factory chimney. The pavement crackles with continuous footsteps, the ragman throws out his call, children laugh.

All I do is listen, listen.

John Dos Passos has affected me. I fall into his language. His *Manhattan Transfer* has haunted me for three days. Unbelievable ugliness, such power, such words, tremendous frankness, a frank-

[1] *"Ragpicker."*

ness which startles and pleases me. There are no veils in his eyes —he sees things painfully sharply, smells real smells, touches things that bleed and ideas nobody dares to touch.

November 13. I had forgotten to mention Enric's last visit. He came in a soft, reminiscent mood. We sat in the library while Mother and Mrs. Madriguera talked in the studio. He saw the photographs of our trips, and we talked about Father, about Manén,[1] Mr. Carl Hamilton,[2] the love of sunshine, the hate of society. Enric said to Hugh: "You know, I thought a lot of Anaïs."

Just before leaving, he kissed my hand and said with an irrepressible laugh: "Oh, I could not do *that* before!"

Indeed, our social laws have made him the gainer by my marriage, and he was quick to see the irony.

He has gone to Nice, seeking sunshine. Though I realize we love many things together, I understand now that this alone does not create love, as I thought before, when I was so sure that I could love only an artist and a genius.

November 22. The only sweet moments I have known lately were at Segovia's concert and on weekends when the Cat was home.

We have found a new ending to all our discussions on Paris: Things, habits, people, may be just as bad in New York, but we are *used* to them, and we can never get used to things here.

Mother sews; Joaquin studies, composes, writes in his journal and reads Amiel; Thorvald writes us descriptions of the cyclone in Havana; Richard's wife has a book of children's stories published; Horace and Frances keep each other entertained; Eugene is silent when I need him most. The Cat is loving, busy, reasonable, helpful. He scolds me occasionally, encourages me, smooths out my wrinkles with kisses, as I smooth his.

Joaquin's journal startles me; it is so much like mine at his age—"I hate bodies," "I need the faith of others," "Such a fine thing exalted me," "Such a person disappointed me," "I need to act more," "Discouragement, dreaminess, aspirations . . ."

November 23. Je deviens de plus en plus sauvage.[3] What I want most now is art and solitude.

---

[1] *Juan Manén, the concert violinist.*
[2] *Enric's patron.*
[3] *I am becoming more and more unsociable.*

My sensitiveness is doing me more harm than good. I cry at concerts, I cry in the middle of discussions when I feel the futility and injustice of everything; active rebellion was nobler than this overflow of bitterness, this outbreak of weeping, this demoralization in the face of facts. The process of hardening is certainly painful, because I want to harden without losing pity and a certain gentleness for other people.

No sooner have I escaped a tea than I am menaced by a dance, and when I have wriggled out of that, I am caught by a concert—Antonio's, which promises to be more of a social than a musical affair. Meanwhile, I cannot dance because our Budget forbids it. I cannot write because Paris depresses me. I can only help Joaquin with his problems, and Richard and others, and keep the Cat happy.

Reading and music emphasize my restlessness and my sense of failure. Segovia, the other night, wrote this phrase in my mind with his guitar: You are not an artist—you will never create. Why do you suffer then? Can you not live like others? Why do you struggle to detach yourself from the stupid life when you have no right to enter the other?

But then, why this conviction of the reality of art, why this feeling for color, for the stage, for costume, expression, gesture, for clay, for rhythms, for music, for movement, for words, for dreams? Why this exaltation at moments, these moments of marvelous faith in myself, why these secret aspirations, this responsiveness to life, this vision into the characters of others, this power of imagination working night and day, why this utter detachment from ordinary desires, ordinary friends, ordinary life, if I am not an artist?

November 26. The East is neglected by the modern crowd. Why? Because the modern spirit is scientific, cynical, energetic and worldly. America and Europe are the center of interest. Europe watches America, and America watches Europe. America is looking for maturity, poise, the power of mockery, knowledge, ancient art and civilization. Europe is looking for energy, scientific and practical advancement, financial art, formulas for material success. While they stand entranced by each other, Hugh and I will slip out unnoticed by the back door to the East.

In the East there is still a slow rhythm, poetry, a sense of beauty, religion, free emotion, dreaming, imagination, ecstasy, contemplation, impulse, a true understanding of eternal things. In the East suggestion still exists, poetry pervades clothes and gestures, nakedness and revelation are kept for love. I have seen America and Europe, and I want the East.

"Horace wants us for a party," Hugh says. "I don't want parties."

"Neither do I."

"How can we refuse him, and not offend him?"

"He should understand."

"He never will."

"And I shall have to see Frances soon," I say. "I can't delay that anymore."

"And you must call up Mrs. N. and pay her a visit."

"Keep Thursday for Mrs. C.'s tea."

Long silence. Then I speak out of a dream—

"Why could we not be so free that tonight, with all these engagements threatening us, we take our valises and go away— go to Algeria, for instance, and never come back, never see these people again?"

"Because that would be merely running away from things, and it would not solve our problems."

"Is it really wrong to run away?"

"It is wrong to run away."

We stayed to face our problems—demands of the bank, demands of friends. What is selfishness? When should one be true to human affections, when to ideals?

Last night I said to Hugh: "You must not think that I fool myself all the time, that I do not realize occasionally that you are no different from other men, that I am just like all other women, that our marriage is like other marriages, that we have our low moments, like others, that poetry and beauty are only a desire which we reach occasionally, that things are not beautiful but we try to believe they are."

"Why do you knock the bottom out of everything?"

"Because that is the only way to find the truth."

"But you know what is *true*—you know that our ideal is the truth, and truer than ourselves. If you don't believe, I shall not love you any more. . . ."

He said this so sadly that I came close to him and said my disbelief was a moment of madness, whereas I know that it is my belief which is a madness—a divine madness like religion.

I'm unhappy. I am unhappy because I know perfectly well that the cynic is a coward. He foresees all barrenness so that barrenness can never surprise him. I began life in the opposite way. I foresaw all beauty so that life could perpetually surprise and whip me. I compromised after a while, believing in nothing except *our* life and ourselves. But my faith is so immense and it is condensed into such a small space that I have moments of terrible doubts, like a man who stakes his soul and wealth and love upon one small coin.

Hugh is braver because he has no time to think. Horace is safer because he has spread himself so much that he can never lose everything at once. Joaquin is the wisest because he lives for art and loves art above all things.

I want to think and be brave at the same time. I don't want to run away. I want to receive all experience without stumbling.

November 27. Antonio's concert the other night, in spite of its extreme classicism and length, was quite successful. He is a sweetly powerful musician and there is a contradiction between his playing and his living. In life he carries out the weaker sides of Eastern philosophy—fatalism, inaction, apathy, pointless dreaming. He disdains sport, health, hygiene, physical beauty and strength and struggle and rebellion. He is calm, nerveless, sweet-tempered, obstinate, learned, unreasonable. Creation for him is a mistake and he does not thwart its plans even when they affect him. He was attracted by Joaquin's originality, by Joaquin's need of education, musical and literary, by Joaquin's talent and goodness. But now, as each displays the tendencies of his character, they become estranged. Antonio wanted to possess Joaquin exclusively, jealously. Joaquin is restless, unfetterable, individual, active. I can no longer help them.

"Men," said the Humorous Banker, "bring nothing to marriage and expect to make something of it. They sacrifice nothing and expect everything."

"Women want all of a man's love," I said, "but still want to keep the admiration of other men. That is why they expose as much of their figure as possible so that there is nothing left secret and intimate for the husband. But if a woman conceals herself, keeps herself for her husband, she has a right to expect that her husband will not go out to admire the nakedness of other women in revues."

"Exactly—and besides, it is only a question of sacrificing vanity. I know that if I tried, I could be admired by other women in order to be able to say, like Horace: 'Oh, I have such a success with women!' But it is a pleasure to sacrifice this satisfaction of my vanity for the sake of our ideal of marriage, and in return for the sacrifices you make."

We serve our ideal with little acts of loyalty, with repudiation of little temptations, with constant efforts to please each other.

December 7. Discouragement while taking care of Mother. Is there anything more difficult on earth? She has been ill with the grippe. Saturday and Sunday were terrible days in which the final decision had to be made—New York or Paris? Radios or antiques? Vacations in New Jersey or in Spain? Bright future in New York without relaxation or delectation, or moderate progress here with enjoyment of concerts, accessible books, beautiful objects and traveling?

The strain of New York life is too great for my banker. I do not want a large fortune at the price of his youth. I don't want him sacrificed to luxury and a fortune—I love him too well. I give up ambitious futures in exchange for his youth and strength.

I shall be *reasonable* about Paris. In that way the remaining two years of Joaquin's studies will not be lonely for Mother. Thorvald is happy in Havana. If we have children, I'll do my best to bring them up as Americans.

Today the sacrifice seems immense. Emotionally, Paris is my calvary. On cool, reasonable days I realize I cannot sacrifice my love to my whims. I shall try to turn my hate of Paris into writing and make it harmless.

December 8. Hugh has suggested uniting my scattery journal writing under the title of "Two Years in Paris," which helps me to know where to begin and where to end. I do my copying in the morning. In three days of strain, when I was asked to do the thinking for my busy banker in order to find out what we wanted regarding our future, I found it difficult to work, even to sew. I think we lost some weight over that decision.

I have kept Ferrero in mind—the limitation of desires in order to live out fully the few truly desired ones. Desires are deceptive. They are often merely a contagious disease, like a desire for the radio or the car or the little moving-picture camera or the large house or the multiplied servants. Every multiplication except that of ideas is a bad calculation and defeats its purpose: too much money for one's own character, too many children for the children's sake, too much ambition to the detriment of a few eternal pleasures.

I have also kept my emotional impulses down. My war with ugliness is not only against Paris—it has to do with all the world. As it happens, I have a larger dose to deal with here, but all the better. It shall be the test of my strength and my sincerity. Anglo-Saxons believe that fighting strengthens you, that it stings you into courage and character. In Scotland, to seek peace is to be too soft and weak. I'll be a Scottish lassie.

December 9. The man I pity most in the world is my husband. What a life I lead him! Not a moment's rest!

"I keep you pretty well stirred up, don't I?" I said last night.

"Oh, but I like it. I would hate you if you let me go to sleep and if I should awake someday to discover that I am a failure, that I have missed all my desires."

He is the only one who can bear to be reminded, who really seeks perfection, who is untiring and sincere.

December 11. Erskine has done a wonderful thing in *Galahad*. He has painted the world in Arthur, Elaine, Guinevere, and the ideal in Galahad, and he has made everybody argue so well that they all seem in the right, from their point of view, and you can take whichever side you wish and feel quite strong and convinced of your rightness.

There are some memorable phrases in the book, some wonderful philosophy, an uncanny wisdom and understanding of character and some crude passages sacrificed to modern taste. Most people read the book for its wit, and that explains Erskine's popularity. But to us he is the oracle of the ideal.

For days his book has upset our life. The first day I read it all through, in my swift impressionistic way. I read it with the eyes of a believer in legends. I wept with disappointment in Arthur, in Launcelot, in Elaine, in Guinevere—oh, above all in Guinevere. I sought the ideal in them, and found it only towards the end in Galahad.

Hugh is like Erskine, and that is why he watches his life so eagerly. Hugh has something of that Scottish dourness and some of Erskine's merciless intelligence. Erskine can make mistakes. He can develop his humanity and his comic spirit too well and become a Balzac rather than the English poet that he is. And he can fall into burlesque.

I am more like Amiel, whose life is lived out. I have observed Amiel's mistakes and do not intend to make them, with the help of Hugh, Erskine and good health. There was no irony in Amiel, and he tempered the sharpness of his vision by kindness. Amiel was softer, tenderer, more affectionate, lived more outside of our world, almost completely in the ideal.

Amiel's mind, echoes of his feelings, live in me perhaps more deeply than in any other being today; and few, perhaps, of Hugh's age understand Erskine as well as Hugh does. We two shall combine and temper and teach each other.

Hugh says my impossible attitude towards Paris is consistent with my true Galahadian spirit and wants me to admit he approved of me before we read our beloved book. There would be no credit due him if he approved of me *now*. Oh, he believes in me, he feeds my madness, he lets me see only one side, the ideal, since this is the only way I can live. He watches me, and I watch him. Neither one can thus escape a glorious life.

Mrs. Erskine wrote me a lovely communicative letter. John is busy changing *Helen* into a play. Anna is too fat. Dr. Fosdick[1] is building a church near them. New York is dirtier and more torn up than ever. They are coming over in the fall of 1927. Oh, to be ready, fully ready, to meet this extraordinary experience!

December 12. When I feel well and energetic, then I must help Hugh with his battle for health. Fog, cold, changes, a low standard of hygiene, make Paris a hospital where one epidemic follows another: consumption, diphtheria, typhoid fever and the grippe. The winter here is a veritable nightmare.

Repetition of old scenes: we sit in the studio addressing Christmas cards for New York. You remember your friends in the order in which they appear in your address book. You make economies on those who failed in the exchange of courtesies last year, and you wish that everyone might frankly abandon the custom which has been spoiled by exaggeration. The original idea was one of thoughtfulness; the modern version is a stilted, expensive flowering of the address book. What has made it so? Hypocrisy, the modern substitute for kindness.

[1] *Harry Emerson Fosdick, pastor of Riverside Church.*

I love the old, true Christmas—the idea of giving, of thinking exclusively of what might give others pleasure, of surprising and spoiling those you love with the very things they do not like to buy for themselves because they seem too unreasonable, too expensive, too selfish—Christmas as a religious ritual which demands a joyous self-forgetfulness, generous giving, reminding people once a year of the delicate thoughtfulness they should practice every day.

The amount of Hugh's family's gift will determine the amount *my* family will get. We are penniless! Fortunately, everybody else is provided for, and it will only be a question of hurrying tremendously for Mother and Joaquin.

I went to an English Montparnassian bookstore and sold them books so as to have money for marketing. It is amusing to be penniless and yet not poor. The usually cross Englishman took an interest in me. Perhaps he suspected a strained situation. I might have started a story right there: "Do you think you might find me work among the artists around here? I am a model." One phrase, and you can begin a new life. Suppose I had said "yes" to my Russian admirer or to the Spaniard or to the painter or to the Cuban millionaire;[1] suppose I had not loved Hugh and was still posing in New York and progressed onto the stage and danced and traveled as actresses travel; or if I had married Enric and lived in Nice now, or married Bob[2] and lived in a suburb, a domestic and stupid life; or married a genius, a writer, as I had intended, and was buried in a library as a secretary. Many, many little gates were opened to me. I made my choice not of the varied worlds but of the man at the gate.

I answered the Englishman's questions patiently. For a moment I glanced into *that* little world—enough to amuse myself during the length of my walk; long enough to risk being run over and followed by a man who thought I was smiling at him.

Is there anything to the Montparnassian life, to those men and women I meet on my walks and who sit at the Rotunde and Dôme cafés, who fill the English Book Shop and the art-supplies shops on Boulevard du Montparnasse, who buy rustic furniture, pottery, modern paintings and attend the School of La Grande Chaumière?

I have heard different answers to my question. The descend-

[1] *This list probably included Boris Hoppe and the Marquis de Avilés.*
[2] *An unidentified American friend who lived near A.N. in Kew Gardens.*

ents of Musset, Baudelaire, Murger, no longer frequent these cafés, which are fake in spirit and serve only to amuse the foreign students in search of atmosphere, who meet there only other students like themselves.

The sincere artists must certainly be too busy to talk as these young people do. But then, French artists are different, and talk was an important occupation in their lives. Where have they gone? And is there really nothing left in our quarter but words and American college boys and men and women who make sport of art? What if I should find out for myself? What has stirred my curiosity is the sight of a woman in Grecian costume walking down the Boulevard Raspail, a handsome blonde whose daring I admired, and then today I saw a man in a sackcloth cape, rich in folds only, wrapped around a magnificent figure, which he carried easily and gracefully on his sandaled feet.

Are they sincere? I know I would be if I donned the costumes I love, to perpetuate styles and ideas I prefer to the modern. I cannot trust anyone to answer me. I myself am going to investigate. I am going to study my quarter, my neighbors, and their life. How can I gain the consent of my jealous Lord? By promising to go out unpowdered and uncurled in order to exclude all admiration from my experiences?

It is easy to make plans on early, bright mornings. In the evening I always regret my curiosities and my excursions. But to live out Erskine's philosophy of action, I must promise to abide by all plans made in lucid moments of courage. Perhaps if Amiel had done this, he would not have failed—and I would not worship him as I do.

Hugh said I should accept the gift of the modern world, of frankness and directness. He said I needed it. He said that, long ago, when I thought I was writing poetically, I was merely writing sentimentally—that I am frank and direct in my thinking now and should write this. Furthermore, he said, all truth is beautiful. But what is truth? That is what I'm looking for.

We have found the key to our most frequent arguments and disagreements. Hugh is fond of speculative thinking, willing to consider and weigh everything. Tell him some preposterous fact: "Well now, let me see," says my Humorous Banker. And he gives it all a hearing, for the fun of speculating.

Tell me the same thing, and I explode. "Impossible! I won't believe it!" Like the story of Wilson's salacious adventure.

"But give me a proof or a reason why it is not so," I am asked. I have no proof, no reason, nothing to justify my protest. I lose the argument, and I keep my faith.

Sometimes I find out I was wrong. But I don't say I was wrong. I say: "Well, if it is so, it *should not* be so." Such a silly argument always remains unanswered.

Isn't it queer? The day is over and I have still some courage and spirit left, even recklessness. Once you begin telling the whole truth and facing everything and everybody, it seems easy to continue. It is like drunkenness.

I wrote the freest letter to Eugene to make him feel the thickness of the crust he is building around himself.

December 15. Letters and letters and more letters. I want to be at peace with the world for Christmas. I am never a bad correspondent. In fact, I write more letters than anything else, which sometimes gives me the illusion that I am working. On my walk this morning (I walk every morning now before sitting at my desk) I pondered this bitter truth: I think that half of literature was made by men who "let go," men who let themselves be pushed and never stopped to bite the end of their penholders or to oil their typewriters. I am impulsive enough, heaven knows, to worry my husband, my family and virtuous men like Richard, but in any writing except my journal, I never let go. A very strange contradiction—a curious trick of consciousness. A sort of stage fright, it seems. Well, I won't worry about it any more. I will keep my mind on my *Two Years in Paris*, which begins dramatically thus:

"Night and day the gargoyles of Notre Dame look down upon Paris with a sinister expression, with derision, mockery, amusement, with hate, fear and disgust. For two years I looked down into Paris, and tried to understand why the gargoyles had such expressions.

"It seemed strange that they should be able to look in such a manner at the lovely river, the graceful bridges, the ancient palaces, the gardens, the majestic avenues, the flowers, the quays and the old books, the bird market, the lovers, the students. What do they see beneath these attractive surfaces? Why do they frown perpetually and mock eternally? What monstrous secrets made their eyes bulge out, twisted their mouths, filled their heads with wrinkles and grimaces?

"I know now."

December 16. Visit to Mlle. Boussinescq very interesting. I did not mind her laughing at me. In fact, I think I joined her in her merriment, and from that moment on we understood each other perfectly. We talked of Erskine and his *Galahad*, of his popularity (too bad! we said unanimously) and of his family. Mlle. B.'s little old mother listened intelligently to everything and contributed with nods, smiles and assents. As Mlle. B. had not yet received her copy of *Galahad*, we did not discuss it very thoroughly.

"One good book I read lately was Irwin Edman's *Richard Kane*,"[1] I said. Mlle. B. jumped from her chair and, bending over her mother, said to her: "Do you remember the albino?" And they broke into merry laughter. "His eyesight was very poor, and he used to tumble down our stairs and stumble about our courtyard and all the way out of our house. Mother and I used to watch him from the window, and feared he was going crazy. He was in a terrible state of exaltation and enthusiasm."

"You knew him!" I said.

"He was so excited about Europe. He said he had never realized how much there was to see, that he felt he had never used his eyes before, that now he was discovering everything, and that it was a tremendous revelation to him."

"Exactly, exactly what he says in his book, speaking through Richard Kane."

"I took him around. He was surprised by the freedom here. He wanted to see a cabaret. We went to one in Montmartre, I think, with smoke and people who sang salacious songs he did not understand, but it pleased him just to have seen these things. I also took him to a little café kept by a man I know. In the back room he exhibited paintings of contemporary artists with the idea that in this way they would be more accessible in price for people who could not afford to buy them through expensive agents and exhibitors. Edman wanted to buy one, but he had no room in his trunk. Everything interested him."

"I'll bring you his book. It will interest you enormously."

"The rascal should have sent it to me," said Mlle. B. "I showed him Chartres with Mr. and Mrs. Sherwood Anderson, and he had promised to write a poem about it and to send it to me."

She also told me that Santayana had an apartment in Paris on a very noisy street where he loved to work, that René Lalou

[1] *Richard Kane Looks at Life.*

was the best guide to French contemporary literature and that we should see the plays of Jules Romains.

I confessed to her that I needed a guide in that world I love so deeply and asked her if she would help me. We made arrangements on a practical basis for talks and teachings. She is poor and has no time to waste. I came away with admiration of her spirit and liveliness and knowledge. My feelings, as usual, were somewhat bruised, but this time they must give way before reason and intelligence.

Over the dinner table, Hugh received the essence and best of our talk. Together we read a criticism of *Galahad* in the Post Literary Review. Hugh pronounced it petty. People seem afraid of looking at large ideas. They pounce upon style, form or the story as material for criticism. But *ideas, ideas* are essential. That is Erskine's gift to us rather than his discovery of a new form. Hugh will write and tell him our opinion and ask him if we have not understood him.

Abel Hermant is quite right in saying (*Figaro* editorial, 14 December):

"Il ... ne haïsait point la solitude, mais il sait que l'on apprend plus de choses et plus vite en société, que l'observation est plus féconde quand elle est contradictoire, que la vérité jaillit par éclairs du choc des opinions, tandis que le penseur qui se recueille toujours ne parle qu'avec soi-même, ou garde un silence dangereux, se complaît et s'enfonce dans ses erreurs."[1]

But we want the society of intelligent people.

Hermant himself counsels the theatre, where you learn much in three hours and do not incur the risk of experimenting among friends whom afterwards you cannot get rid of.

What egoism, n'est ce pas? What conceit, what selfishness, what coldbloodedness, what calculation! I admit everything. Emerson went further (and he had more right than we have); he naïvely went looking for people of an intelligence equal to his own. The Literary Review discovers this monstrous egoism in his Journal.

---

[1] *"He did not hate solitude, but he knew that one learns more and more quickly in society, that the observation is more productive when it is contradictory, that truth sparks like lightning at the confrontation of opinion, while the thinker who forever withdraws into himself, communicates only with himself or keeps a dangerous silence, dotes on and sinks deeper into his errors."*

Of course, it is a ticklish affair to measure the size of one's intellect and of other intellects, and to then try and form a friendship between them. I shall measure nothing but our sincerity. We are, for instance, more sincere than Horace in our worship of thought and art, and this will be the justification of our desires.

December 17. Parties with Horace and Frances are impossible. The two of them together jar on us too much. Horace alone we can stand, and I like to see Frances alone, where the contrast between us is amusing, but it becomes too strong when Horace and Hugh carry on their own clashes, at least, while ideas mean so much to us—and we happen to be at that unfortunate stage.

Today Frances and I took an hour's walk through the Luxembourg. Her breeziness, her experience, her laugh, her easy way of assimilating everything, her comfortable lack of philosophy—all these things are exactly opposite to myself, and that is why I admire her. We have formed a friendship after her own style— half serious, understanding, tolerant, human and therefore frail and defective. She thinks I am a most curious mixture of maturity and childishness, and I think of her in precisely the same way. She is old where I am young, in actual experience of life, but she is young where I am old, in thinking, reflection, intuition.

She is superior to Horace in being whole and a character; she is inferior in intellectual ways. She is superior to me in knowledge but inferior in the capacity to feel. In liking her, I tend to dislike Horace. Because, since they like each other thoroughly, Horace identifies himself more with her spirit than mine. What I don't mind in her, because it is sincere and consistent, I despise in Horace because it is a simple surrendering to one side of himself, and he is neither entirely sincere nor loyal to her spirit, any more than to mine. Loyal to nothing but a new fancy. Of all four, he is the most inglorious.

December 19. The rather insipid peace of Sunday, with a pale, roseate sun, a crisp, frosty air and flower vendors selling holly and mistletoe. You feel the tenseness of holiday preparations interrupted, and a certain impatience—at least, we do. I cannot sit still anywhere, stung every moment by memories and regrets for other Christmases. I regret the cheerful days in Richmond Hill shared with Miguel, Eduardo, Charles and Enric. I believe I miss their companionship.

Perhaps it was two letters from Enric and my answer to them which brought back those regrets. Perhaps it is the realization that I must be more dignified in my demonstrations and less impulsive. Whatever it is, I feel lonely and Hugh understands that I need friends. He is busy working concretely for our ideal. I must work for it spiritually. He has asked me quite positively to do the thinking for the family, but I cannot think all day and then subdue myself in the evening to provide a restful shelter for my Love's figure-worn mind. I understand that my questions, my excitement, tire him and that he feels unfit to guide or criticize or respond to me. But I will relieve him of this task. I shall live a life outside of ours, for the sake of ours. I shall give him not the struggle and drudgery of ideas, but their essence. I shall bring him not problems but discoveries, such as he gets from good books. He has wisdom. I like to consult him, but I shall have to get wise without him.

December 27. On Monday the Guilers' gift arrived, and the shopping started. Until Friday evening I lived on the streets. Mother had also received her money and kept equally busy. Friday evening we dressed up the little tree, filled the apartment with holly, mistletoe and red candles and brought all kinds of packages from secret hiding places. Then Hugh sat down and wrote me his second Christmas poem—a beautiful piece of writing. Meanwhile, I slept. At 11 o'clock we all went to the midnight Mass. It was a bitterly cold night; the music seemed touching to me, though pronounced bad by the Musician of the family. I wished there had been snow on the ground and more piety in my heart.

Sunday we invited Horace to dinner. I'll write fully about this when more in the mood for it. For me, days of excitement, pleasure, noise, bring a reaction of sadness, always. I am in a very bad mood, and struggling to come out of it. See what stilted, sulky writing I have done. As a punishment I'll write the whole story over again tomorrow.

We had another gift for Christmas which I should appreciate. In fear of losing Hugh, the Bank Manager raised his salary 75%. We stay in Paris, comfortably, able to help Mother, able to save for the future and to build up the life we desire. In all our discussions I influence Hugh, and if we stay, I have only myself to blame. I think we are making a wise, practical, brave, romantic, spirited and mature choice.

1927

January [?]. I made no resolutions for the New Year. The habit of making plans, of criticizing, sanctioning and molding my life, is too much of a daily event for me. Joaquin made an amusing list of his accomplishments, however, an original deviation from the traditional faultfinding, regrets and humble promises. In that optimistic viewpoint, I will follow him. He mentioned the number of his compositions. My record is kept by my Journal, my only work. He read 30 books during the year.

I read 75 books.

I recopied about 300 pages from my Journal.

I made 6 decorative pillows.

I re-arranged the books in the library about 10 times.

I went to church only on Christmas Night. (Oh, that is something wrong. I was writing good things.)

I wrote about 200 dutiful letters.

I went to 61 parties and visits.

I went of my own free will to meet Mlle. B. again.

I sacrificed my dancing lessons and sculpture to an anemic budget.

I kept all our accounts faithfully.

I reconciled Joaquin and Antonio.

I made the studio pretty at a small expense, mostly by work.

I pleased my New Family.

I learned to manage servants firmly and to keep my eyes open on every detail of housekeeping.

I forced myself to rest and relax, thereby gaining a little weight.

I wrote faithfully about all our trips.

I earned a poem from my husband at the end of the year.

I faced and accepted Paris as a test of my courage and to accustom myself to suffering.

I faced and accepted French literature and tried to appreciate their talents through characteristics personally distasteful to me.

I lived up to my ideals about society by evading its lighter sides as often as possible. At the same time I offended no one.

I am ready at any time to admit that I have many faults. So as not to discourage myself I won't mention them today.

January 5. Another industrious, dutiful day: sewing buttons, pillows; binding old music and old books; balancing accounts; tidying library, papers, bills, quotations; putting away holly, mistletoe, and the Christmas tree; taking my daily French and Spanish dictation; making plans for improving the housekeeping, the house decoration, and for making new clothes (out of old ones).

While I was ennumerating my labors, Joaquin came to rest from *his* work and to talk. He likes to rest on my new pillows, to finger the stuffs I am working on, to discuss the life of musicians, his own, and mine.

January 6. Another good, stupid day, half of it spent in bed because I didn't feel well. But I am satisfied, because I have not wasted any time. I go from one thing to another, shirking nothing, postponing no prosaic details, which I am fond of doing "some other day." I conquer my inclinations, curb my whims and therefore kill my imagination. But not permanently, for the devil has a million lives. Then, when I have peace, through saintliness, I hate it.

Joaquin is celebrating the arrival of a baby grand piano to replace the unresponsive "tin can" which he has endured since September for the sake of economy. These are the comforts Hugh is providing with his work. It is only fair that I should keep his buttons sewn on, at least.

The other day, walking down the boulevard, when Hugh was admiring the long, nickel-plated automobiles, I said that they reminded me too much of Eversharps.[1]

Joaquin and I found another similarity in our characters. At night he dreams so much, so intensely, so continuously, that he feels as if he had not slept. We mind loud talking around us, "scenes," the inquisitive staring of the Parisian. We never push our way through a crowd. We both give our seats to old people in buses. We don't bear criticism very well; it stings our ancestral pride. We like distinction in manners and clothes, and quietly run houses. What we want, we want immediately, and would walk into the sea after it. What we don't want, nothing but a Scotsman can make us take, or an appeal to our too soft hearts.

January 7. Terrible mood, from which I cannot free myself. Oppressed by a tea given at home by Mother to insincere, bored and

[1] *Eversharp pencils.*

boring people. Joaquin played badly, Mother sang badly and nobody listened. Our Danish cousin[1] arrived in the middle of it, the sincerest person among them, and they laughed at her with their eyes. I served tea but could not talk. Joaquin said afterwards I needed more society to lose my timidity.

Lord, is there anybody who understands?

Yes, Hugh.

Moods are moods and not an idea arrived at through reasoning. They can only be fought and conquered by another mood. Let us seek another mood then.

January 8. I conquered my mood by serving others, by accompanying my Danish cousin on her shopping in the afternoon and having all the family to dinner in the evening. Now I'm safe because it is the weekend, and my Love is near me, and I'm *good*, sad-eyed but cheerful. Sweetness of temper with me is an effort sometimes. I'm not naturally gifted.

January 16. I have not had the time to think over carefully the last events: a visit from Horace, Molière at the Odéon, a talk with Frances, an afternoon with Mlle. Boussinescq and an evening of music and two new books. Or perhaps I have thought too much about them when I should have been writing.

The talk with H.B. is what I treasure most. I understand her better and admire her intensely. I was about to say that I had misjudged her. But no, I merely judged her as well as I could a year ago. Since then, the change is in me and not in her.

I had termed her a matter-of-fact person. Except for the tears, her impression of *Galahad* was like mine. Erskine had demolished a mystic, and made the ideal ridiculous. He was expressing his epoch, developing towards that French tradition—Voltaire, Rabelais, Anatole France—which she did not like, she the worshiper of Chartres and the Middle Ages.

I leaned over to catch every word; in the end, we were talking together at the same time, saying exactly the same thing.

We passed into confidences—estrangement between her and Erskine. I tried to explain this. He hoped to find in her a representative and a guide for the one French tradition he loves—that of Anatole France—which she doesn't like. He was perhaps slightly

---

[1] *A.N.'s maternal grandfather was Danish.*

disappointed to find her sharing her interest between modern literature and Chartres. Pure speculation. Erskine, the marvelous sage, is full of his own miracles and, like a true artist, seeks only what helps him. Unconscious egoism. With me he showed the most delicate intuition. What estranged him from H.B.?

Fortunately, she finds more kinship in her friendship with Sherwood Anderson. "A simple, sincere man who never learned to make literature, who broke away from his work, his business and gave up a fortune. Il veut tout comprendre, tout connaître. Il est tendre, si humble envers les choses, si sensible."[1]

After talking for three hours, we went out together and I accompanied her home. I came back tired, elated and full of admiration for her opinions, her spirit and her character.

That night Antonio and a violinist played. The music seemed an accompaniment to my life. I followed its ascensions and inflections with intense vibrations of thought and feeling.

The difference between the sonatas of César Franck and d'Indy struck me as the chief difference between people of intelligence: César Franck had unity, coherence, a whole personality. D'Indy was varied, multicolored, moved by too many influences, broken, scattered, contradictory. Le premier chante, le deuxième cherche.[2] I prefer the simple assurance of Franck. D'Indy expresses, instead, the general character of French intelligence, which sees too much.

The Victim, who was specially created to suffer in the hands of Life because she expected such fantastic perfection from it, has now reached the third stage in the progress of her understanding. After being scourged with Evil in its worst form, the Parisian expression, she is beginning to smile bravely, to rationalize, to go forward in the meeting and mastering of it. She is showing a spirited resignation, a pitying smile, and continues to carry about a wistful face, but the eyes are no longer reproachful, nor the mouth unforgiving.

But I shall gather in myself those ideals I can't find in others. I shall make them—in character, deeds, thought, written words, clay, dancing, furniture—in everything I touch. I desire perfection and beauty with all my soul.

[1] *"He wants to understand all, to know all. He is sensitive, so humble about things, so sensible."*
[2] *The first sings, the second searches.*

January 17. I am made to reach ideas through suffering, through emotion. Is that right?

It brings, first of all, confusion, pain, unnecessary intensity. Feeling is struck first, tears burst from it, the idea is born out of struggle and tragedy. What kind of idea? The same, on the whole, which others arrive at by calm reasoning, by rationalizing, by unconcerned judgment, by a natural labor of intelligence.

This was perfectly developed in the case of Molière's *L'Avare*, seen at the Odéon, with Darras in the title role. The audience laughed. I couldn't. My heart tightened—the more exaggerated the burlesque, the stronger my sense of its emptiness and childishness. What was wrong? I didn't know. But the Miser's ridiculousness, the overacting, jarred on me. I might have screamed with an instinct resembling madness: there is something wrong with this play.

Our phlegmatic Danish cousin was looking on unmoved. The little boy in Hugh, the little boy I love, who laughs at the circus, at Charles Chaplin and Buster Keaton, laughed, but I knew why and knew also that his laugh was different from the others.

Coming out, my cousin said calmly: "They emphasized the burlesque too much. They willed the ideas. A Frenchman in Copenhagen is fighting against this interpretation of Molière as 'bouffonnerie.' "

"A sound, shrewd criticism," said Hugh.

Simple, harmless, not worth an evening of suffering. Yet how can I give up the instinct and emotion which lead me to the truth? Could I arrive at it by some other way? I must. I am a good critic, I know. I have the flair and the courage. But I must use my intelligence, not my emotions. Sometimes I hate my Spanish ancestry.

Guinevere fooled herself. She believed in ideal love, and she believed that it was for the sake of it that she loved Arthur, and then ceased to love him, and loved Launcelot and then Galahad. But we know that she sought a triumphant expression of herself, a glorifying mastering of men by her beauty. We know that she wanted to be loved faithfully, although intellectually. And we know she often wore new dresses.

How much coquetry or vanity there is in my own attitude towards men, I don't know. Until now I truly believed in beautiful love. I sincerely tried to inspire Eduardo, Enric, Marcus and the others. I naïvely believed that since men would do something for the sake of my prettiness that they would not do for the sake of other things, I was justified in using my prettiness for the service of the ideal. I admit I wear a lot of new dresses, but I have also obtained idealistic results. For selfish reasons? For self-glory? But I want to be real, and God knows, I thought I *was* real. But so did Guinevere. I can't be as false as that.

Hugh thinks me real. But he may be caught by the illusion. But what *is* real—my passionate instinct for beauty, my desire to spread it around me, my spontaneous gestures towards others, beckoning, urging them onward, or that moment spent before the mirror, which seems the key to my life but never an end to it, never the object of it?

This self-doubt teases me at a moment when I seek frankness, utter clarity, utter intelligence, courage, truth.

And Guinevere's falseness mocks and taunts me—Guinevere and her new dresses! H.B. is the very opposite of Guinevere. She was the first to see through her. She hasn't the faintest coquetry. Plain hair, plain dresses, flat shoes. Is that being real? But in that case I prefer falseness, and I shall look tolerantly upon my vanity as inevitable and human.

January 21. Having finished my owl-brooding upon last week's ideas and people and occupations, I gave a few days to practical duties, to letter writing, mending, dress fittings, visits, errands, by which I gain nothing but a peaceful conscience. I read the two books assigned by H.B., marked and criticized them, suffered and judged, and this afternoon comes the second talk with H.B., the glorious point of my week.

It is snowing with Parisian mildness. Joaquin is ill, as I am, through an excess of mental evaluations. Je ne plaisante pas.[1] We wear out ourselves and others. He dreams of symphonies, I dream of plays. Notes dance in his head, words in mine. A new piece takes his appetite away, and a new book keeps me awake. Then we get a cold, or rheumatism, and everybody thinks it was due to wet feet.

January 24. H.B. pounces on my American ideas as if I had no right to them, or at least as if they were out of place in one born in Paris. I said something about not wanting to waste her time.

"Oh, but that's an American idea. I *believe* in wasting time!"

"But not badly," I said, alluding to my ignorance.

[1] *I am not joking.*

"Any way at all is right. Time was made to be wasted."

Some men live regretting the past epoch, or looking forward to the new. Some are contented with their own epoch. Some belong to none.

I belong to two. I am trying to reconcile them. I hold on to the best of Romanticism and admire the frankness and strength of our modern language. They will be fused in my life, my ideas, and my work—not harmoniously, but out of the struggle there will be born a supreme idea, the Ideal perhaps.

Because I keep what is today despised, sweetness and enthusiasm, my face seems young to the hard-eyed people around me. But I know I am not young inwardly, because I am living in pain and struggle, because two epochs meet in me, because my head belongs to old paintings and my spirit lives in the modern world, because one of my hands is pretty, smooth, decorative, and the other energetic, tense and strong, because my hair is long. I would choose long dresses if I could, and yet my phrases are short and my thoughts sharp, and my legs free and swift. I have nothing but an instinct to tell me what is beautiful. I cannot support all my choices with rational thinking.

Sensualism seems ugly to me—or rather, sexuality, as they call it now. A harmonious and total sensitiveness of the senses is beautiful. An excess of sexuality is ugly when it is the mere satisfaction of an appetite. It deadens the spirit, it destroys the finer senses and even the sensitiveness of the body.

I seek a new name for my religion which I know is not puritanism. My intense love of beauty separates me from puritans. With me, it is not a question of what is wrong and right. I live too fully, too richly, too intensely, too sincerely, to live by the force of shadowy words and laws. No, it is something else I feel.

Dante, Botticelli, Wagner in his *Parsifal*, Bain[1] in his Hindu stories, Beethoven, Bach, César Franck, Unamuno in his *Tragic Sense of Life*—they all found expressions for it. I am not alone.

I like Waldo Frank's *Rahab*. He gives that precious mixture of soul and love, human passions pushed by divine desires, woman seeking herself and truth through struggles and physical blunders —ideas, moving perpetually through the flesh, flesh tormented by the spirit, flesh teaching the spirit.

Frank breaks the hard surface of cities and shows their inner life. He breaks through the hard secrecy of men and women and

[1] *Francis William Bain, British author.*

shows their souls. He places knowing fingers upon their warm
bodies, their illnesses, fevers, stumblings, defeats, surrenders, sacrifices, and watches with all-seeing eyes the struggles of the flames
to keep alive. He is a true poet because he sees those flames in
everything, where others would only see the ugliness. For that I
like him.

I suppose I must confess that I have incurable preferences. In a
country, I choose the exceptional people; the crowd does not interest me. I lean in taste towards the aristocratic, in interest
towards the individual, in art towards the personal. When I travel,
my eyes are arrested by details. I do not give up my mind to the
whole. I listen to the impressions which burst from my personal
reaction. I experience the emotions dictated not by others, books
or traditions but by my own clear-voiced intuitions. I choose the
isolated places, the unmentioned roads, the forgotten book, the
despised man.

I have always believed in the exception. What America is as
a whole doesn't interest me so much as the small, small groups
who combatted materialism, who rebelled against standardization,
who thought much and alone and against the currents.

I prefer Amiel to Shakespeare, Guérin to Molière—not to be
consistently contradictory, but because I prefer them instinctively
and sincerely.

I am not original. There are thousands like me, but we shall
never know each other because we want to be alone. If we met,
we would be a large group, and we don't approve of groups. We
would seek some other way to be isolated. We live in exile from
society. We live in sighing, pitying ourselves, lamenting our loneliness and working obstinately to maintain it. We give trouble to
the leveler of spirits and minds, to the peacemakers, to the seekers
of lethargy and contentment. Our wails, our egotistical wails,
keep everybody awake.

At last I see myself as part of the Universe and this Universe
is moved by a vast and undiscovered Plan. I see that Father had
to come from Spain with his heritage of music, culture, intellect,
in order to find Mother, the essentially good, born of a strong,
firm, honest Northern man and a soft, coquettish, beautiful Frenchwoman, so that out of these two natures where generosity mixed
with supreme selfishness, goodness with intellect, simplicity with
culture, honesty with hypocrisy, softness with hardness, three
children could be born.

And Mother had to suffer so that we would possess the heritage of art and intelligence without the evil influence of our father's presence; so that we might know her courage, her power of sacrifice and her devotion; so that she might go to New York, where I would meet Hugh. Tia Coco's living in Kew was instrumental, for it attracted us there. Johnnie was instrumental with his party-loving nature, which brought him to a certain Peggy's house, where my own party-loving brother took me, where we met and from which Johnnie went home to praise me to his serious brother.

I take it that everything worked for our marriage from which something wonderful might come. But I do not believe everything worked *only* for us. In turn, I was to be instrumental in the birth of Eduardo's artistic nature, and Hugh's position in the bank was to be in favor of Joaquin's life in Europe, and Europe was to send progressive Thorvald running off to Havana.

I see the chain now, moving invisibly. I do not know the object of the movement yet, the final end, but I see some sense to it, some reason, some logic.

H.B., at our second talk, was clever and just. She is the perfect critic. I can safely read the books she likes and meet her friends. She understands my questions and laughs only at my romanticism. Oh, she has found traces of it—she pounces on it, not to destroy, but to make me realize its absolute death. We laugh together. She gave me *Rahab* to read and revealed Louis Jouvet to me in *Au Grand Large*. I had the impression of a fine actor with an intellectual forehead, sensitive, witty.

The play was astonishing. It realizes the supernatural (it gives a substance and image to death). It may be simple, and many do not take it seriously, but then they did not see through the symbols. I suffered in it, felt it, believed it. The ultimate idea haunted me. It strikes the imagination, it runs deeply and shakes the peaceful foundations of life.

Jouvet is courageous. And he gives back to the theatre the antique flower it seemed to have lost. All the other plays I have seen were sillier than life, more sentimental, more farcical, more futile, more ridiculous, emptier.

February 7. Busy enjoying the New Budget. Music, plays, books, literature lessons, Spanish dancing lessons, gothic furniture. I was never so happy, so well, so spoiled by life and Hugh, so grateful, so full of pity for others, so understanding of the world, so gentle, so deeply alive. Music is the only art which can now describe the fullness of my life. With all this, our love blooms, deepens, gains in richness, ardor and color. Our fourth year of marriage is a chant of triumph.

February 18. Impossible to fill the gaps. I'll build a skeleton, somewhat the weight of my own body, for instance, and hope the flesh will come on afterwards. First of all, at the Ursuline Movies, near the Schola Cantorum, we saw two remarkable pictures: *Jazz*, in which fantasy and symbolism were startlingly expressed; and then *Rail*, without words, all concentrated acting, a study of the drama in still life.

The day after, a humorous play for my little Scottish boy, *Potash and Perlmutter*. After that, duties—shopping with helpless, infantile American girls, shopping for my lovable sisters, a harrowing visit to Mrs. G[uicciardi], with all her worldliness and insincerity, a lunch with Flying Friends, a campaign to help Hugh get accounts for the bank, movies again, my first visit to a Beauty Salon and submission to massage and an unnecessary "wrinkle cream," "dress rehearsals" at my dressmaker's, castanet lessons, literature lessons, furniture shopping for a comfortable armchair, movies again . . .

Entr'acte. I minute: Jeanne,[1] who had succeeded Elizabeth, is thrown out. The house has to be disinfected to make up for her two months' presence. During the transition I worked so hard that I caught the grippe. I took it with me to the theatre on Sunday with H.B., where we saw *Mignon*, with incidental music by Schumann, translated by a friend of H.B.'s.

Evidently the grippe planned a revenge. Hugh and I quarreled for three days, and on the fourth I went to bed, too late. Today I am conquered, but Marie is here, the new maid, clean, pretty, affable, slow, southern, at least so she seems at first. My first judgments are always useless.

A letter from Eduardo should have cured me if I were still so romantic. Instead, it saddened me. A weak, trickly, feeble little letter. He remembered me in connection with spring.

The Cat's birthday was of course celebrated, with 29 candles and a stool for his guitar playing.

[1] *The maid.*

The Skeleton lacks animation. I guess it is due to the grippe. I even wonder if the anticipation of new experiences will prevent it from gaining weight. Look at the future! Tia Antolina and Baby are coming in the summer, Tia Julia and Tio Enrique, friends; Frances is staying; the Bank is giving a dance. In summer we go to New York for a month, and a month to Tunis and Algeria. In the fall, the Erskines. Enric Madriguera must be coming back from Nice. Another cousin, Gilbert,[1] has taken Eduardo's place.

March 11. Almost a month, not of forgetfulness but of intense activity. The Bank keeps us in suspense. Are we leaving for New York on April 1? Or for the mountains to rest?

Whatever we do, I have kept the cleaner, seamstress, dyer, shoemaker, etc., busy. And then with the three-day trip to Lille "on business," visits, entertaining of "friends," lessons, etc.—well, I have lost weight.

My Humorous Banker is tired and cross. At this time last year we were preparing for Italy. We need to go away again, we need calm, solitude, clean air, peace, meditation.

I have no desire to write, though I never stop thinking. It is curious that although I love a rich life, I hate an overcrowded life. I believe in rumination and lose half the beauty of all things when I am deprived of the time to ruminate. What is the use of a stirring talk with H.B. if I cannot sit for two hours recreating it? What is the meaning of a letter which has to be tucked in a drawer a minute after reading it? Why can I not see two persons or so a week instead of seven?

I gain nothing but physical weariness, and my observations are half buried through lack of words, which usually accompany them.

Why aren't my thoughts smooth? Because of infinitesimal irritations. Unmentionable, except by men like Pepys, unconquerable except by saints:

A missing button on Hugh's vest the day of his speech before the bank officers.

A taxi man who cheated us of 10 frs.

The maid, who burns the toast every morning.

The cleaners, who lose the collar of my coat.

The art shop, who won't order 20 pages of gold paper I need

[1] *Gilbert Chase.*

for my windows because he wants to wait until the "blue paper is all sold."

The grocery, who sends mildewed prunes.

The fly in a bottle of wine.

Rain on the day I wear my new shoes.

Well, I imitated my detested Pepys. Now let me imitate the saints: heaven, which sent the little trials of everyday life, please give me a dignified and worthwhile trial so that I may find glory in it. I would prefer an immense test of my courage and endurance to all these humiliating little tasks. Are they *really* necessary?

The light in the studio comes now through sculptured, gothic frames. Our eyes dwell pleasurably on the long table and on the credenza, on the two high-backed chairs. Hugh has an armchair which receives him with softness and flexibility. It rains only every other day. Oh, we now are spoiled by life and by each other.

March 16. Monday morning I bought paper and charcoal and entered the portrait class of the Académie de la Grand Chaumière (in reality, de la Grande Poussière[1]). A woman of thirty stood naked on the platform. I had never drawn anything but stick figures. And yet something that guides my fingers and my eyes can be trusted so well that on the second morning, after eight attempts, I received a compliment from the teacher on his tour of criticism. Am I studying drawing? I don't know. I have long had the suspicion that it is people and character I seek through all these expressions. I think as much about the life of my little dancing teacher as I do about the steps she teaches me.

My drawing class began with an emotional experience. The first day I noticed something in the way the model climbed the platform to resume her pose—a shy gesture of the hand as if protecting herself from the first moment of nakedness—and something gentle in her acceptance of commands from the students and something inexperienced about her posing. She has not done this very long, I said, observing also, with a tightening of the heart, that her body showed weariness and that dark circles under her eyes betrayed not only weariness but unhappiness. The students despised her. They spoke to her only to scold her for moving or for a change in the pose. I smiled at her. I was disturbed and felt a terrible pity for her which I could not explain. All day I

[1] *. . . of the Great Dustiness.*

thought of her, all day and throughout Antonio's concert, despising myself for my impressionability.

The next morning, in the middle of the pose, she touched her head with her hands, turned pale and with vague phrases slipped to the ground.

"Oh, now she's tired," said a student impatiently.

I ran up to her and, putting my hand on her shoulder, asked her what was the matter. She began to cry and in very bad French exclaimed to me that she had not eaten for two days. I ran out of the school to a café and came back a few minutes later followed by a waiter carrying a big cup of coffee and brioches. By that time a gray-haired lady had taken up a collection for her, and my poor model was hysterically pouring out her story: a Russian woman, knowing little French, out of work, her nurse's diploma useless, her rent due and no money for food . . . She cried, talked, ate and, much later, resumed her posing, her body still shaking occasionally with a sob.

This morning she looked happier. All the students were kinder to her. They remembered to give her moments of rest. A German boy fetched her a glass of water. My feeling of pity made me shy and I spoke to her only once.

Drawings of her body are now tacked on the studio wall. A body—muscles, proportion, curves—meaning nothing. But her face, I see her face, shyness, suffering, tears, swollen eyes and red nose, quivering mouth, shame, hunger. I see her picking up her coat upside down and I hear the money that was given her falling out of the pockets and rattling on the stand. I see her breasts rising when she sobbed. I see her bending over her coffee, her kimono partly opened on a blue, shivering body. I see the swollen veins on her hands, her eyes lifted up against the harshness of the students, some of them fearing to approach her as if she were ill.

"Don't forget that arms have muscles," said the teacher, breaking the smooth line of my drawing.

Bodies have feelings—bodies suffer, bodies stumble and tremble. Am I learning drawing?

"Vamos! Uno, dos, tres!
    "Ay, ay, ay, se equivocó!"[1]

[1] *"Begin! One, two, three!*
"Ay, ay, ay, you made a mistake."

She is small, plump, she loves garlic, she dances in a cabaret. Daylight does not suit her. Her eyes are puffed—she is hardly awake; you can count the safety pins on her and the fresh layers of rouge over the old ones. Someday I will find jam on her hands, as you do with children. But she can dance better than most people walk. But am I learning dancing?

Joaquin has a New Friend.[1] I was going to let him keep his new friend all for himself and for his own journal, but I know now this cannot be because he will be partly mine, too, I feel. The first evening he came he interested me immensely. He is American and Spanish but looks decidedly Spanish. He is, first of all, a kind and affectionate, high-minded man and then a man of clear opinions, of knowledge, of keen observation, of rare intelligence.

Emilia [Quintero] sent him to us, and he expected another boring visit. He was disappointed in that. Since then he and Joaquin have had long, long talks and have gone to concerts.

We all went together to Antonio's concert. That was the evening I realized I would have to write about him myself because we have a strong interest in common, or a vice, if you want: he has kept a journal from the age of seven.

Horace shrinks, shrinks, shrinks. During our last visit I realized Frances's tolerance was serving as a sleeping potion. Horace fools himself, but not others, about himself. He uses some of her words to cover the futility of some of his experiments. Physically he dissolves. Arms, legs, head, eyebrows, all hang in different directions rather limply. When he gets up, I always fear he will forget a portion of himself. So many people hold the strings of his Self and pull without consulting each other. I have dropped my string completely, out of pity for his wild gesticulations.

March 17. Mornings given to sketching. Every other afternoon, dancing. One in between for H.B. Thursday a visit, usually. Weekends for the Cat. What time have I for brooding? After a visit, such as I received this afternoon, I find it hard to come within myself again. People hurt me. I know no one who has yet resisted the temptation to "harden me." Something in me brings out the destructive spirit in men and women. "She is too blithe, too interested, too eager, too tense—that's bad. It must be cured." I see

[1] *Irving Schwerke, a music critic.*

these words in their eyes. Sometimes they act out of kindness: "Poor innocent thing, let us make her wise." "Poor poetic fool, let us teach her."

Why don't they leave me alone? I love life; why do they disapprove of that? I love art; why should that annoy them? I like to be busy and mostly alone; why do they smile at my intensity and devotion to things? Well, I am childish today, and my anger is futile.

My drawing is improving day by day. I fear sometimes that the love of lines might take the place of my love of words. Will my journal become a sketchbook? Every new form of art seems a new life and a new soul. But I mustn't seek too much and love too many things. Why is our life so unbelievably short?

March 28. In the High Place. Sun, wind, scattered thoughts, unfinished phrases, flying leaves, vague plans. Oh, I want peace. I want to stop living, just for a little while. I am tired.

Next week I give up sketching to shop. I continue the dancing so I will know at least a Sevillana before I leave. I will see H.B. up to the last minute, between sewing and dress fittings and housekeeping (my *fourth* maid is beginning Monday).

I am reading Giraudoux and do not have the patience to praise him in the phrases his rich style deserves. I have heard music and am too broken up mentally to speak of harmonious things. I live mechanically, preparing for new experiences, preparing clothes, cameras, sketchbooks, gifts, books, journals. My trunk, valises and my mind are overpacked.

March 30. A surprise, a shock, a strong impression—two days of unforeseen suffering. Enric comes back unexpectedly. I help him with his shopping. We tramp arm in arm in the rain. Our talk is light, teasing, uneven. Then suddenly in a taxi, coming home late in the afternoon, the confession. He still loves me. Why does he feel me closer to him when I am further than ever? "Oh, Anaïs, I can't realize you are married. I can't believe it. . . . But you don't feel anything. You are cold."

"No, I am not cold any more. I understand, I feel. See, here is the hand I never gave you before."

"You never liked me."

"That is not true. But please understand—I was a child *then*. I felt nothing. I *did* like you. I like you better today: you are stronger and older."

"May I keep your hand? . . . I feel you understand, I feel you are closer. . . ."

We are dazed, I by his hunger for affection, he by my new tenderness, by my gentleness.

That night, we went, the three of us, to the movies. He caressed the fur of my sleeve with thin, pathetic hands. His hat was rumpled and soiled, his coat a bit too long for him. His eyes were very hungry, though I know other women spoil him. Why must *I* spoil him?

And yet we met again this morning, sat in the Café de la Paix in a rare moment of sun between showers. We saw him off. I miss him. His tone, his eyes, his voice haunt me. His caressing way of saying: "Tu, Anaïs."

My gentleness with his suffering seemed disloyal to Hugh. I couldn't sleep last night. Have I a right now to make up for those years when I never laid my hand on a fevered and restless head, when every act, every glance, every word, was jealously preserved for One?

April 4. Terrible moods since that moment I last saw Enric's face on the train and came home to my dancing lesson.

"But you *must* smile," said my teacher. "Smile while you dance. Look happy and carefree."

I couldn't smile. I could hardly dance. I wanted to write Enric, and then I decided to beware of my impulses, to beware of myself, of my sentimentality. I haven't written yet, nor will I for a long time.

We had a businessman to dinner Saturday—such a long, sad evening full of talk on banking. We went to the theatre, and on Sunday for walks and tea. There were moments of sunshine and even of forgetfulness. Today I worked in order to free myself. When all was done, when I had had my dancing lesson, and my "goûter"[1] with Mother, I found myself in a dark, desperate moment: it was the end of my courage, of my pretense. What is wrong, eternally, with me? If I am left alone with myself, I'll go mad. I telephoned Hugh to come home early, and then I sat down to face my mood and conquer it if possible.

Where is the strength and clearness of my beautiful days? Can my reason be so easily disturbed? An impression should pass. One's intelligence should understand the cause of it and dissolve it.

[1] *Snack.*

I have been, as so often before, ridiculously impressionable. I have been wax in Enric's thin, pathetic fingers. Does nothing but feeling animate me? Have I no spirit, no wisdom, no reason?

April 10. Soft weather, a walk with Hugh in the park, sleep and love, dreams of the vacation to come, these things have soothed and cheered me at the end of a strenuous week.

Miguel Jorrín came to see us. He, also, shared our life in Richmond Hill, the walks through the fields, talks with Eduardo and Enric by the fire, parties, dinners at home cooked by Mother and served by me, our carefree and simple weekends. But *his* coming did not disturb me. He has matured only in intelligence and not in character. He is paradoxical and fond of bantering, not too sure of himself but pretending, and has acquired the habit of never saying quite what he thinks.

We are going out, all three, tomorrow night. I did not offer to help Miguel with *his* shopping (no more of those adventures for me until I grow harder).

Out of all the mad, full week I remember with pleasure only Joaquin playing Schumann at the Schola concert on Friday, though he failed to interpret Beethoven, through lack of character. He has progressed musically, technically, intellectually, but has now come to a stop. His *character* and individuality must develop. He is too gentle, too apathetic at moments, too nice, too easily loved and admired. I help him only by intuitive criticism, which he feels keenly and to which he responds bravely.

July 20. Paris. I took a new diary book with me to Luchon[1] and wrote in it up to the day we saw the Erskines in New York, and then lost it in a valise which disappeared from the pier, lost it with my nightgown, slippers, cold cream and other necessities. I had sometimes paused to consider such a calamity and had often wondered how I would behave when it happened. Today I am glad it happened because it helped to prove to me that I am not easily discouraged. I grieved exactly two days, and this was probably due in part to seasickness, and then I cheerfully rewrote as much as I could remember during our trip home. I did not think Luchon important enough to rewrite, even though I did a lot of thinking there and observed rustic life, the characteristics of mountain peasants and farm animals. I may leave a few pages for

[1] *A spa in the Pyrenees.*

Luchon, however. After that I shall merely copy from my small black notebook what I wrote on board ship. And then everything will continue as usual, except that I must admit Richard was right when he advised the use of the typewriter and carbon copies.

The trip to New York on the Mauretania was a combination of roughness, cold, exquisite food, bad music, uninteresting passengers, general luxury and, above all, speed, so that we had no time to finish Will Durant's *Story of Philosophy*. But we saw Chamberlin[1] crossing the ocean in his small, frail plane, a unique sight and one which stirred in me a real enthusiasm for the modern expression of courage. I enjoyed the contrast between inward luxury and the sea—between dime-sized rolls and the taste of salty air. I enjoyed sitting at our softly lighted table in an evening gown and walking around the deck in a thick coat, to be whipped by the wind and bitten by the spray. I enjoyed studying the passengers' profiles against the sky as they walked back and forth. I also saw the defiant tail of a whale. And I saw a woman who wore a silk dress with fringe on deck. It was just then that the waves got rough.

[Editor's note: To preserve the chronology, A.N.'s rewritten diary entries are presented first, followed by her shipboard notes.]

[June 6?] Besides the New York family, Eduardo was there to meet us—my handsome and romantic cousin, with a deep, rich voice and a graceful, inimitable way of bowing and stretching out his hand. We agreed to meet the New Family later at Forest Hills and went off with Eduardo in a taxi to Richard's apartment. The keys were given to us without hesitation. We walked into the well-remembered studio, so immense, so soft in coloring—too soft, I thought this time. The first things we saw were the plaster casts on the table, the statuette and the bust.[2] On a sculpturing stand, in the best light, we saw the bronze reproduction which had been on exhibition all winter. I changed from my suit into my Russian dress and hat—black and red. Eduardo was immediately impressed by my clothes and my "steadiness." The three of us went to Child's for lunch—that queer, clean, shiny place which looks like a hos-

[1] *Clarence Duncan Chamberlin, American aviator, who made a record nonstop flight from New York to Germany, June 4–6, 1927.*
[2] *Both of A.N.*

pital where they are trying to cure you of the love of meat. The menu contains proofs that most great men were vegetarians and adds a few facts about their lives and accomplishments. If they really survived a vegetarian diet, it was because they didn't eat in Child's.

We told Eduardo all about France. We said, We don't want to deprive you of your illusions—but get rid of the *usual* illusions about France, and we'll give you something to take their place, a real understanding and appreciation. It took us the duration of a lunch to do both things. It took me less time to find out that Eduardo was earnest about his work, very sincere and serious, more emotional and sensuous than intellectual, more sensitive and impressionable than thoughtful. Withal, terribly appealing, with eyes equally soft for *all* ladies and all ladies' eyes soft for him. From here it is easy to add that he reads Proust and the Russians and yet he has managed to keep a candid soul and childlike seriousness. In fact, I was teasing him with my new-found irony, and he did not understand. It is remarkable that when I become mocking everybody else gets serious, and when I am serious everybody seems to be laughing at me. That day I laughed gently at Eduardo. Six years ago that would have seemed impossible to me. Yet it happened at Child's over a vegetarian lunch.

That very afternoon at Forest Hills the Parisians received a different reception. Johnnie [Guiler] thought we had lost our American pep. He himself was full of pep and so worn out he couldn't relax. For the second time I was admired for my clothes. Eduardo had found them full of character, but he had noticed the inward change, too. Apart from Eduardo and Eugene, [everyone seemed to think that] clothes were the only things I brought back from Paris. Towards the end of our visit the opaqueness of Americans began to irritate me. Nothing was demanded, or expected, of me but sweetness. I felt I was living among children and at moments I felt stifled. The most important parts of me, of my life—maturity, wisdom, thought—all these were out of place.

I took what I found in New York—energy and life, the spirit of medieval builders, the giant strength and courage and obstinacy, the comforts, the pure milk, the honesty, the delightful laugh and good humor of the colored people, the prompt and expensive service and the plays—but they came later—oh, not so much later, I remember now, because we began that very Saturday [June 11] by attending the last performance of Joel Harris's *Spread Eagle*, in which Eduardo was acting the part of a lazy Mexican worker.

Eduardo's voice was rich and dragging, his acting perfect. I was very proud of him.

[Beforehand] we had had lunch with Eugene—Eugene matured after two and a half years of life in Bellaire, Long Island, in a house like ten thousand other American houses, as old as we are after two and a half years of Europe. Of course, he had gone to Florida on business to look over bananas and oranges. And we give credit to Europe for everything. Steady, human, clear-eyed Eugene, still holding his forehead with his right hand when he speaks.

[June 12.] We went to the Waldorf to see Baby and Tia Antolina. Baby has developed character and principles and a sound understanding of life. After taking Baby out to lunch we went to Forest Hills. Edith and Ethel [Guiler] took us to the tennis club. We sat on the terrace and were spoken to by several young men, so Pussy became worried and marched us all down the grass tennis courts ostensibly to watch Johnnie play.

The dinner with the Guilers was cheerful. Hugh's father is sincere, but his mother isn't—she is fond of people of wealth, of social life, and unintelligently fond of her children. She cannot understand me. I am refined but not conventional. I am something entirely foreign and unstable and unsafe. And then I have, after all, stolen her son. She tries her best to love me, but she can't. I try even harder, and I can't love her, alas, but I do love Hugh's father, with his kindness, intolerance, sincerity, goodness and hardness and narrow-mindedness.

[June 13.] I saw Uncle Gilbert—pathetically thin, harassed, desperate. His situation at home is maddening. Tia Coco is influenced by Christian Science and is in danger of losing her daughter and her money. Uncle Gilbert is at war with C.S., appealing to the law to protect his child. Tia Coco, guided by C.S., struggling to shift the ground of dispute and separation to a question of money in order to evade a sectarian scandal. Terrible scenes take place frequently in which each accuses the other of madness. Nothing more terrible in all the world, nothing more criminal than an illogical, unreasoning woman against whom nothing can prevail—no patience, logic, ideal or fear of violence. I have known moments when such a person has given me a desire for extreme violence. Poor Uncle G. has such temptation now.

That evening, dinner at Forest Hills with the New Family—Scottish jokes, the characteristic Guiler laugh, hearty and real, the sweetest trait in the family.

Went to the city with Mother G. and the girls to see *Annie Laurie*. Lillian Gish is my favorite, and more so in that story, where her delicacy was in such contrast to the Scotsmen's roughness—a roughness I also love. Forgot to mention that curious moment when we first stood at Pennsylvania Station, waiting at the gate for our train. Place, time, smells, colors, crowd, all the same as two and a half years ago. We couldn't believe we had been away, and had an uncanny fear of having merely dreamed Europe.

[June 14.] It rained. I stayed home to unpack, to wash stockings and mend them, to write the Maynards, and I wrote melancholic pages in my journal. In the evening we met Baby and Tia Antolina for dinner at the most beautiful of restaurants, inspired by old Italy and executed by Alice Foote McDougal with a truly American sense of selection, harmony and decorative beauty. I couldn't remember the food, although its poor quality made an impression on my epicurean Cat.

The comedy we saw that night, *Her Cardboard Lover*, was marvelously well acted by Jeanne Eagels.

[June 15.] Eduardo came to say good-bye; he was leaving for a summer resort with his father. We had a sharp, tense talk in which we tried to cover the story of three years. It is nearly impossible to consciously fill such gaps. The most important facts, the elusive ones, escape such brutal condensation. But we did gain some knowledge of each other. We agreed that we were both living fully, with all our senses. He told me about his work, his cultivation of his voice and of his entire body, all expressive and necessary in acting; the command he has now of a once weak memory because he needs to remember old impressions and emotions for his acting. He expressed fear of writing a journal in case it might someday be published, since an actor's life is public property. He asked me to destroy his old letters, as he had destroyed his first journal, because he looks down upon his youthful thoughts (he can't see they are but the necessary details to the whole). And of course, I didn't promise. At the door I asked him, "Must I still take care of Frances for you?"

"I don't care any more," said my fickle cousin.

"Good-bye, Eduardo, don't write me."

"But I will!"

"Don't lie!"

I saw him again, just before we left, but with his family. Nothing worth recording, except that I was able to confirm my suspicion that he loves the Russian, that he is a Russian. Physically, I observed, his eyes are less beautiful and less prominent in his face—he is all mouth now, a very rich, full, sensuous mouth. Body and face are harmoniously expressive of sensitiveness, sensuousness, languor.

What a contrast with Uncle G. when I saw him that same day—all eyes, all suffering, body tense and desséché.[1] Added to his other sorrows, he is now a man conscious of not having fully lived. His first effort to approach warmth, pleasure, spontaneity, led to his marriage, and even now, standing on the ruins of it, he is grateful for his union to the Latin race, whose warmth and lovingness has brought him joy. He forgets the sorrows brought him by the other face of that warm impulsiveness—cruelty, passion, injustice.

I took my good, patient, gentle, open-minded, harmlessly radical uncle to the theatre. We saw *Broadway*, an excellently acted play, but showing innocence to be still a sentimental illusion among Americans, the heroine a symbol of it, a virgin among chorus girls, a dutiful girl, a child-faced woman.

We had dinner with Eugene (in a fake French restaurant). He had experienced exactly what I did when reading modern literature—a great sense of freedom and power—a sense that knowledge of all things dispels fear and the haunting mystery of ugliness, that clearness and frankness give strength. But Hugh asked: "Where are they bound for? What do they express and do with this freedom and power for which they struggle?" "Why," I said, "must you always seek an end and use to all things? Is there any end except the struggle itself? Books have never revealed anything to us but the struggle. They have always promised a final revelation but have never given it, even the greatest of them—the Bible—and modern literature can't do more than the Bible. Books approach and discover life, a new life, but they can't show us its end." Eugene agreed with me.

After dinner we took a walk along Riverside Drive, where I had spent a great part of my childhood mending stockings and writing in my journal and watching Joaquin playing. Eugene told us about the novel he and his father had written. We did not read it, after all, but I was glad to know he had been writing. He was delightfully responsive, not only to deep ideas, but to little human things as well. His voice was steadier and richer.

[1] *Desiccated.*

[June 17.] I had lunch with Baby and went to the movies with her. Saw *La Dame aux Camélias* in modern American dress —her lover in bell-shaped trousers—terrible. With what pleasure *Le Figaro* would have pounced on this production, that paper which so lovingly collects sarcastic anecdotes on Americanisms and smacks venomous lips over American manners, plays, books, etc.

[June 18.] In the evening we went to the famous new movie house, the Roxy, a gigantic and repulsive building, overornamented, noisy, oppressive and with an idiotic program. That and the Paramount are proofs that American greatness is sometimes a mere inflated balloon.

Edith and Ethel made friends with Baby, but this attempt to bring the families together brought out the fact that the Guilers did "not want the introduction of Catholics into our family until the girls are settled down and married." This showed me the real foundation of intolerance and ignorance lying beneath our reconciliation and estranged us both from them, secretly.

[June 19.] Edith and Ethel came to see the studio. They went wild over Richard's paintings and the studio. We turned on the radio (oh, America!), the girls danced the Charleston and the Black Bottom and I showed them part of my Sevillana. Ethel wore some of Richard's old costumes and looked quaint and lovely in them. She has a small face, a rather calm and skeptical nature, real talent for drawing and dancing and may not end by marrying a tennis champion.

[June 20.] In the morning I saw Frances Schiff—now a reporter for the *Tribune*. She hasn't changed so much—the same conflict between a soft, kind, feminine woman made for marriage and an odd, skeptical mind seeking something else. The oddness is disappearing year by year. She is clever, but not enough herself, and too respectful of men. I did not feel at home with her; I tried hard to understand her life, but she could not understand mine. Everything I told her she took literally. We could not talk long enough for me to make her understand or at least suspect there was something she is missing. And why should I explain? It would be like the telling of traveling to someone who can never hope to travel, to spread restlessness where there is peace. So we showed each other our new dresses and she told me about her work. Reporters, like actors, live under high tension and often resort to strange vices as a result of very unsteady and disturbing lives— didn't I take to smoking while in New York? Well, they take to drink, Christian Science or love affairs. Eduardo has told me the same thing. Frances hasn't taken to anything yet except a nonchalant way of speaking of a "companion" for a trip—not a husband.

Q.[1] came to see me that afternoon. His eyes, his pathetic hands, his solitude, disturbed and moved me. I was kind and soft and soothing and made him happier. That evening we went to hear Edith play at her teacher's apartment. Giggling girls playing nicely, prettily, disgustingly. The teacher was charming but not a musician. Tragic ignorance, lack of genius and intelligence and musicality—a nursery of children who will never grow up. My only pleasure that evening was a selfish one—wearing my evening dress, for which I chose the stuff and made the design, and receiving many compliments on it and being told I had the face of an old cameo.

[June 21.] Lunch with Baby and movies at the Paramount. That evening was the only quiet one we spent at home. I lay on the green couch and smoked. Hugh turned on the radio. In the middle of some good music I said: "Suffering is part of our peace —let us hear it to the end! I want all of life and fear no part of it."

[June 22.] Posed for Frances's sister Helen. As Helen painted silently, I fretted and grew impatient to continue my "active life." In the afternoon I had my hair raised by a mystery play Baby took me to. In the evening we were invited to the apartment of Hugh's Aunt Timmie for dinner, and we took her afterwards to the best play we were to see in N.Y., *The Silver Cord*.[2] A domineering, sentimental, devoted, cruel mother. Among other things a brave, clear-speaking girl tells her mother-in-law just what kind of illness prevents her from appreciating her. The fearlessness and frankness of science dispelling fogs, uncovering the once terrible secrets of human behavior, making those dark and fearful and unknown things simple and curable.

[June 23.] Father G. came to see us, and some of the family tangles were again superficially straightened. He is so absolutely sincere that I can't help being generous with him.

I had lunch with Uncle Gilbert; heard an unbelievable story of mental torture and struggle. I supported his sound reasoning and view of the situation, helped him to act on his perfectly just and intelligent plan. He was comforted and encouraged, but I

---

[1] *Someone A.N. chose not to identify—most likely Enric.*
[2] *By Sidney Howard.*

knew that as soon as he got home, emotions, uncontrollable feelings, would destroy the clarity of his thinking, and he would go on hopelessly turning around.

In the evening we took Tia A. and Baby to the theatre. Saw a delightfully cynical play and was amused to observe that having created a type—blasé, cynical—they did not know what use to make of him and so dropped him on the lap of a rich woman who took him to the Riviera. The last act remains unwritten.

I found a delectable cynicism in all the plays—not the ashy, destructive cynicism which kills action and the desire to live, but a lively and creative one. To Americans, knowing the worst of human nature is not a reason for ceasing to live—it is only the beginning of life, it clears the way for richer living. Criticism and cynicism here are spurs to greater efforts. How I have loved this shedding of wise, sarcastic phrases instead of tears.

[June 24.] A conventional lunch at the McAlpin with the Guilers. Conventional evening spent at a musical comedy—*Rio Rita*—worse than I remembered musicals to be; only the fact that we were guests kept me from burning down the theatre. From there to an after-theatre supper with more entertainment. A terrible evening.

[June 25.] We went on a bat with Eugene. We had lunch and saw two plays—the second as a retribution for the first. *Saturday's Children*, in the style of Bernstein's *Felix*—a faithful and unimaginative copy of mediocre people's lives. Jane Cowl was exquisitely clever in *The Road to Rome*, though the play itself was but a poor and vulgar imitation of Erskine's *Helen*. I was grateful to have seen her act and pray I may see her again.

In between the plays we had a wonderful talk with Eugene. He understood my change and stared a lot either at the change or at my face—to the point of worrying Hugh, who was even more worried when he discovered I liked Eugene better for it all.

[June 26.] Dinner at Forest Hills and quiet evening looking at childhood photographs of Pussy and his family. Pussy at 10 in his kilts—adorable. I wish I had known him then.

[June 27.] Spent in preparation for the greatest Day. Clothes examined and pressed, camera loaded, hair washed and curled, long talk with Hugh over things we wanted to tell Erskine—and early to bed.

[June 28.] At 9:15 we left Grand Central Station for Wilton, Conn. Erskine met us with a most cordial smile. I had promised myself not to be afraid of him, and I was still a little, but it was a wonderful day. We learned more about him, his work, his ideas and his life. Later I will return to this day and all that he said. We had nothing to give him but a book of Godoy's poetry and what we thought worthwhile in our last year in Paris—a few ideas, a few books, a few plays, a few high days. He made us dissatisfied with ourselves by the sheer beauty and energy of his own life. Yet at the end of the day he gave us encouragement by writing in his book of *Essays* "In admiration and affection." And we went away knowing him better, loving him more and determined to deserve his friendship.

[June 29.] We saw Ethel Barrymore in *The Constant Wife*. Splendid actress and excellent play.

[June 30.] The Maynards came out of the elevator just as we were about to go downstairs for dinner. Richard was unchanged and fussed. Lorraine was even lovelier and more demonstrative. "So much to say—we don't know where to begin!" So we began sensibly by going to dinner at the chop suey. We learned that Lorraine's book on a child movie star was coming out in the fall, that Richard had started a novel and wanted to abandon painting forever, that we should stay in New York for good, that we were both looking healthier and happy.

[July 1.] I was up early. Pussy had already gone to the bank. Richard read me the beginning of his novel. It was really an introduction, a sort of credo of his technique and intention—a curious way of beginning a novel, by making himself as conscious as possible—a way which would kill any novel I might attempt.

After lunch I began to pose for a new painting. Richard prepared the chair and the canvas and struggled to get the right light. He asked me questions about our life in Paris, and I found myself drawing an intensely interesting picture, full of color, movement, rhythm, meaning and beauty. And unexpectedly, I was struck by the conviction that the life in New York could not hold me, that I longed to return to Paris.

Richard told me what Lorraine had said about us—that Hugh inspired confidence and would certainly be Bank President someday and that I was an artist in living. Living artfully won't satisfy me, except temporarily, but I am glad people think I do that well, at least.

In the evening the four of us had dinner together and then went to the movies. During the movies Richard tried to "figure out" the curious space between my eyes and the exact shape of my nose in preparation for the next day's work (which was very embarrassing).

[July 2.] We didn't really get to work until afternoon, and then Richard was in a good vein so that in two hours he had made marvelous progress. Though he didn't see the change in me and refused to admit one, in spite of Hugh's insistence, the face in the new painting is *altogether* different from the old.

That evening we were invited to Forest Hills for dinner and dance at the inn. Johnnie led me through all the modern, dislocating steps, and I took pleasure in finding out I could do them easily. Since I follow modern literature, it is right that my body should be equally supple, free, and jolty. Only, I must say, ultramodern dancing is ugly.

[July 3.] In the afternoon, Lorraine and Richard took us riding in their blue car, and we went to Richmond Hill. I saw Mother's house and the bungalow and nearly cried. I regretted the past, not because I wanted to live it over again, but because it is something lovely and forever lost. Richmond Hill was overrun with new houses but otherwise unchanged, peaceful and stagnant. I lived a rich inner life there, but how much richer now.

[July 5.] In the morning I made a pretense of posing and Richard of working, but we talked sadly. Richard wished we were not going away because we were their only real friends; he deplored the necessity of letter writing, the fact that we hadn't talked enough, and he told me again how much faith they had in both of us.

I felt very sad when I saw them go off in their car and realized that in those four days they had won my affection, that I would not forget Lorraine's smile and the story of her life. Nor would I forget Richard's pathetic eyes; his eagerness to make life more beautiful and romantic; his evasion of sorrow; his dislike of fatalism, of tragedy, of Mrs. Wharton's books; his utter unconsciousness of irony; his gentle and kind sense of humor; his utter incapacity to live by his emotions rather than by principle, to do things out of pleasure rather than out of an inexorable sense of duty, to do spontaneous sketching and living—all that I call living repressed, so tightly and hopelessly. Dear Richard, with his old tan linen hat for automobiling, his distress at my not wearing rubbers, his armful of raincoats for all the family, his slowness, his bewilderments, his distress before my quickness, his frowns upon the elasticity of my thinking—and Lorraine's smile and her understanding of his qualities and her patience. Well, they were gone.

We had lunch with Eugene downtown, told him all that Erskine had said, which brought out interesting commentaries. Eugene is not entirely won over by Erskine, but he will be, because I had the same objections at first, and I was finally and utterly convinced of his greatness.

[July 6.] Good-bye to Frances and Helen Schiff, lunch alone, French Line for visa, last-minute shopping, frantic packing, a moment's rest and I was off with Pussy to Forest Hills for the last evening.

July 7. Terribly sad day, parting from family, friends and New York.[1] The loss of one of our valises containing our diaries added worry to sadness. I am grieving over the loss of those diaries. I had copied out a great part of Hugh's journal on my typewriter, but not all, and the story of Luchon, our trip and New York is lost.

Seasickness completed our day. In between, I unpacked, brooded, re-read old letters, made plans for work in Paris and tried to make Hugh laugh in spite of my gloom. Have remembered Q. too much. For once feeling only guided my actions, and I do not regret my softness.

July 8. Hugh had another bad day. I had lunch and dinner alone in the dining room, two dismal meals, and spent most of my time hoping for news of the valise. If I don't hear about it today, tomorrow I will start rewriting. Our fellow passengers are impossible. I like people individually, but en masse they are offensive.

Have been depressed and self-centered and critical. Such a familiar mood had to come after a month of insouciance and action and exhilarating fullness.

July 9. It is strange, but seasickness is the only thing which subdues my love of life. Sitting here on deck with a pale, unshaven Cat at my side, I find it impossible to recall the keen excitement of our month in New York.

July 10. When we first sailed we were so despondent that we wished a storm might sink our ship. But now Pussy is well, the sea is smooth, the sun is out and we live again. Life on board is a

---

[1] *A.N. and Hugh returned on the* De Grasse.

hotel life, and in a hotel personal life is out of place. Under the eyes of so many people we must be stoical. I try to appreciate the absence of housekeeping, the fact that Pussy doesn't need to go to the bank, that we can sleep late and drowse and smoke—for I have taken to smoking.

I began the morning we arrived in New York, facing that unique and beautiful skyline. I was tense with memories of another arrival four years ago[1] and trembling with expectation of what this visit would be. I smoked a cigarette, stoically, deliberately. Now that I have come as far as the smoking of a cigarette on that steaming hot morning of our arrival in New York, I believe I have the courage to continue.

[July 12?] We are in the train. I have many cheerful things to think about but I can't remember them at the moment. Greenness, houses and telegraph poles do not interest me, neither did Le Havre. Returning to France pleases my intellect and stifles my heart—perhaps because I am tired.

Hugh said last night that when he traveled with me he always felt as if he were bringing in contraband. This is certainly the most original compliment I ever got. It took a Scotsman to sum up my value so realistically.

At home, facing Paris, friends, life and myself again. I found Paris soft, small, quiet, delightful, found that I understand my friends better, found our life becoming more and more wonderful and stayed awake the whole of the first night with excitement and anticipation.

---

[1] *After their marriage in Havana.*

❧ Index ❧